Management and Organisations in Social Work

Management and Organisations in Social Work

SECOND EDITION

TRISH HAFFORD-LETCHFIELD

Series Editors: Jonathan Parker and Greta Bradley

LearningMatters

First published in 2006 by Learning Matters Ltd.
Reprinted in 2007

Second edition published in 2009

British Library Cataloguing in Publication Data
A CIP record for this book is available from the British Library.

ISBN: 978 1 84445 216 3

Cover and text design by Code 5 Design Associates Ltd
Project Management by Deer Park Productions, Tavistock, Devon
Typeset by Pantek Arts Ltd, Maidstone, Kent
Printed and bound in Great Britain by Bell & Bain Ltd, Glasgow

Learning Matters Ltd
33 Southernhay East
Exeter EX1 1NX
Tel: 01392 215560
info@learningmatters.co.uk
www.learningmatters.co.uk

Contents

Acknowledgements

This book is for the lovely Ted and Katie, Mum and Dad who continue to give me unrelenting and selfless support. A special thank you is overdue to my colleagues Kate Leonard, Jill Yates, Anna Nelson, Alison Higgs and Louise O'Connor for their constant encouragement and help to make working life both interesting and fun.

Introduction

Social care organisations are required to constantly respond and adapt to the shifting social, legislative, economic and political influences prevalent at any given time. This inevitably leads to major changes in the way in which social care services are organised and managed. These in turn have impacted on how the social work profession has had to respond and continuously develop its knowledge base, values and skills in practice to meet new roles and challenges generated by social and political structures. As a profession, social workers have been constantly engaged in contemporary debates about the nature of social work and the role that it plays in the diverse range of organisations in which it now finds itself operating. One of the drivers behind the new degree in social work was to equip social workers to meet these new challenges. Since then, there has been a further trend, reinforced by government policy, towards blurring role differences and loosening boundaries between professional disciplines (GSCC, 2008) in which social work roles have become more elastic in order to respond to new policy aspirations, expanding knowledge and rising public expectations about care services. As a practitioner, it is critical that you are able to understand and operate within these often complex environments. A thorough and critical understanding of the issues that arise, whether you are working in the statutory sector, the third sector or a private organisation, is essential to help you develop and achieve effective practice. Exploring, understanding and being active in maximising the potential of the relationships between government, organisations, management, employees, service users and the community are critical to achieving the delivery of high-quality and successful services. Not everybody involved in this chain will necessarily be able to recognise or deal with issues they are presented with, all of the time. This book therefore aims to give you the foundations to assist you in becoming more active in the process.

Recognising that we do not work in a vacuum, the book addresses some of the key issues underpinning the constant changes and challenges for providing effective social care services now and in the future. It attempts to locate some of the responsibility for managing change and challenges with staff working in organisations by clarifying what these processes are and the role of staff within these. The effective delivery of social care depends on being able to identify and apply some of the essential key research, knowledge and evidence base about organisations and management systems to the environment in which you are working. You also need to be able to integrate these into the practical skills required in day-to-day practice. In essence, collaboration between staff, management and service users at all levels in organisations is crucial to successful delivery of services.

The overall aim of this book is to assist you in your professional and practice development as an active participant in the organisations you work with. More importantly, through recognising and taking responsibility for your role you should be able to become a more satisfied member of the organisation and a better advocate and representative of the people you serve within the wider environment. Much of how an organisation operates can be analysed and explained in terms of many different aspects of power and its enactment.

Critical reflection can help to examine power relationships relevant to organisational life (Fook, 2004, p. 58). Once you understand how your position, practice and role within an organisation are affected by power relations and your ability to act on these, there is an increased potential for effective organisational change. I would also argue that one of the roles of social work education is to better prepare social work professionals for management positions that enable you to take advantage of more progressive management practices in a climate of constant public sector reform.

Requirements for social work education

The study of management and organisational studies are strongly related to the curriculum and requirements for social work education and training. These are contained within the Department of Health's prescribed curriculum for competence in each of the six key roles for social work (www.skillsforcare.org.uk).

Key Role 1: *Prepare for work with people and assess their needs and circumstances.* This book will address the relationship between organisations, the wider society and political structure, the community and individuals within it by examining the basis on which services are provided.

Key Role 2: *Plan, carry out, review and evaluate social work practice.* There will be an examination of the methods and approaches used to undertake this role within the organisational setting, such as through service user involvement, quality assurance and performance measurement.

Key Role 3: *Support individuals to represent their needs, views and circumstances including advocacy and involvement in decision-making forums.* The role of organisations and management in promoting and facilitating service user involvement is considered. There will be an examination of the impact of resource management on service provision, looking at how management and leadership theory and styles underpin ethical and effective decision-making.

Key Role 4: *Manage risk.* This relates to the relevant Health and Safety legislation, polices and procedures and their role in facilitating safe and professional working relationships within the organisational setting between employers and employees as well as between the organisation and its service users and carers.

Key Role 5: *Be accountable with supervision and support for own practice.* Ways of achieving this through complaints and representation procedures and staff support frameworks in the form of supervision and staff development will be examined. Ethical issues in relationships between personal practice and institutional practice in challenging and promoting equality are important here.

Key Role 6: *Demonstrate professional competence in social work practice.* We will look at the concept of learning organisations and the way in which management and organisations recognise and support professional development.

The General Social Care Council's (GSCC) Code of Practice for Social Care spells out the specific standards that must be met by both employees and employers in social care (www.gscc.org.uk). The code recognises the interdependence of both parties to meet standards for good practice by spelling out the duties of the employer to support the employee and are very relevant to the topics explored in this book.

Social care workers must:

- protect the rights and promote the interests of service users and carers;

- strive to establish and maintain the trust and confidence of service users and carers;

- promote the independence of service users while protecting them as far as possible from danger and harm;

- respect the rights of service users whilst seeking to ensure that their behaviour does not harm themselves or other people;

- uphold public trust and confidence in social care services;

- be accountable for the quality of their work and take responsibility for maintaining and improving their knowledge and skills.

Social care employers must:

- make sure people are suitable to enter the workforce and understand their roles and responsibilities;

- have written policies and procedures in place to enable social care workers to strengthen and develop their skills and knowledge;

- put in place and implement written policies and procedures to deal with dangerous, dis-criminatory or exploitative behaviour and practice;

- promote the GSCC's codes of practice to social care workers, service users and carers and co-operate with the GSCC's proceedings.

The study of management and organisations draws on various academic disciplines such as social policy, political science, sociology, psychology, social work theory, social work law and ethics. All of these topics have direct impact on social work practice in the organisa-tional setting. The topics explored in this book will also meet the subject skills identified in the Quality Assurance Agency academic benchmarking criteria for social work (www.qaa.ac.uk). These were originally published in 2000 alongside those for social policy and administration and were revised in 2008 to reflect co-terminosity with professional training and the acquisition of the protected title of 'social worker'. This interface entails close links with professional, regulatory and statutory bodies. The subject benchmarks require an understanding of the nature of social work and the development of problem-solving skills under the following headings:

1. Managing problem-solving activities;

2. Gathering information (including searches and presentation of findings);

3. Analysis and synthesis;

4. Intervention and evaluation.

In summary, each chapter in the book will incorporate knowledge, research and case studies to illustrate how the underpinning requirements of the social work degree have been met.

These topics will also be relevant and of interest to people following management development programmes in social care such as NVQ Level 4, and practitioners following the post-qualifying framework or wishing to progress to management roles.

Book structure and learning features

This book has four main aims:

1. To provide an introduction to the study of management and organisations for students following the social work degree, management development programmes or practitioners who want to refresh or develop greater knowledge of this particular subject area. Each chapter can be read as a stand-alone topic but makes clear links to other concepts and specialised areas developed in subsequent chapters. The aim is to stimulate both a wider interest and understanding for readers looking at their practice at both macro and micro level and an enthusiasm for more knowledge.

2. To enable readers to translate the theories, concepts and ideas presented in each chapter into a framework for practice which can be activated in the reader's own organisational setting. There will be a number of case studies and reality-based interactive material which encourages the reader to investigate and transfer knowledge to their own unique setting. Readers will be encouraged to develop and utilise their own tools and capabilities to challenge and improve practice in a way that meets their individual learning needs.

3. To stimulate debate and critical reflection. Whilst the text will highlight and encourage readers to be proactive, open-minded in their attitude and professional practice within the organisational setting, complex questions, ethical dilemmas and problems will be raised which are known to be the root cause of many dysfunctional organisations and management teams. Readers will be encouraged to consider ideology, professional and personal values, judgements and decision-making and the role these play in organisational structure and culture.

4. To give you a flavour and a summary of dynamic literature and current research to draw on. Through the presentation of case studies, considering examples of best practice in the field of social care, we can consider the evidence base to support critical reflection and in evaluation of the situations we find the most demanding and complex. Pointers will be given towards web-based learning materials and other literature to develop the readers specific interests in this area.

Chapter synopsis

Throughout the book references will be made to how each chapter links or draws on key topics discussed in other or previous chapters. **Chapter 1** will start by looking at the nature of organisations delivering social work and social care. We will look at theoretical models used to describe organisations and using these, identify the key elements of any organisational structure and its relevance to contemporary organisations. We will explore the historical perspective on how organisations have developed since the post-war period right through to the current reformation and restructuring of service provision in key areas such as children's and adults' services. This will take account of social, political and economic factors driving these changes. The development and relevance of 'business' culture to social care organisations will be discussed, referring to the ethical issues arising for those affected.

Chapter 2 introduces theoretical models of management and leadership and how these relate to change management theory and practice. This chapter will emphasise the differences and similarities between managing and leading and identify the specific and unique roles of managers in social work and social care. The concept of transformational leadership and its role in change management will be explored. Change management theory will be explained and you will have the opportunity to engage with a change management model using a case study to illustrate the change process. You will be invited to identify the key elements for successful change and the roles that different people in the organisation play. The chapter will conclude by summarising the key skills, knowledge and practice that social workers need to work effectively with their management teams, focusing on promoting ethical practice in the workplace.

Chapter 3 explores the basic concepts underpinning approaches to performance management and the role of inspection and regulation in social care. You will be introduced to the concept of quality assurance and asked to consider what constitutes 'quality' in care services from the perspectives of different stakeholders. We will look at the development of quality assurance systems from the post-war period onwards to help you understand the current emphasis on performance management and how these are implemented through contemporary inspection and regulation regimes. A critical evaluation of the usefulness of performance management to social work environments and the complexity of developing appropriate tools will be examined. You will be invited to consider how you might go about developing meaningful measures of social work services using a case study and an example of a national performance indicator to illustrate this. We conclude by looking at the future of quality assurance systems and the role of social work practice in developing and enhancing these.

Chapter 4 builds further on ideas about quality assurance, focusing specifically on organisational frameworks used to involve service users in the design, delivery and evaluation of social care services. From a strategic perspective, we will discuss the theoretical models for increasing participation of service users and carers at different levels in the organisation. You will be encouraged to consider the policies and decision-making processes that make organisations successful in engaging or involving service users effectively with reference to the relevant legislative and policy frameworks. The second half of the chapter will focus on the role of customer care policies, specifically customer complaints and representation procedures, and how these are implemented in organisational settings. You will be invited to consider the issues involved in making a complaint and we will look at the essential elements of a local procedure. We will evaluate different forms of advocacy and rights-based approaches to service delivery.

Chapter 5 will examine the context in which social care is resourced and delivered and the complex challenges for organisations to balance needs, demand, costs and quality within the current legislative and policy framework. We will discuss current government social policy initiatives, demography, projections of 'need' using census and research information to help identify challenges and issues arising for organisations and required responses. Focusing on the commissioning and contracting process, you will be invited to consider how decisions about purchasing services are made and the role of social work practitioners within this. Equality issues will be highlighted and an introduction to costing services will develop your understanding of balancing costs and quality in service provision.

Chapter 6 analyses the organisational equalities framework, looking specifically at institutional forms of discrimination and how these manifest themselves. Strategic approaches to promoting equality in social care will be outlined. There will be a review of the literature on discrimination and oppression and an exploration of terms such as 'institutional discrimination', 'equal opportunities', 'direct' and 'indirect discrimination' with reference to the legal framework. There will be an evaluation of the research evidence relating to the under- or over-representation of oppressed groups in care services as well as employment practices in organisations demonstrating the presence and impact of institutional discrimination. Using a case study you will be asked to draw on knowledge from previous chapters on organisational structure, culture, policies and procedures. You will be able to apply some of the principles already covered in relation to quality assurance, service user involvement and effective resource management and look how these contribute towards promoting equality in social care organisations.

Chapter 7 looks at the legislation, policies and procedures organisations have in place to ensure dignity at work, exploring issues such as violence and aggression, stress management, bullying and harassment in the workplace and the research findings relating to these. You will be given brief scenarios to help you analyse and develop strategies to deal with difficult and complex situations as well as to identify the role of management. There will be an introduction to policies and procedures used by organisations to improve staff performance and ensure a safe and respectful working environment. This will include supervision, training and personal development and work–life balance initiatives that promote effective relations between management and staff. The role of collective bargaining and trade union or professional bodies will be highlighted and there will be an opportunity for you to construct your own personal action plan to improve dignity at work.

Chapter 8 summarises the more positive aspects of successful organisations and good management practice that have been discussed throughout the book and links these to the concept of a learning organisation. The complexities, demands and difficulties of working effectively, flexibly, innovatively and proactively in organisations delivering social care will be highlighted. Theoretical models of what constitutes a learning organisation will be presented by reviewing the different roles played by government agencies and national bodies, as well as those played by management, staff, stakeholders, users and carers. You will be asked to explore organisational strategies that encourage informal learning alongside education and training as a key to employability and personal development.

Useful websites and recommendations for further reading will be indicated at the end of each chapter.

A full glossary of terminology is provided at the end of this book so that a more detailed explanation of the jargon and terminology used in individual chapters is given. Words and terms explained in the glossary will be indicated in **bold** in the main text.

Lecturers' resources

Each chapter has a companion set of PowerPoint presentation slides summarising the key points and brief lecture notes. These can be accessed through the Learning Matters website at www.learningmatters.co.uk.

Professional development and reflective practice

Great emphasis is placed on developing skills of reflection about, in and on practice. This has developed over many years in social work. It is important also that you reflect prior to and during practice. This book will assist you in developing a questioning approach that looks in a critical way at your thoughts, experiences and practice and seeks to heighten your skills in refining your practice as a result of these deliberations. This can be even more difficult to achieve when thinking about broader ideas of management and organisations which can feel far removed from what you do every day yet have such an important bearing on how you practise. The book has a number of learning activities that encourage you to break down these broader issues into more tangible areas that have a direct relationship with your practice.

Reflecting about, in and on your practice is not only important during your education to become a social worker. It is considered key to continued professional development. As we move to a profession that acknowledges life-long learning as a way of keeping up to date, we need to reflect and contribute to how that culture is prevalent in the organisations that we work in. Knowing the organisational context in which we learn as well as our individual professional development needs is clearly shown by the emphasis given in the National Occupational Standards and the General Social Care Code of Practice for both employees and employers.

Chapter 1

The nature of organisations delivering social work and social care: structure and cultures

A C H I E V I N G   A   S O C I A L   W O R K   D E G R E E

This chapter will help you achieve the following National Occupational Standards and General Social Care Council's Code of Practice.

Key Role 1: Prepare for, and work with individuals, families, carers, groups and communities to assess their needs and circumstances.

- Inform individuals, families, carers, groups and communities about your own, and the organisation's duties and responsibilities.

Key Role 5: Manage and be accountable, with supervision and support for your own social work practice within your organisation.

- Manage and prioritise your workload within organisational policies and priorities.
- Contribute to identifying and agreeing the goals, objectives and lifespan of the team network or system.

Key Role 6: Demonstrate professional competence in social work practice.

- Review and update your own knowledge of legal, policy and procedural frameworks.
- Identify and assess issues, dilemmas and conflicts that might affect your practice.

General Social Care Code of Practice

Code 6.7: Recognising and respecting the roles and expertise of workers from other agencies and working in partnership with them.

It will also introduce you to the following academic standards as set out in the social work subject benchmark statements:

3.1.3 Social work services and service users

- The relationship between agency policies, legal requirements and professional boundaries in shaping the nature of services provided in inter-disciplinary contexts and the issues associated with working across these boundaries.

3.1.2 The service delivery context

- The complex relationship between public, social and political philosophies, policies and priorities and the organisation and practice of social work including the contested nature of these.
- The issues and trends in modern public and social policy and their relationship to contemporary practice and service delivery in social work.

3.1.3 Social work theory

- Social science theories explaining group and organisational behaviour, adaptation and change.

3.1.4 The nature of social work practice
- The characteristics of practice in a range of community based and organisational settings including group care, within statutory, voluntary and private sectors, and the factors, influencing changes in practice within these contexts.
- The factors and processes that facilitate effective inter-disciplinary, inter-professional and inter-agency collaboration and partnership.

3.2.2.3 Analysis and synthesis
- Employ understanding of human agency at the macro (societal), mezzo (organisational and community) and micro (inter- and intra-personal) levels.

3.2.2.4 Intervention and evaluation
- Build and sustain purposeful relationships with people and organisations in community-based and inter-professional contexts including group care.

3.2.4 Skills in working with others
- Act within a framework of multiple accountability.

Introduction

This chapter looks at the nature of organisations delivering social work and social care. We will start by looking at theoretical models used to describe organisations and identify the key elements of organisational structure and culture that are relevant to contemporary organisations in social care. We will briefly explore historical perspectives on how organisations have developed since the post-war period (1940s) to the current restructuring and transformation of children and adult services. This will enable you to take account of the main social, political and economic factors that affect organisational development. Debates about the structure and culture of public sector organisations often make reference to characteristics, trends and features adopted from, or traditionally associated with, private business sectors in the UK (Dominelli, 2002; Healy, 2002; Tsui and Cheung, 2004). We will look at the relevance of these debates to how organisations go about delivering support and care within an increasingly demanding and diverse public service sector environment. These debates will then continue throughout the book in relation to different topics related to modern social care organisations and management practice and explore the sometimes controversial relationships that can develop between organisations and their **stakeholders**.

Theoretical models of organisations in social care

The study of organisations draws on disciplines such as sociology, political science, economics, social policy and psychology as well as from its own discipline, research traditions and networks. Organisational theorists are interested in the study of three interrelated questions: what are organisations trying to do? how do they try to do it? and why are they doing it in a particular way? To answer these questions, we will start by considering three interrelated elements: strategy, structure and culture, all of which should be considered simultaneously (Payne, 1996).

Organisational strategy

Strategy describes the means by which social care is organised, resourced and delivered. Having a strategy enables organisations to manage changes to secure their future growth and sustain success (Clegg et al., 2005). Without a clear strategy, organisations will drift; strategic plans enable the organisation to steer its way ahead and are often associated with the task of management at the top of an organisation. The origin of strategic theory comes from ideas of competition in relation to quality, performance, product, cost or price. Whilst social care organisations are not traditionally perceived as competitive organisations, we will see later on in this book that the way in which they have had to respond to the government's modernisation agenda encourages competitive activity. Numerous legislative and fundamental policy shifts have required social care organisations to also collaborate towards the delivery of seamless and holistic services in the community within a financially demanding environment. Strategic plans emanate from these shifts and determine which changes are needed to organisational structure and environment to accomplish this. Changes in the environment in turn create a need for new strategies. As new strategies are developed, they require new organisational structures to adapt, setting up a cycle of continuous change which drives the organisation (Chandler, 1962). Chandler argued that as businesses enlarge, they have to cope with a greater volume of business and therefore modern organisational forms evolved as a necessary strategic adjustment to market conditions. Strategic action directs and shapes an organisation's relationship with its environment: by forecasting changes, planning responses, and making these a reality. Modern management thinking sees the role of strategic thinkers in an organisation as defining the big picture, steering the organisation with a strong grasp. On the other hand, the lower levels of the hierarchy are said to realise and implement instructions from above. We will explore any controversies about this concept in Chapter 2 when we look at management and leadership styles. In the meantime, if you want to find out more about organisational strategies you will find evidence of it in the way in which services are planned and designed, in documents that state the intended outcomes of how the organisation operates, and through the way in which managers organise and direct activities within the organisation.

Organisational culture is also an essential element in this chain of events and our experiences of behaviour, rituals and jargon in the organisational setting are all manifestations of organisational culture. Therefore, making changes to an organisation's strategy and structure alone will not guarantee success in achieving government's objectives. Processes and attitudes also need addressing and this is the joint responsibility of politicians, managers and professionals (Cabinet Office, 2000). In conclusion, the culture that precedes, develops and emerges through organisations embracing changes is vitally important and management has a unique role in nurturing and influencing organisational culture.

Organisational structure

The ways in which organisations are physically structured play a significant part in shaping people's relationships to it, for example in their attitude and behaviour. An organisation is defined by its external boundaries, such as those with the locality, the nature of the building it inhabits and its area of business. Likewise, internal boundaries such as job descriptions, units of work, and the titles used to describe teams or services within it, provide a means of organising work and communicating with people about the job they are expected to do within the organisation. Roles played by managers and employees, customers and service users are in turn influenced by any external constraints or demands on them; for example, the resources available, legislative and policy requirements as well as internal constraints from the decision-making process and support available. If you were to take a more psychological approach to understanding organisations, you would look to the internal or individual factors which determine human behaviour in organisations. In summary, organisational strategy and structure can in turn determine or influence culture.

ACTIVITY **1.1**

Take five minutes to come up with your own definition of an 'organisation'. What words come to mind and what metaphors or images might you use for thinking about organisations in social work? It might help to think of an organisation you are already familiar with such as a children's initial assessment service, community centre, women's refuge or a service user led organisation. Try to draw a diagram or chart that shows the structure of the organisation you are thinking of. How would this be different for different organisations?

One definition of an organisation is:

> *A social arrangement for achieving controlled performance in pursuit of collective goals.* (Buchanan et al., 2004, p. 5)

With the government's drives towards more joined-up government, organisations with rigid or fixed structures have to become more fluid or chameleon-like in order to adapt to their new environment. Government policy continuously creates new sets of organisational enclaves, for example in response to cross-cutting social policies around particular service user groups away from more traditional functions such as health care or housing. Examples of these enclaves can be found in Drug Action or Youth Offending Teams or care trusts around particular service user groups. For professional staff delivering services, different practice protocols and service models can pose major barriers to effective and efficient joint working, for example to meet the needs of children who leave care or people with complex mental health problems. Such ingrained professional practices cannot be changed overnight and harmonising or simplifying joint approaches to social issues is bound to require a longer-term effort (Pollitt, 2003).

Models of organisations

In Activity 1.1, you may have concluded that there is no such 'one size fits all' when describing organisations. The purpose of organisational structure is firstly to divide up organisational activities and allocate them to sub-units and, secondly, to co-ordinate and control these activities so that they contribute to the overall aims of the organisation. The role of a manager is to support and facilitate these two functions.

One way of depicting the structure of any large organisation is that of a pyramid or triangle, showing its vertical and horizontal dimensions, as in Figure 1.1.

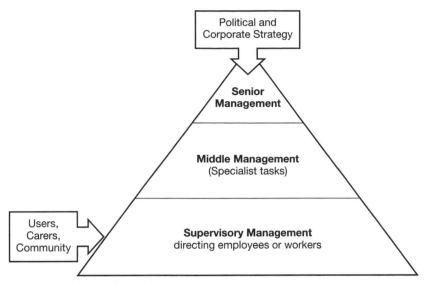

Figure 1.1 A typical hierarchical bureaucratic structure

In this structure the vast majority of employees are located at the operating core of the pyramid, undertaking day-to-day work and delivery of goods and services. It is through these people who have direct contact with service users that the purpose of the organisation is realised. Reporting relationships exist between these, up towards the strategic apex where senior managers co-ordinate, motivate and control employees so that they work together to achieve overall organisational goals. Management at the middle of the pyramid are responsible for ensuring decisions are executed and manage and monitor the resources of the organisation. You may recognise this type of structure in a large care trust. These generally operate as rigid bureaucracies led by a senior management team (Morgan, 1987). This type of organisation can be slow, but efficient, with a rule-bound structure where a senior management team makes the majority of decisions and departmental heads are responsible for decisions in their specific areas of specialism. The term 'bureaucracy' often carries negative connotations. It was originally coined by an organisational theorist, Weber (1976), to articulate a form of organisation design defined by a number of characteristics. These include centralised power and control held by a small executive group which establishes formal relations between people of authority. A hierarchy of ascending authority attaches to certain positions, rights, responsibilities and entitlements with mechanisms in place to monitor and control. In bureaucratic organisations, activities are based on the formal rules; one type of bureaucracy Weber described was the 'rational-legal' where values and principles are universally applied without favour or prejudice.

Straightforward classifications of organisational structures are problematic, but provide a starting point to help us understand the importance of roles, rules and procedures within organisations. Examination of decision-making, issues of accountability, legitimate or otherwise, helps us to relate to the organisational structure and vice versa. This may be formal like the one described above or much more informal as often seen within community-based or social enterprises, co-operatives and mutuals both large and small. Formal organisations will have explicit structures made up of designated groups led by management teams which determine how they will work together. Informal structures, however, rely more on an unintended network of interactions between stakeholders which emerge in order to respond to the same or different needs. In user-led organisations which aim more towards sharing power and decision-making, the structure may be more likely to resemble a matrix where equal weight is given to different roles and aspects of work of the organisation. As a result, each individual's expertise contributes to specialist and overall aspects of the work. The role of the management team, if there is one, is to provide operational support, facilitate people and set the general strategic direction.

These different models of organisational structure demonstrate how unrealistic it is to distinguish between work designs on the one hand and organisational design on the other as these are inevitably linked (Procter and Mueller, 2000). Mintzberg (1989), another well known organisational theorist, identified five key dimensions which were seen to inform the type of organisational structure required as follows:

1. **Degree of job specialisation**, including horizontal and vertical division of responsibilities and accountability. These would be relevant to generic and specialist functions in an organisation and determine whether the management control was flat or very hierarchical.

2. **Criteria by which jobs are grouped together** and the links between these different roles.

3. **The degree of formalisation of rules and regulations** and to what extent these are written down, for example through policies and procedures or customs and practice.

4. **Types of integrative mechanisms and lateral linkages**, meaning the way managers and specialist work together, the presence of project teams and collaborative, liaison arrangements between them.

5. **The extent of centralisation of the decision-making structure** and how far decision-making can be delegated down to those directly delivering the service.

Classical and scientific theories of organisations and management structure

Having considered what organisations might look like, we now turn to theories about how they might function and what makes them tick. Classical theorists have had an enduring and worldwide impact on organisational thought and management practice. The term scientific management theory (SMT) was coined by F.W. Taylor at the turn of the 20th century (1911). Taylor described management techniques for bringing greater discipline into manufacturing, clerical and professional work and it has been strongly argued that scientific management is having a wider and more pervasive impact on society today than it did back in Taylor's time (Pinnock, 2004). SMT likened organisations to machines where employees are merely cogs in a process carrying out single specialist tasks. In this paradigm, the organisation is concerned with continuous processing and mass production. It has a top-down approach to planning, monitoring and controlling the work of others in its span of control. You may think that this is rather an old-fashioned idea as it presents organisations as rigid and predictable but some academics have compared this with current approaches to delivering aspects of social care. The care management process, for example, and performance management systems have been identified as systems which emphasise efficiency in the style of SMT, relying mainly on numerical objective measurement (Coulshed and Mullender, 2001; Munroe, 2004b). Likewise, systematic approaches to formal purchasing and provision of social care where each care plan is broken down into clear mechanistic tasks to meet service users' needs can also reflect an SMT approach (Powell and Hewitt, 2002; Malin et al., 2002).

Taylor's method gave no scope for imagination or creativity and was based on his five principles of management:

1. Clear division of tasks and responsibilities between management and workers.

2. Use of scientific methods to determine the best way of doing a job.

3. Scientific selection of the person to do the newly designed job.

4. The training of the selected worker to perform the job in the way specified.

5. Surveillance of workers through the use of hierarchies of authorities and close supervision.

(cited in Buchanan and Huczynski, 2004, p. 429)

Taylor did, however, emphasise that relationships between managers and workers should be co-operative rather than adversarial and encouraged them to work together productively for mutual benefit.

ACTIVITY *1.2*

Can you think of any examples of the scientific approach in an organisation you are familiar with? How relevant is it today? What might be the advantages and disadvantages to this approach to social care and organisations where social work is practised?

You may have identified that the scientific approach doesn't take into account the motivation of employees, their personal aspirations, achievements or need for job satisfaction. It tends to neglect their psychological needs, individual potential and capabilities, as well as the need for interpersonal relationships at work. Taylorism has been criticised for its simplicity and assumptions about human motivation, neglecting the subjective side of work as well as ignoring the impact of work groups.

Further analysis of Taylor's work by Braverman (1974) looked at the 'deskilling' issues arising from such an approach, highlighting the way in which it encourages fragmentation, rationalisation, mechanisation and institutionalisation of work. Organisations with this type of management approach would be less likely to exercise any discretion. Creativity or innovation is stifled and subverted to the overall aims of efficiency, predictability and control. Braverman's ideas were later taken up to some extent by Marxists and trade unions concerned with employee exploitation. In contrast, organisations taking an 'upskilling' position place more importance on employees than on physical assets and profits. This approach promotes investment in the workforce through the provision of education and training to help workers cope with greater complexity of work tasks and hence greater productivity.

Humanistic and motivation theories
The human relations school which emerged in the post-war period specifically addressed the failure of management to consider social relations, social order and collaboration

7

needed to sustain individuals' psycho-social needs at work. People like Mayo (1945), Barnard (1938) and Mary Parker Follet (1868–1933) believed that organisational authority depended on its individual members having co-operative attitudes. They stressed the need for more informal relationships to help the formal and informal systems within organisations merge and to develop effective communication systems (Clegg et al., 2005). Leadership and democracy in organisations were seen as essential ingredients to efficient and effective business and are reflected today in concepts such as the 'learning organisation' (SCIE, 2004). Similarly, theorists such as Maslow (1954) and McGregor (1960) developed theories about motivation and the importance of recognising motivational factors which underline the way in which employees relate to the vision, values and goals of the organisations they work in. Table 1.1 shows a summary of McGregor's X and Y Theory. McGregor believed that managers who believe in Theory X are more likely to be remote from their staff and tend to meet with them only to give instructions or reprimand. Theory X managers believe that staff respond to a carrot-and-stick approach. In contrast, managers who believe in Theory Y are more likely to consult and collaborate with staff and are more active in giving and receiving feedback. Theory Y managers believe that staff are intrinsically motivated to do their best at all times.

Table 1.1 McGregor's X and Y Theory of Motivation (1960)

Theory X	Theory Y
• The average person inherently dislikes working • People must be constantly directed and driven • People are unambitious and uninterested in work achievements • Money is the main motivation to work • Most people are dull and uncreative and require leaders to take key decision	• Work is as natural as rest and other activities to people • People enjoy being given responsibility and can be self-directive • Anyone can be imaginative and creative if they are encouraged • Money is only one benefit of work and people are driven to improve their quality of life • Managers are there to facilitate and collaborate with staff

Source: McGregor, D (1960) *The human side of enterprise*. NY: McGraw-Hill. Reproduced with permission of the McGraw-Hill Companies

Theories of employee motivation are often used to develop tools for managers to encourage best performance by promoting autonomy at both the individual, team and service level. We will explore this idea throughout this book when we look at how we interact with performance and regulatory frameworks for social care (Chapter 3), the management of diversity and equalities in the workplace (Chapter 6) and the concept of dignity at work (Chapter 7). In conclusion, humanistic theories as opposed to scientific theories demonstrated and emphasised the major impact of social factors on work behaviour: in particular, the motivation of people working within the organisation and the need for team co-operation. They established the relationships between job satisfaction, group morale and the actual 'output' or quality and quantity of the work done related to the influence of particular management styles and structures.

ACTIVITY *1.3*

How do you think these ideas relate to organisations in social care? Think of some of the roles that people play in providing care, for example within residential care for older people. What are the key issues for managers and employers in motivating and developing their staff? How do you think this impacts on the experiences of service users?

Systems theory

We will conclude this section by considering systems theory as a way of describing organisations, based on the ideas of Lewin (1951) and the Tavistock Institute of Human Relations. It is an organic model, integral to which organisations can only exist through transactions across its boundary. Each organisation is a complete system in itself, comprising sub-systems which interact with each other and the external environment, tending towards an internal equilibrium.

The boundary of the organisation or system may be permeable or closed. The boundary separates inside systems from outside, across which the organisation exchanges with its environment. Inputs are fed into the system and these could comprise a profile of community needs, legislation and government policy and service plans. These inputs are then assessed, processed and transformed into outputs which could take the form of different information or services provided back into the community. The activities required to perform the task of converting the inputs into outputs are provided by constant interaction with the organisation's sub-systems, examples of which might be human resource management, inter-agency work and finance systems. In complex organisations, there will be a number of open systems operating simultaneously, each performing its own specialised function. Organisations providing human services often have multiple tasks or conflicting and competing sub-systems. How to allocate resources and prioritise different activities is determined by the primary task, which must be clarified and performed if the organisation is to survive (Zagier-Roberts, 1994, p. 29). The role of managers in the systems approach is to manage the sub-systems, the boundary and the interface of the larger total system with the outer world. Accurate analysis of the primary task can highlight discrepancies between what an organisation says it sets out to do and what is actually happening and helps to redefine its enterprise as a whole.

Critiques of systems approaches

Systems approaches do not prescribe any particular organisational design and are criticised for being politically neutral, functionalist and normative, taking little or no account of the interplay of power dynamics within the organisations (Coulshed and Mullender, 2001). As we will see in the next section, when we take an overview of the historical development of social care organisations, these factors are inevitable in the way social care organisations are influenced by the wider agenda as well as the way in which they influence organisational culture. Before we do this, we will turn to the third element in understanding organisations by looking at the phenomenon of organisational culture.

Organisational culture

ACTIVITY *1.4*

Trying to identify or define organisational culture is not easy. What sort of things do you think constitute culture in an organisation and how might it show itself?

Schein (1997) defines culture as the deep, basic assumptions and beliefs that are shared by members of an organisation which are often hidden and unconscious and represent the way in which an organisation perceives itself and its environment. Put simply, culture is learned, shared and transmitted. It is a combination of assumptions, values, symbols, language and behaviours that manifest the organisation's norms and values. Objective aspects are tangible, such as rituals, leaders and stories about the organisation. Subjective aspects are related to assumptions, shared beliefs, values, meanings and understandings of 'how things are done around here'. In social care organisations, culture is particularly shaped by the structure, management and leadership functions especially in relation to decision-making. It is contingent on relationships between service users, staff and managers, which in turn interact with a wide range of dynamic factors such as professional status, class, ethnicity, gender, sexuality and so on.

There may be several sub-cultures flourishing within an organisation. The cultural network is the primary informal means of communication. Lysons (1997) likened this network to an iceberg: what you see above the surface is the formal organisation, consisting of structure, spans of control, rules and procedures and job descriptions. However, below the surface lies the informal and invisible organisation made up of grapevines, informal leaders, group norms and sentiments, emotional feelings, needs and relationships. These ideas will be developed further in Chapter 2 when we explore how management and leadership shape organisational culture. A sound philosophy, vision and management and leadership styles that model values and create a system where staff feel valued and rewarded are important to creating a healthy organisational culture.

The role of emotions in organisations

Before moving on to look at a brief history of the evolution of organisations themselves, it is worth dwelling on some of the latter ideas around the relationships between structure and culture that I have outlined above. Menzies-Lyth, a psychoanalyst and social scientist (1917–2008), conducted action research within a number of organisations in which she applied ideas from her discipline in order to change the culture of institutions. Her research into hospital settings (Menzies-Lyth, 1988) for example, identified a number of institutional defence mechanisms that enabled members and the management team to contain anxiety arising naturally from the distressing daily work that people undertook. These defence mechanisms included the adoption of ritual task performance, the use of depersonalised language to describe patients and service users to emphasise their difference and a sense of professional detachment and denial of feelings inevitable in the work they did. Similarly, managers were found to respond in a highly critical and repressive way using tactics to remove decision-making from frontline staff and through reduced responsibility and constant checking of practice. Menzies-Lyth concluded that the needs of an organisation's member for social and psychological satisfaction and their need for support in dealing with anxiety were an underestimated influencing force coupled with the role of task and technology which is often overexaggerated. Menzies-Lyth (1988) concluded that while structure and primary tasks within organisations provide an essential framework for functioning well, within those limits, culture structure and mode of functioning are also strongly determined by the psychological needs of the members of an organisation. These themes are very much contemporary in today's organisational environment. Cooper (2004), for example, has examined the nature of the link between organisational structures as a result of policy change and the nature of practice that goes on within them. In his examination of the report on the circumstances of the death of Victoria Climbié, Cooper highlights what he calls the 'surface and depth' of its findings and identifies the links between the 'extensive' concern of policymakers and the actual conditions that affect practice (the 'intensive' concerns of practitioners in their direct dealings with service users). Any prevailing organisational culture that emphasises structure, procedures and protocols thus prevents a more searching inquiry into the fundamental failures in safeguarding work and the adoption of surface instruments that focus on bureaucratic instead of human factors (Cooper, 2004). Thus both commentators emphasise the importance of relationships within organisations that are rewarding and participatory. Both point to the importance of analysis of policy change and enquiry that engages staff and their managers in the development of useful and realistic systems and structures.

> *Every organisation is an emotional place because it is a human invention, serves human purposes and is dependent on human beings to function . . . Emotion is what creates and sustains a system in its current form. Individuals and groups continually organise themselves both on the basis of their emotional responses to organisational issues, and on the basis of avoiding emotion.*

> (Reynolds and Vince, 2004, p. 447, cited by Morrison, 2007, p. 256)

A brief history of the evolution of social care organisations

The previous section has demonstrated that no one model or theory is adequate to understand social care organisations. As key providers of welfare services, social care organisations have been subjected to differing forces and directions of change since the post-war period (1940s onwards). This brings into question how far the boundaries of contemporary and modern organisations in the 21st century will be reformed, modernised or replaced (Clarke, 2004, p. 106). To explore this further we will now briefly examine the historical sequence in which the need to develop more flexible, quality-orientated and responsive organisations has taken place. These have been in response to a constantly changing social, economic and political environment which has largely displaced large-scale social services hierarchies and bureaucracies. The extent of policy changes across health, education, social services and housing, for example, has shifted the balance towards far greater integration of traditional organisations as we know them. The development of **care trusts** and emphasis on partnerships and planning between statutory, third and private sectors have directed organisations towards a greater focus on autonomy and independence of service users within a social inclusion framework (DoH, 2000a). Government policy has identified the potential to empower a wider range of people with support needs through increased community involvement to develop approaches to care in which people themselves become genuinely part of their own caring communities (Means et al., 2003). This philosophy fits with the strategy for regeneration, neighbourhood renewal and social inclusion. How social work practitioners move away from bureaucratic processing of service users and their communities towards putting service users first will be also be dependent on the structure and culture of the organisations they work in (Means et al., 2003, p. 221). Tensions have arisen where these ideals conflict with the increased demand for service at a time when economic pressures have forced a reduction in expenditure, forcing social workers to balance needs and resources and towards more defensive practice (Lymbery, 2004).

The post-war welfare state

Prior to the creation of the British welfare state after the Second World War, the main means by which vulnerable groups in society or those without means could survive was via the public workhouse and public assistance institutions created through the Poor Law 1930 and charities. The subsequent establishment of the NHS in 1946 and the Health and Welfare Committees who provided residential accommodation under the National Assistance Act 1948 by local authorities (LAs) led to a complex patchwork of provision which was not easily available and unevenly developed (Means et al., 2003).

The implementation of the 1970 Local Authority Act led to unified social services departments (SSDs) which developed client group hierarchies, mainly children's and elderly people's departments, with emphasis on residential provision and limited community-based services as described in the National Assistance Act 1948, the Chronically Sick and Disabled Persons Act 1970 and some voluntary and private sector residential provision. Large institutions for the mentally ill and people with learning disabilities were designated as hospitals under the new NHS. Whilst LAs had some responsibilities, there was minimal expenditure on any prevention and after-care of patients. The implementation of the Mental Health Act 1959 helped to develop a complex infrastructure of LA-provided services such as hostels, day care, social work support and sheltered employment. According to Oliver (1990), this production process of employment meant disabled people in particular came to be regarded as a social and educational problem and became more segregated in institutions of all kinds.

Seebohm and the Local Authority Social Services Act 1970

The initial tasks of social services departments introduced via the LASS Act 1970 was to draw together a variety of disparate functions previously carried out by the children's department, the welfare department and mental welfare services to meet the needs of different client groups. The *Seebohm Report* (1968) emphasised how public sector services were organised and delivered by clarifying responsibilities and accountabilities and contributed to the growing institutionalisation and the bureaucratic nature of social services in particular (Bamford, 2001, pp. 3–4). This process confirmed the ascendancy of the traditional statutory SSD and the growth of welfare services as large bureaucratic structures. This was also a period of optimism in social care with the influence of the radical social work agenda leading to the development of a diverse range of organisations to respond to grassroots needs in the community.

The introduction of community care and the market economy

Two concerns, financial and organisational, informed the changes brought about by the NHS and Community Care Act 1990 (NHSCCA). Firstly, criticism of welfare professionals and concern about rising costs of care and, secondly, concerns about the 'disciplinary' state and recognition of the importance of the service users' voice in shaping services from disabled people's organisations and survivors of psychiatric care (Beresford et al., 1999). The user movement challenged ideas on dependency and advocated change and the right to citizenship. Simultaneously, the Conservative government's concern to control growing public expenditure on health and social care, especially in residential care where expenditure grew six-fold between 1978 and 84, meant that they took a critical view of waste and inappropriate targeting of resources identified in various reports (Audit Commission, 1986; Griffiths Report, 1988). Organisational bureaucracies were seen as inefficient, inflexible and unresponsive to consumers (Clarke and Newman, 1997). The idea that market efficacy rather than collective planning was the best way of ensuring efficiency, accountability and choice in health and social services was at the heart of government policy objectives. To achieve this the 1990 NHSCCA separated **purchasing** and **providing** functions in the NHS and SSDs and defined the role of SSDs as 'enabling' authorities, as purchasers and contractors, and worked to secure delivery of services away from their traditional role of direct provision. Major structural changes to SSDs took place with the development of care management, **commissioning** and purchasing functions. LAs were now responsible for preparing community care plans for the locality, assessing individual needs and arranging packages of care. The principles of market competition likewise affected traditional voluntary sector organisations (since known as the independent sector, together with the private sector), and radically altered traditional relationships of statutory services with them. The voluntary sector has to some extent had to compete to provide services and equip their organisations with the skills to do so whilst reducing their campaigning role, which can weaken its position as an external impartial critic (Jones and Novak, 1999).

In an attempt to address some of these inequities, in May 2006, the government set up the Office of the Third Sector (OTS), which incorporated the responsibilities of the Active Communities Directorate in the Home Office, and the Social Enterprise Unit in the Department for Trade and Industry (DTI). This decision was taken in recognition of the increasingly important role the third sector plays in both society and the economy. The third sector comprises organisations that share common characteristics such as being non-governmental, value-driven and who principally reinvest their surpluses to further social environmental or cultural objectives. The sector encompasses voluntary and community organisations, charities, social enterprises, co-operatives and mutuals both large and small. Some of the issues relating to this mixed economy of care will be explored in more detail in Chapter 5 when looking at resource management.

Managerialism

The drive to externalise services to the private sector were seen as offering better services for the same or reduced costs. Application of businesslike approaches to welfare provision raised issues about the quality of care and safeguards where partners from the private sector were principally concerned with profit making. The new commissioning role of social services was described as a strategic activity of assessing needs, resources and current services and developing a strategy of how to make best use of available resources to meet needs (DoH, 1995a).

Social care organisations have also been affected by political perspectives on public service management. Through the application of market principles including outright privatisation, management techniques from the private sector were also introduced to support the development of market mechanisms within public services. The roots of **managerialism** emerging through the 1980s represented a view that the public sector should be more businesslike, led by the belief that efficiency, value for money and getting more from less could also be delivered by stressing the customer or consumerist orientation, a strong hierarchy and performance management. There has been great criticism made of managerialism as a set of beliefs and practices that assume better management will resolve a wide range of economic and social problems and reflect the dominance of market capitalism in the world (Dominelli, 2002). Tsui and Cheung (2004) have identified the following principles as underlying the ideology of managerialism:

- The client is a customer (not service consumer) and encouraged to define the quality of service provided.

- The manager is the most important person in the organisation and efficiency and effectiveness is all important.

- Knowledge and expertise in management are dominant and supersede expertise in specialist areas or professional practice and professional staff are likewise expected to undertake managerial tasks within the organisation.

- The quality of service and performance in human service organisations can be improved through the use of managerial skills.

- Elements of the market economy determine decision-making over the overall organisational or community interests.

- Quality is greatly emphasised and equated with standards and systems to measure efficiency rather than effectiveness.

(Tsui and Cheung, 2004)

ACTIVITY 1.5

What do you think are the main advantages or disadvantages of applying business principles to the delivery of social care? What are the implications for managers, staff and service users?

There is no simple answer to this question; however, the introduction of business principles into social work practice warrants serious discussion to ensure that the relationship between marketisation and improvement in quality and costs of services is not just assumed. We will unpick some of these assumptions in detail in later chapters. Features of the market economy include an emphasis on using output measures to allocate funding and an increased emphasis on evaluation of the performance of services and individuals. The implications for managers are that they have the specialist technical knowledge and skills to achieve this such as accounting, managing complex financial arrangements and detailed knowledge of the market in social care. Demands in this area can conflict with managers' role in promoting social justice and equity in provision of care and the need to develop collaborative relationships as well as competitive ones. This potentially creates conditions where managerialism can flourish. Staff also need to be conversant with these approaches whilst striving to achieve outcomes for service users consistent with the value base of social work. However, knowledge of the complexities of service users' needs can be a vital asset in decision-making and resource allocation. For service users, there are advantages in relation to increased choice and quality of services, but there also needs to be a pragmatic recognition of the limited capacity of service organisations to meet their individual and community needs and more participatory approaches to delivering care.

The independent (third) sector

One of the impacts of applying the contract culture to social care can be seen in repercussions for the voluntary sector. The rules about how LAs could purchase services using the community care grant had the deliberate effect of stimulating the private, for-profit sector. Voluntary organisations previously offered services funded by a combination of annual support grants and local fund-raising activities. Locally based voluntary sector organisations had traditionally been seen as part of the network of active citizenship underpinning statutory provision. These groups saw the changes brought about by the 1990 NHSCCA and subsequent reforms as a compromise to their independence signifying a retreat by the state from its responsibility for direct provision. Two significant models of provision subsequently developed in the late 1990s by larger voluntary sector organisations: the development of arm's-length trusts to manage residential care and development of care services by housing associations (Bamford, 2001). For smaller providers, however, the increasing burden of registration requirements, pressure of costs and the mechanism by which services are purchased have led to the need for more political sensitivity by LAs to ensure that grassroot organisations unable to compete in the open market can survive. Critics of the reforms in the late 1980s and 1990s have highlighted how greater use of voluntary agencies to deliver services at zero or subsidised costs have been required by the state through the new 'contract culture' (Badham and Eadie, 2004). Feminists criticised the development of informal welfare which relies on family, carers and reinforced sexual divisions of labour (Dominelli, 1997; Foster, 2004). On a larger scale, subsequent partnerships with the voluntary sector through local government social inclusion units and 'new deal for communities' has enabled the development of mutualism, **communitarianism**, **civil society** and **social capital** (Blair, 1998, cited in Powell and Hewitt, 2002).

As stated earlier, in 2006, the government established the OTS and following the White Paper *Strong and prosperous communities* (HM Govt, 2007a) set out its expectations that the sector should be a key partner within local government in creating stronger and more prosperous communities. The government is attempting to recognise the value of the diversity of organisations in the third sector as a means of providing a voice for under-represented groups, in campaigning for change and in promoting enterprising solutions to social and environmental challenges and in transforming the design and delivery of public services. However, some evidence has identified that while there is already a high level of interaction between public-sector commissioners and third-sector providers, within the market economy, there remain fairly low levels of tendering activity among TSOs as they continue to experience lack of resources in order to engage in this activity (Iff Research Ltd, 2007).

Modernising social services – collaborative approaches to social care

In 1997 the incoming 'New Labour' government had a mandate for a programme of social and economic reconstruction connected to the ideas of user choice, equality, citizenship and empowerment which were part of progressive social work discourses in the 1990s (Davis and Garrett, 2004, p. 22). At the same time, there was a continuing privatisation of welfare and promotion of managerialism in social work organisations. The welfare state was required to transform from its provision of passive support to one that is more active in supporting people to promote independence (Blair, 2000). To deliver this agenda, a range of initiatives was designed to address inequality, poverty and social exclusion. The modernisation agenda (DoH, 1998a) effected significant change on the social care landscape with particular emphasis on the benefits of inter-professional arrangements, such as

---

RESEARCH SUMMARY

Between 1996 and 2003, every council in England (except two) had a **Joint Review** of its social services. Controversially, no link was found between how much a council spends on social care and how good its services are. The quality of leadership and management were said to be the key factors driving improvement and where councils adopted a modern businesslike approach. The Audit Commission (2004a) in its document *Old virtues, new virtues* summarised the changes achieved during this period (1996–2003), as is set out in Table 1.2 below.

Table 1.2: How are organisations changing?

Old Style	New Style
Traditional social services departments	A variety of structural arrangements that seek to integrate social care functions across the council
Patchy, corporate and political interest in social care	A higher corporate profile for social care
Professional leadership	Managerially driven: strategic direction and business planning
Passive and paternalistic approach to users	Enabling and empowering
Council main provider	Council as commissioner
Annual budget planning. Finances monitored and controlled centrally. Value-for-money focus	Longer-term financial perpective. Delegated authority. Best Value approach
Little information on costs and activity	Robust performance management
Aim for good relationships with partners	Strategic joint commissioning and integrated structures
Single profession	Major workforce pressures but more skill-mix and integrated teams

Source: © Audit Commission *Old Virtues, New Virtues*, March 2004, p 33

---

in the creation of youth offending teams and proposals to create unified care trusts to further integrate health and social services (Lymbery, 2004, p. 44). According to Lymbery (2004) this has led to a significant reorientation within social work whereby social workers can no longer assume that they will be working in a unique and supportive environment which solely supports social work practice. Social workers began to be employed in different organisational frameworks such as care trusts for mental health and learning disabilities and other joint service initiatives aimed at achieving holistic delivery of services. At the same time, it has been argued that the pressures of organising and funding statutory services reduced the variety and diversity of services and that the morale of social workers within SSDs became observably poor (Jones, 2001).

Whole-systems approach to service delivery in social care

Public sector reform in the decade from 2005 looks set to connect services more directly to people and shape them around their personal needs. Long-term transformation of social care services and its partners is evidenced in the policy and legislation for children's and adults' services, both of which have 10–15 year implementation programmes. These transformations were initially spelt out in the following documents: *Every Child Matters* (DoH, 2004a), The Children Act 2004, *Independence, Wellbeing and Choice* (DoH, 2005a), the Mental Health Bill 2005 and *Youth Matters* (DfES, 2005). These documents provide a parallel focus in political, structural and managerial terms. Firstly, in local government, the appointment of directors of children's services responsible for co-ordinating and managing the provision of local children's services across education, health and social services to ensure a co-ordinated approach to meeting the needs of all children and young people. This has built on the many initiatives already in place such as Sure Start, Connexions, Head Start and is characterised by a tight and ambitious implementation timetable over 10 years. Secondly, the adult services Green Paper and the subsequent White Paper, *Our health, our care, our say*, proposed changes for adults with social care needs and their communities by making social care more responsive to the needs and expectations of service users, their families, carers and the wider communities (DoH, 2005a, p. 7; DoH, 2006). These papers were used to stimulate debate and encourage stakeholders to engage in a process that transforms the way social care is viewed. Social care has increasingly been delivered by a range of providers, many of which now lie outside the direct line-management structure of social services and have amended the statutory function of the director of social services as defined in the LA SS Act 1970. These structural changes in social care and the need to influence a range of service providers beyond the immediate scope of SSDs is necessary to deliver the vision for the future for both children and adult services. Joint appointments of directors with other organisations such as primary care trusts have promoted strategic responsibilities for the planning, commissioning and delivery of social services for all adult client groups.

According to Hudson (2005), reform of organisational strategies and structures in social care uncritically endorses the concepts of 'choice' and 'autonomy', which sits uncomfortably with parallel concerns about ensuring cost-effectiveness. Implementation strategies to make these ideas a reality have to ensure that the identified outcomes are underpinned by the means for which a coherent joint approach is required. This starts with inter-agency **governance** at a national level, moves down through integrated strategy and process to the front line where delivery of services takes place through social care, education and health specialists.

Summary of the government's key outcomes for children and adult services in the next 10–15 years

Outcomes of *Every Child Matters: Change for Children* (DoH, 2004a)

- Being healthy

- Staying safe

- Enjoying and achieving

- Making a positive contribution

- Achieving economic well-being.

White Paper, *Our health, our care, our say: A new direction for community services*:

- Improving health and emotional well-being

- Improving quality of life

- Making a positive contribution

- Increasing choice and control

- Freedom from discrimination and harassment

- Achieving economic well-being

- Maintaining dignity and respect.

Personalisation of care services

Since the above reforms, and the Comprehensive Spending Review in 2007, the government has gone even further in order to respond to the demographic challenges presented by both an ageing society and the rising expectations of those depending on social work and social care for their capacity to lead more full and purposeful lives. This has included the need to explore options for the long term funding of the care and support system, to ensure that it is fair, sustainable and unambiguous about the respective responsibilities of the state, family and individual (HM Govt, 2008). *Putting people first* (DoH, 2007b) and the *Children's plan* (DfES, 2007) stress the need to get away from standard 'one-size-fits-all' provision and to personalise services in a way that it can respond to the circumstances, strengths and aspirations for particular children, adults and families (GSCC, 2008). Both require joint strategic needs assessment by the relevant statutory bodies which actively engages other stakeholders in a local area agreement and that supports social enterprise and sustainable community development. This is a challenging agenda, which cannot be delivered by social care alone, and to achieve this sort of transformation involves working across boundaries in social care such as housing, benefits, leisure and transport and health. In organisational terms, every area is expected to create forums, networks and task groups to involve staff across the sectors and service users and carers as active participants in the change process, particularly in the design stage. Working across the sector with partners from independent, voluntary and community organisations should ensure a strategic balance of investment in local services. These range from support to those with emerging needs, to enabling people to maintain their independence. Supporting those with high-level complex needs, involves looking at resources spent through mainstream services as well as those spent via social care budgets (DoH, 2008b). Within children's services a new Department for Children, Schools and Families has been established with ambitious goals for 2020. This has meant new leadership roles for children's trusts in every area and a central role for schools at the centre of communities. These radical changes have many implications for where social work situates itself. The roles and tasks that social work needs to develop in the twenty-first century, involves helping people achieve joined-up solutions by responding to demands for more personalised solutions (such as the provision of individualised budgets) and to be flexible and adaptable to people's changing situations. It has huge implications for the development of the future workforce and the capacity to empower people who use services.

The developments within the personalisation agenda are not without controversy, as some critics such as Ferguson (2007) have argued. Ferguson argues that its popularity is congruent with key government themes of individualising social problems and increasing personal responsibility and the transfer of risk from the state to the individual. He highlights the potential for social workers and the organisations in which they practise to neglect further structural issues affecting communities such as poverty and inequality. Therefore, the philosophy of personalisation should not be accepted uncritically in the reality of how care services will be delivered. That the present organisational arrangements for social work in the UK will continue to change and alter is clear. Increased levels of formal multi-disciplinary working where social workers operate alongside other professionals, offer opportunities for social work to consolidate its position in a more integrated environment. On the other hand, the continued drive to separate assessment of need from provision of services may have an overall impact in fragmenting the pattern of service delivery requiring social work to redefine its core roles and tasks so that it is able to survive in different organisational locations (Davis and Garrett, 2004). As we saw from our earlier examination of the relationship between structure and culture, the effort required to merge structures can actually distract from a focus on the user and equal attention to organisational culture is needed to secure overall improvements. These are things over which you may feel you have limited influence but understanding organisational culture is the key to understanding the dynamics of workplace stress (Thompson et al., 1996). Needless to say that social work is an evolving profession, and its contribution to the environment in which it works will be constantly affected by new policies, the need to expand its knowledge base and rising public expectations about the role it plays.

ACTIVITY *1.6*

What do you think are the implications of personalisation for social work practice. How can the profession respond?

CHAPTER SUMMARY

The future of social care organisations

The transformation of social care organisation looks set to continue into the future. On the one hand, continuing a theme already laid down by the Labour government to reduce the top-down 'command and control' model of policy management and ending the monolithic, one-size-fits-all approach to services in favour of devolved power and greater autonomy to innovate at local level (Henwood, 2005). On the other hand, emphasising the rights of consumers and putting powers in the hands of the patient, the parent and the citizen (Labour Party Manifesto, 2005, p. 8). Mapping these objectives is complex and involves other government departments and reference to wider policy objectives which cut across issues and departmental boundaries. This means achieving a coherent agenda across children's services and adult social care at the interface with communities and neighbourhoods which will no doubt lead to wholesale radical restructuring of social care organisations.

Social workers operate in a complex and fluid legislative and policy environment with ongoing legislative and policy developments across the spectrum of social care services. As we saw at the beginning of this chapter, social work has tended to operate a hierarchical line-management structure influenced by the LA context in which the majority of services have been commissioned or delivered. New management and leadership approaches will be needed that are not wholly tied to the line-management relationship but which provide professional support and supervision and support staff development within a framework of sound governance. Structures that make it easier for social workers and staff to move between the voluntary and statutory sector would also promote skill development and those entering management.

This chapter has aimed to give you some fundamental knowledge to help you understand the relevance of organisations' structure, strategy and culture. When working effectively, the organisational context is an important resource for support and authorisation for decisions made. Your understanding of how an organisation functions in the community it serves, including the political dilemmas it faces, the tasks it performs, the relevant policies, procedures, how to access information and support, will help you to be more critically aware of issues within it. These will be explored in more detail in the relevant topics in this book.

FURTHER READING

For a fuller account of the social, political and organisational contexts of practice **Lymbery, M and Butler, S** (2004) *Social work ideals and practice realities*. Basingstoke: Palgrave Macmillan, looks specifically at conflicts and demands on social work practice in a realistic and optimistic way.

Jordan, B with Jordan, C (2001) *Social work and the third way: tough love as social policy*. London: Sage, for a lively debate and analysis of the relationships between New Labour's programme and the implications for social work practice.

WEBSITES

www.dfes.gov.uk

The children's plan, building brighter futures (2007)

This plan sets out the government's strategic objectives and agenda for children, their families and communities for the next ten years http://www.dfes.gov.uk/publications/childrensplan/downloads/The_Childrens_Plan.pdf

www.dh.gov.uk

Putting people first: A shared vision and commitment to the transformation of adult social care (2007)

This spells out the government's protocol for improving adult care and its strategic objectives up until 2011.

Chapter 2

Management, leadership and change management in social care

A C H I E V I N G   A   S O C I A L   W O R K   D E G R E E

This chapter will help you achieve the following National Occupational Standards and General Social Care Council's Code of Practice.

Key Role 3: Support individuals to represent their needs, views and circumstances.
- Enable individuals, families, carers, groups and communities to be involved in decision-making forums.
- Present evidence to, and help individuals, families, carers, groups and communities to understand the procedures in and the outcomes from decision-making forums.

Key Role 5: Manage and be accountable, with supervision and support for your own social work practice within your organisation.
- Develop and maintain effective working relationships.
- Contribute to identifying and agreeing the goals, objectives and lifespan of the team network or system.

General Social Care Code of Practice
Code 3.4: Bringing to the attention of your employer or the appropriate authority resource or operational difficulties that might get in the way of the delivery of safe care.
Code 6.3: Informing your employer or the appropriate authority about any personal difficulties that might affect your ability to do your job competently and safely.
Code 6.7: Recognising and respecting the roles and expertise of workers from other agencies and working in partnership with them.

It will also introduce you to the following academic standards as set out in the social work subject benchmark statements:

2.1.2 The service delivery context
- The contribution of different approaches to management, leadership and quality in public and independent human services.

3.1.3 Values and ethics
- Aspects of philosophical ethics relevant to the understanding and resolution of value dilemmas and conflicts in both inter-personal and professional contexts.
- The conceptual links between codes defining ethical practice, the regulation of professional conduct and the management of potential conflicts generated by the codes held by different professional groups.

3.1.4 Social work theory
- Social science theories explaining group and organisational behaviour, adaptation and change.

3.2.2.1 Managing problem-solving activities
- Manage the processes of change.

Introduction

This chapter will introduce theories of management and leadership and their relevance to social care. Within the turbulent and constantly changing environments of public sector services (as outlined in Chapter 1) and the evolving knowledge and evidence base of social work, it is unsurprising that the meaning and parameters of management are also changing. Increasingly, there is less distinction between what are considered to be managerial tasks and work of other staff groups. This distinction has become blurred by the effects of technology, de-layering and decentralisation of problem-solving and decision-making in social care organisations or other organisations in which social care services are delivered (Harrison, 2005). Frontline staff have become more involved in team management tasks, whilst managers occupying middle management positions find themselves increasingly involved in business functions and the strategic process. Therefore it will be helpful for you to understand, identify and appreciate these different roles.

'Leadership' is a term that we tend to equate with positions of power, influence and status. However, acts of leadership can be observed at all levels of the organisational structure. In flatter structures and team-based work, in virtual and networked organisations, traditional leadership positions based on hierarchy are less dominant. In understanding the qualities that leadership embodies, this chapter will help you to consider your capacity to develop your own professional leadership skills and to become an effective organisational operator (Thompson, 2003, p. 198). Thompson defines an effective **organisational operator** as someone with the knowledge and skills required to work effectively within an organisation in order to maximise opportunities for promoting equality. Achieving confidence in this area should also help you to manage any tensions you may experience between promoting social justice principles that guide social work professionals and the effects of managerialism. It will certainly help prepare you for your own future role in management, if so desired.

We will revisit the concept of managerialism and explore how this might impact on social work practice. We will identify potential strategies to help promote your assertiveness, personal and professional boundaries which may become compromised in the changing nature of social care environments. Towards the end of this chapter we will examine the effects of organisational change on professionals and service users and how power relationships and 'authority' in organisations can affect social workers' realm of influence over decision-making. The negative effects of managerialism can lead to avoidance by some organisations in addressing ethical issues or to breaches of the GSCC codes of practice through increasing use of formal procedures to overshadow compassionate, ethical and professional practice (Lonne et al., 2004). Research substantiates that ethical dilemmas are emerging as a major factor emanating from the reconstruction of the welfare state (Banks, 2001; Lonne et al., 2004; Charles and Butler, 2004). Your practice therefore needs to be proactive, in seeking out and advancing your own knowledge and professional ethical practice in the workplace by investigating and developing support networks within an equalities framework. Understanding change management theory and the process of change can help with this and this will be the last topic in this chapter. There we will identify the key elements and roles that different people in organisations play to make change management a successful process.

What is management?

Management is essentially a practical activity. All managers use a range of skills that cannot easily be categorised yet need to be integrated into their practice. This integrative task involves achieving synergy, balance and perspective (Harrison, 2005). Most management activity is undertaken through complex webs of social and political interaction involving a continuous process of adaptation to changing pressures and opportunities.

Management has to operate across many internal and external boundaries to fulfil the government's emphasis on partnerships, strategic commissioning and the demands of the market economy in care services. This means knowing who they need to collaborate with and how to achieve the vision of the organisation. According to Kearney (2004, p. 103), managers are also the mediators of standards and quality of social work practice. Managing practice involves combining available knowledge of external standards, statutory requirements and organisational procedures with internal knowledge and skill of how these operate. These knowledge and skills provide integrated support to individual and collective good practice to social work teams. First line managers are particularly important as we depend on them to manage services, interpret thresholds, juggle resources and deliver policies, not to mention the essential people-management aspects. Managing practice in social care has much in common with other professionals such as head teachers and locality nurse managers who hold similar responsibilities. However good organisations are at strategic planning, strategies can only be delivered through informed and committed first line managers. This has been recognised by the development of management and leadership standards in social care (Skills for Care, 2004) and the national training strategy for managers embedded in the National Vocational Qualification (NVQ) and Post Qualifying (PQ) Awards framework for social work (www.skillsforcare.org.uk, www.gscc.org.uk). Managers also need to know how to manage themselves. This begins in professional training with the social work degree through developing and consolidating reflective practice and professional ethical awareness not only at an individual level but at an organisational level.

ACTIVITY 2.1

What do you think are the main roles and responsibilities of managers in social work and what skills and knowledge are needed to manage people effectively?

Many researchers have attempted to define the key elements of management; Hales (1993) and Mintzberg (1989) undertook extensive studies of management work in a range of sectors over a long period and although there are some variations, below is a summary of their findings on similar elements of all managers' roles.

Interpersonal roles
- Acting as a figurehead or leader of a work unit and acting as a point of contact;
- Negotiating with staff at different levels, with other managers, other work units and people external to the organisation.

Informational roles

- Monitoring and disseminating information flowing in and out of the work unit;
- Forming contracts and agreements and liaison with others.

Decisional roles

- Innovating, identifying and establishing new objectives and methods to improve the overall work of the unit;
- Monitoring flow of work by handling disturbances, solving problems and dealing with disruptions;
- Allocating resources, financial, material and human;
- Directing and controlling the work of others;
- Planning what needs to be done within timescales.

Mintzberg's research also suggested that, in practice, leadership is just one dimension of a multifaceted management role. The GSCC codes of practice for employers clarify the role of management in setting standards for social care workers and echo some of the roles identified above. The following codes specifically relate to management tasks:

Code 1.4 Giving staff clear information about their roles and responsibilities, relevant legislation and the organisational policies and procedures they must follow in their work.

Code 1.5 Managing the performance of staff and the organisation to ensure high quality services and care.

Code 2.2 Effectively managing and supervising staff to support effective practice and good conduct and supporting staff to address deficiencies in their performance.

Code 2.3 Having systems in place to enable social care workers to report inadequate resources or operational difficulties which might impede the delivery of safe care and working with them and the relevant authorities to address those issues.

(www.gscc.org.uk)

Skills for Care (2004) have identified a number of distinctive things that social care managers do and, according to them, make good social care managers:

- inspire staff;
- promote and meet service aims, objectives and goals;
- develop joint working/partnerships that are purposeful;
- ensure equality for staff and service users driven from the top down;
- challenge discrimination and harassment in employment practice and service delivery;
- empower staff and service users to develop services people want;
- value people, recognise and actively develop potential;
- develop and maintain awareness and keep in touch with service users and staff;

- provide an environment and time in which to develop reflective practice, professional skills and the ability to make judgements in complex situations;

- take responsibility for the continuing professional development of self and others;

- demonstrate an ability to plan organisational strategies for workforce development.

(Skills for Care, 2004).

Differences between managers and leaders

Other theorists have suggested that managers and leaders are quite distinct in their role and functions (Kotter, 1996). As you may have deduced from the previous section, management is mainly to do with planning and organising whereas leadership is associated with creating, coping and helping to adapt to change. In Kotter's view, the biggest challenge for leadership is that of transforming people's behaviour and changing their feelings through the development of **emotional intelligence**. This challenge is sometimes referred to as **transformational leadership**. Boydell et al. (2004) agree that management is about implementation, order, efficiency and effectiveness, whereas leadership is concerned with future direction in uncertain conditions. In conditions of relative stability management is sufficient but in conditions of complexity, unpredictability and rapid change, leadership qualities are required. There is no doubt, however, that whilst the two functions are distinct, there is an overlap between them. The development of leaders and managers therefore needs to be an integrated process, set in its organisational context and shaped by particular challenges facing an organisation. As employees, most of us want to contribute something to those challenges based on our own perspectives. We also need acknowledgement of our own knowledge, skills and experiences. Managers who value this in the people they work with and look on employees as colleagues rather than subordinates are more likely to exhibit leadership qualities and be able to inspire others through making them aware of the importance of their role to the success of the organisation. We often refer to the presence of these virtues when we talk about management style. Managers who carry out their functions in a competent, professional, understanding, compassionate and appropriate way will be able to develop their own leadership qualities and those of their staff. We will see later on that the ability to do this can sometimes be compromised by the dynamics within the organisation and the conflicts caused by power struggles and institutionalised negative behaviour.

ACTIVITY 2.2

Think of a person you know who is in a management position. This could be somebody from your practice learning placement, your university or in a previous job. Consider how effective they were as a manager by focusing on aspects of their practice that you found either helpful or unhelpful. Once you have done this, list the main tasks and responsibilities of that manager.

We will now compare your list with the perspective of others. Below is an overview of the research that Hales (1993) conducted into the activities which he thought typical of how a manager works:

1. reacting and responding to events and requests as opposed to initiating them;

2. being concerned with *ad hoc*, day-to-day activities, often short, interrupted and fragmented tasks;

3. negotiating and bargaining in relation to the content, style and boundaries of work tasks;

4. taking an eclectic approach and being able to commute between different activities;

5. being able to think in action, by making decisions and planning even whilst engaged in other activities;

6. being interactive, with a high level of interpersonal skills and communication;

7. being practical and concrete, rather than concerned with abstract ideas.

(Hales, 1993)

Hales thought that the diversity of responsibilities managers have is dependent on their working context and expectations of the organisation and individuals within it. In social care, however, there are a number of additional qualities that we expect from managers. These are based on professional values and ethics and the way in which these interact within different levels of the organisation, for example between individuals, teams, service units and the senior management team or management committee.

> Basic to the profession of social work is the recognition of the value and dignity of every human being, irrespective of origin, race, status, sex, sexual orientation, age, disability, belief or contribution to society. The profession accepts a responsibility to encourage and facilitate the self-realisation of each individual person with due regard to the interests of others.

(British Association of Social Workers, 2003)

If you recall from the discussion on humanist theories in Chapter 1, the essential task of an organisation's formal or strategic leadership is one which inculcated in all its members a belief in common purpose. Whilst developing vision and strategy is very much a role allocated to management at the top of formal hierarchical organisations, the way in which this is communicated, shared and developed with other stakeholders will determine how successfully this is implemented. Partnerships between social work and management disciplines at all levels can provide a bridge for professionals to work purposefully while feeling valued and sharing the values of the service.

Strategic leadership

Strategic leadership defines those people whose specific job it is to lead an organisation. Strategic leaders are the people who provide the overall vision and co-ordination that drives the organisation forward. They have prime responsibility for developing a language

RESEARCH SUMMARY

Drawing on in-depth interviews with managers in the non-profit community services sector in Australia, Healey (2002) explored the contributions made by social workers to social welfare management and documented their perceptions of threats and opportunities posed to progressive management practice in a climate of reform. I have summarised her findings as:

- the central importance of social justice principles and participatory and consultative approaches to involving stakeholders, especially service users and service providers, in the management process;

- the importance of collaborative and participatory management processes;

- securing the co-operation of external business sectors for the future in terms of providing financial resources and technical knowledge such as accounting and legal information. The managers' appreciation of the value base and complexities inherent in professional practice and how this is valued is a vital asset to the organisation in decision-making and resource allocation;

- concerns about threats to the diversity of community service organisations because of economies of scale and administration of funding through contracts and their capacity to bid for these;

- increased pressure to delineate service goals and outcomes (also seen as a means of valuing public service delivery by acknowledging its potential contribution).

(Healey, 2002, pp. 527–40)

and organisational identity that binds everything and everyone together and inspiring them towards collective action and loyalty to the organisation's mission. Senge (1996) described strategic leaders as the social architects of their organisations, designing purpose, vision and core values and working with broad-based groups. Their membership stretches beyond the traditional elite of senior managers so that they can design policies, strategies and structure to translate ideas into business decisions. The key tasks of strategic leaders are to build and sustain shared vision and high ethical values which provide a compelling, engaging picture of where the organisation wants to get to, whilst also communicating an accurate picture of current reality. This would include working with a wide group of people to build strategies and overseeing the implementation of those strategies as well as making sure that resources are allocated to achieve them. One of the main challenges for any strategic leader would be to achieve a quality of life in the organisation that will generate and sustain commitment of the internal and external stakeholders to its goals. Effective leadership and management of change helps to develop a healthy organisational culture which involves service users, carers and the community through to employees, the management team as well as those who fund, contract with and have any interest in the organisation.

Management or managerialism?

If you recall from Chapter 1, a managerialist perspective focuses on a narrow range of issues of perceived importance to managers concerning management control and performance by pushing other issues off the agenda or preventing a more critical approach to management practice. Bureaucratisation of professional judgements and decision-making can cause professionals to cease considering the specific issues of service users, or providing holistic services that seek to promote change and facilitate the decision-making capacity of service user/carers in contributing to their own empowerment. Dominelli (2002) suggested that managerialist approaches perceive social work professionals as merely another unit of flexible and redeployable resource to be managed. This curtails professional autonomy and pre-empts the potential for either strategic or tactical alliances between professionals and management to overcome their own sense of powerlessness. Managerialism can have a detrimental impact on the content and quality of professional supervision (Dominelli, 2002; Tsui, 2005). The focus can become more concerned with whether practitioners are meeting administrative requirements at the expense of time spent looking at casework in which frontline staff are helped to stand back and review critically their assessments and plans or to look at relationship dynamics (Rushton and Nathan, 1996). Munroe (2004a) has suggested from her examination of numerous child abuse inquiries since 1990 that the types of solutions adopted to try and improve frontline social work have predominantly taken the form of bureaucratic solutions which seek to formalise tasks through greater managerial oversight and control over all levels of work without necessarily improving the quality of actual practice. According to Munroe, the subsequent stream of reorganisations, at both local and national level, has not been shown to make any significant difference to standards of practice except to make it more visible for monitoring and audit. Managerialism has therefore increased in social work as a response of social care agencies to defend themselves from public criticism (Hood et al., 2000).

RESEARCH SUMMARY

A study of why staff leave social care was undertaken by the Audit Commission in 2002 and six key factors were identified as influential:

- the sense of being overwhelmed by bureaucracy, paperwork and targets;

- insufficient resources leading to unmanageable workloads;

- a lack of autonomy;

- feeling undervalued by the government, their managers and the public;

- an unfair pay structure;

- a change agenda that feels imposed and irrelevant.

(Audit Commission, 2002, section 3)

Reflective management

There are a number of issues affecting recruitment and retention of staff in social care organisations. The role of managers in providing quality support to staff and service users incorporates five core characteristics: consistency and fairness; acceptance and respect; integrity and honesty; reliability and trustworthiness; empathy and understanding (Audit Commission and SSI, 2000, p. 4). Managers at all levels need to continue to develop greater level of skills including new ones to respond to the changing policy environment within which social care is delivered. Likewise, social work practitioners need to be able to confront and engage in micro dilemmas to avoid demoralisation caused by constant organisational upheaval and to manage conflict effectively. Work done by Charles and Butler (2004) provides a framework to enable social workers to utilise personal, professional and organisational devices to challenge managerialist practices fundamentally at odds with social work values. The authors question the scope for practitioner-led approaches to organisational change and identify the dilemmas confronting social workers in bridging the gap between their ideas and the practical realities of practice (Charles and Butler, 2004). Using Schön's reflective cycle (1991), the authors encourage social workers to take a more reflective approach. Some dominant organisational environments can cause workers to have difficulties in actively or visibly challenging problems and where the unconscious processes operating within agency structures do not allow emotional expression. Charles and Butler highlight how this can engender feelings of stress, abandonment and disappointment which ultimately have a cumulative effect on self-respect and integrity. However, developing skills for reflection in action can enable social workers to identify the different levels within which they can accept, influence or control their situation. By analysing issues at each level, a framework or strategy can provide social workers with the opportunities to exercise personal, professional and organisational devices to exert more control. If you want to read more about this approach then I refer you back to the further reading at the end of Chapter 1 (Lymbery and Butler, 2004).

Managers who use a wide range of leader behaviours are viewed as more effective than those who use a more limited range (Ahearn et al., 2004). A perspective shared by many organisational theorists is that work environments are inherently political and to be effective, the use of 'political skills' helps managers become more adept at using interpersonal skills and information management skills to more positive effects (Ahearn et al, 2004). Mintzberg (1985) defines political skill as the ability to effectively understand others at work, and to use such knowledge to influence others to act in ways that enhance one's personal and/or organisational objectives. By working with and through others, managers can become more effective at networking, coalition building, and creating **social capital**. According to House (1995), leaders who network are in a better position to secure more resources for their units and are valued more by their teams. The accumulation of friendships, connections and alliances allows them to leverage this social capital to facilitate change.

Sources of power in organisations

So far we have been examining different styles and forms of management and leadership and you may have recognised that the appropriate use of **power** and authority in social care has an influence on how this is perceived by those being managed or led. Organisations are made up of formal and informal rules that co-ordinate actions of different people. But how do they make sure people from diverse backgrounds, with particular interests and different understandings, comply and benefit from these rules? Raising these questions means addressing fine lines between the exercise of power and **ethics** (Clegg et al., 2005). Clarity in matters of authority, leadership and organisational structure is essential for the competent functioning of any organisation.

Management authority

'Authority' refers to the right to make ultimate decisions, and in an organisation, it refers to the right to make decisions which are binding on others and are derived from one's role or power within the system. This will not be true for all organisations; for example, the voluntary sector may distribute authority in a different way as we saw from matrix structures described in Chapter 1. Obholzer (1994) talks about authority being sanctioned from 'below' where, by definition, by joining an organisation, a person willingly delegates their own personal authority to those in charge. This can subsequently be affected, however, by undermining or sabotage, consciously or unconsciously. Authority can also come from 'within' the person who holds it, as the attitude of the authority figure is crucial in affecting how, to what extent and with what competence institutional roles are taken up. Obholzer concludes that 'good-enough authority', at its best, is a state of mind arising from a continuous mix of authorisation from the sponsoring organisation or structure, sanctioning from within the organisation and connection with one's inner world of authority (pp. 40–1).

Management power

Power is a concept that encompasses the mechanisms, processes and dispositions that try (not always successfully) to ensure that people act according to the rules and hence is a central concept in both management practice and theory. French and Raven (1958) identified five main bases of power. These are reward, coercive, referent, legitimate and expert and are represented in Figure 2.1. The figure also lists a sixth source of power: affiliation.

The exercise of power should not always be perceived as negative, nor is it necessarily something just held by those in authority. Externally, power comes from what an individual controls and from the sanctions they can impose on others. It is derived from social and political connections. Internally, power comes from an individual's knowledge and experience, strength of personality and perception of themselves. You may be familiar with these ideas from social work theory and the dynamics involved when working with service users and carers and their experiences. You may be able to identify in your own practice both with service users and within your own organisation, some of the sources of power that you personally hold as well as the sources of power held by others. Within the organisational context, these ideas can be expressed in the type of language we use to describe people's jobs and functions or in the language used to describe service users and colleagues. Furthermore, a match between the concepts of authority, power and responsibility is required. As professionals, we have responsibilities for our own practice and are

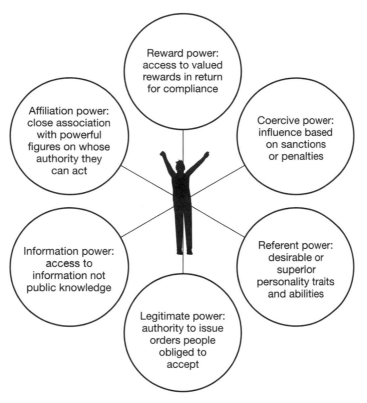

Figure 2.1 French and Raven (1958) Sources of power. Ann Arbor, MI: University of Michigan Press

accountable to those higher up in the organisation as well as in our own mind. This is the way in which personal and professional values and ethics operate. According to Obholzer, assessing the nature and functioning of an organisation by clarifying the nature, source and routing of authority, the power available, is time well spent by any social worker or manager (2004, p. 43).

ACTIVITY 2.3

Now reflect back to Activity 2.2 in which you were asked to consider the qualities of a manager you were familiar with. Using French and Raven's categories, can you identify the sources of power that you perceived the manager to have? What examples can you think of as to how the manager used their power and authority and what effect did it have on the people they worked with in the organisation?

You may have identified that the way in which managers use or abuse their authority or power will be significant to the way in which they manage change. Therefore we will now go on to look at change management and the role of managers within this process.

Managing change in social care organisations

The ability to adapt and redesign structures in response to the government's change agenda is critical to the success of organisations delivering care. Change management theory often explores change from the perspective of those initiating or responsible for change. Change creates anxiety, uncertainty and stress whether you are committed to it or not. The success of change is also very dependent on whether the softer 'human' issues are considered, and how these are integrated with 'hard' structures and systems (Buchanan and Huczynski, 2004). In social care organisations, the healthier and more user-focused the culture, the more constructive and engaged will be the response to change agendas. Closed and controlling organisational systems may simply assimilate new agendas where existing attitudes, practices and services lead to little real change except on the surface (Morrison, 2000, p. 372). Lewin (1951) developed a theory of change management which described a process during which the organisation needed to unfreeze, move to its new desired state and then refreeze and stabilise any changes achieved. However, it is now generally accepted that this refreezing process is no longer possible given the constant nature of change within public sector environments. Instead, organisations have to adapt to a pattern of frequent and complex initiatives impinging on it which will affect work and organisational design, resource allocation, systems and procedures in a continuous attempt to improve performance. In this scenario, it is often difficult to evaluate how effective change actually is or to study it in terms of the process or consequences. Strategic imperatives, i.e. social, economic and policy shifts in social care, mean that organisations have to be more creative, flexible, adaptable, fluid and responsive. All of this takes its toll on everyone within it, so much so, that theorists have characterised this response as a 'coping cycle' similar to that used in understanding bereavement and loss.

CASE STUDY

Ajoda is a well established voluntary sector organisation providing domiciliary care, information advice and advocacy services to African older people. Ajoda receives a core grant from the LA and some small charitable grants for its information, advice and advocacy services. The majority of its funding, however, comes from annual contracts with the local social services and the primary care trust for domiciliary care services. With four months to the end of the financial year, the LA has announced that with increased uptake of direct payments in the local community and their strategy to implement personalised budgets, they will be reducing their block contract for domiciliary care service with Ajoda by 40%. They also want Ajoda to provide more assertive outreach services to older people with dementia. Ajoda's own internal review has also identified that uptake of the information and advocacy project is very poor. A user survey has identified that people require outreach services in their own home and there is a need for more carers' support. The management team has set up a three-month project team to review these changes and draw up an action plan which will inevitably involve some restructuring of the service overall. The last Ajoda staff newsletter also announced that the organisation was heading for a projected overspend of £32,000 this financial year.

In your examination of the above case study, what are the triggers for change? Try to separate these into 'external' (those impinging on the organisation) and 'internal' (those internal to the organisation).

Who do you think should be involved in the project team and what do you think should be their immediate priorities?

It is important to identify the depth of the change intervention required, which depends on the extent of the organisational problem being addressed. The external factors impinging on Ajoda are legislative and policy changes as a result of the Direct Payments Act, 1996 the impact on the personalisation agenda and the local demands and needs of its stakeholders, for example its service users and funders. Internal factors are a shortfall in the budget to meet the day-to-day requirements of the service and the provision of services that are not being fully utilised. Leaving aside these circumstances for one moment, we will look at three types of change identified by Mabey (2001, p. 9) which she differentiated from the literature.

1. **Incremental change.** This approach requires making an improvement in the way things have been done with the aim of doing them better. In the above case study, service users and carers may not be using the information and advice service because it is not meeting their needs. This may not be related to the quality of the service itself but the way in which it is being provided. As a single service within a range of services to African older people, the information and advice service could be more community based and practical by providing information and advice in people's own homes or be decentralised to the other services in the overall organisation. Implications for change could involve: retraining the existing workers, reviewing terms and conditions of their jobs and setting up a system to accurately identify and monitor the types of issues that service users need assistance with and how best to meet them.

2. **Transitional change.** This approach involves the implementation of new strategies and requires the rearranging or dismantling of previous methods. For example, reduced funding for the domiciliary care service does not necessarily mean reduced demand. Alternative marketing strategies of the service may involve being more proactive in 'selling' its services direct to the community over a period of time, especially to those who may now have more choice through the increased take-up of direct payments or who did individualised budgets, they may prefer to purchase care from organisations who they feel are in tune with their own community. The domiciliary service may also need to diversify and provide a wider range of services that older people need and this would be very dependent on more consultation and user involvement which could take up a lot of resources in the short term. This type of transition requires careful management as it involves a transitional period during which a number of issues need to be balanced and controlled.

3. **Transformational change.** This approach is usually the most profound and traumatic and is so described because it implies comprehensive change at several levels and the outcome can be unpredictable. Transformational change usually involves radical reform of mission and core values, an altered distribution of power and dramatic change to the organisational structure and decision-making roles. This type of change management

process would be seen in the integrated whole-systems approach to services around service user groups that we looked at in Chapter 1.

Strategies for change

In the second stage of Activity 2.4 you were asked to identify the priorities for the project team to take the change forward. One influential approach to change is project management, which revolves around the concept that change follows a life-cycle with a sequence of clearly identifiable and discrete steps to achieve it. Kotter (1996) outlined eight steps that draw together these key ingredients of successful change management and which I have presented as a continuum in Figure 2.2.

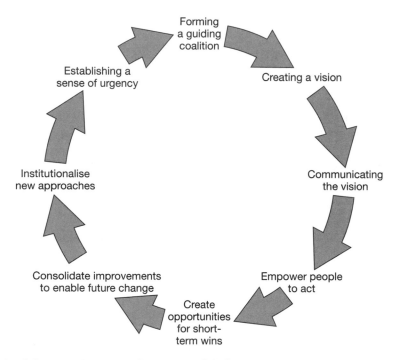

Figure 2.2 Eight steps to managing successful change (Kotter, 1996). Reproduced with permission of Harvard Business School Publishing

The priorities that you identified will need to fall in with these steps and find practical and realistic ways of achieving them. At a practical level, people affected by change need to be given sufficient information in a way that makes the issues explicit and creates conditions under which they can engage in the vision being created and their individual role within it. Theorists on change management emphasise that above all, an organisation needs a vision of where it wishes to go, a strategy of how it intends to get there, and a way of monitoring and evaluating where it is at any point in the process. However, having a clear vision and strategy alone will not guarantee that the change will be implemented successfully. Whilst the logic and reasons for change may be clear in business terms, everyone may not see it that way. In the case study Ajoda's current services may not be viable in the longer term particularly with insecure funding but designing and implementing a new service requires the active engagement of the team members affected and their representation in the project team. Managing change is therefore as much about managing the process as content and requires sound understanding and skills in people management.

The literature on change management stresses that people's reactions to change will include an emotional element and one such model is that of a five-stage transition, from denial and resistance to exploration, acceptance and commitment (Handy, 1993). In this model, people initially feel threatened, deny or become angry and put up resistance. Leadership needs to achieve a shared vision together with a sense of urgency. Sharing proposals with staff at an early stage is vital, along with consultation and updates on progress. At the resistance stage, managers have to work with people's responses and provide support and encouragement. Change should be as transparent as possible with enough short-term gains to keep up commitment and energy levels to avoid burnout. Change is a necessary part of a continuous process of organisational development and there should always be opportunities to address the following as illustrated in the case study:

- Structural changes in management or team responsibilities.

- Changes in organisational culture, values and ways of working by involving service users and new stakeholders such as carers in the design and provision of services.

- Improvement in systems and the management of process.

- The need to move individuals in and out of posts. With Ajoda, the information advice staff may need retraining and negotiation of new work conditions which help them to be able to go out into the community and undertake outreach work in a safe, competent and confident way.

C H A P T E R   S U M M A R Y

This chapter has looked at theories of management and leadership and how these overlap and interact with the roles and functions that they fulfil in social care organisations at different levels. We have looked particularly at the role of management and leadership in creating and sustaining the need for organisational change. As a critically reflective social worker, where managers in your organisation have justified the need for change, you will need to ask how the opportunities that change brings will be fully exploited for the benefit of service users, carers and the community as well as for practitioners delivering services. Managers in social care organisations have an important role to play in managing tensions between different sectors of the agency, balancing views and the professional input of staff against the needs to control standards within a legislative and political framework. Social workers likewise have to manage the paradox, realities and conflict in balancing issues of care and control whilst keeping a focus on the rights and needs of individuals with the needs of their carers, families and wider community. This chapter has given you an insight into some of these dilemmas, to help you develop your expectations and strategies to get the best out of your organisation's management teams.

FURTHER READING

For a full guide to the management and leadership standards in social care, visit Skills for Care at **www.skillsforcare.org.uk** available on CD-Rom.

Menzies-Lyth, IEP (1988) *Containing anxiety in institutions: selected essays.* London: Free Association Books.

This book provides a formula for thinking about social structures as a form of defence and how organisations and bureaucracies fail to contain high levels of anxiety and stress that affect individuals that work within them.

http://www.scie-peoplemanagement.org.uk/resource/

Social Care Institute for Excellence – people management website

Contains a large database of resources, including good practice information, about common areas of leadership and management practice.

Chapter 3

Working within the organisational performance and regulatory framework: quality assurance systems

A C H I E V I N G   A   S O C I A L   W O R K   D E G R E E

This chapter will help you achieve the following National Occupational Standards and General Social Care Council's Codes of Practice.

Key Role 2: Plan, carry out, review and evaluate social work practice with individuals, families, carers, groups, communities and other professionals.

- Prepare, produce, implement and evaluate plans with individuals, families, carers, groups, communities and professional colleagues.

Key Role 5: Manage and be accountable, with supervision and support, for your own social work practice within your organisation.

- Manage and be accountable for your own work.
- Manage, present and share records and reports.
- Work within multi-disciplinary and multi-organisational teams, networks and systems.

Key Role 6: Demonstrate professional competence in social work practice.

- Work within agreed standards of social work practice and ensure own professional development.
- Contribute to the promotion of best social work practice.

General Social Care Codes of Practice

Code 6: Be accountable for the quality of work and take responsibility for maintaining and improving knowledge and skills.

It will also introduce you to the following academic standards as set out in the social work subject benchmark statements:

3.1.2 The service delivery context

- The significance of legislative and legal frameworks and service delivery standards (including the nature of legal authority, the application of legislation in practice, statutory accountability and tensions between statute, policy and practice).

3.1.5 The nature of social work practice

- The process of reflection and evaluation, including familiarity with the range of approaches for evaluating welfare outcomes, and their significance for the development of practice and the practitioner.

3.2 Gathering information/analysis and synthesis/intervention and evaluation

- Take into account differences of viewpoint in gathering information and assess the reliability and relevance of the information gathered.
- Analyse information gathered, weighing competing evidence and modifying viewpoints by relating to particular tasks, situations or problems.
- Monitor, review and evaluate outcomes.

3.2.4 Skills in working with others

- Act within a framework of multiple accountability.

Introduction

This chapter explores approaches to **quality assurance** (QA) and **performance management** in social care. We begin by defining QA and what this means in social work. We will then go on to examine the chronological development of national and organisational frameworks for measuring and assessing the quality and effectiveness of social work and social care services. There will be a detailed examination of current inspection and regulatory regimes and an overview of debates on the effectiveness of these, concluding with a discussion of the future of QA, inspection and regulation in social care.

Familiarity with the ideas behind performance measurement will increase your understanding of local policies and procedures relating to these in everyday practice. These are there to ensure standards in social work and social care are established and maintained. In this chapter there will be an opportunity to look critically at your own role as a practitioner, in your team and service area by applying some of the principles underpinning quality assurance to the practice setting. You will be invited to analyse one example of a national standard and **performance indicator (PI)**. This is intended to help you appreciate how a potential contribution towards achieving **'quality'** in social care may be made at every level in the organisations you work in.

QA is not only dependent on the existence of organisational systems and procedures but relies equally on social workers recognising the purpose and value in evaluating the effectiveness of their professional practice and role within this. Chapter 4 will therefore go on to look at QA from the service user perspective. This highlights the importance of the way in which organisations may involve service users in the development, delivery and evaluation of services which lies at the very heart of any effective QA system.

The relevance of quality assurance and performance measurement to social work practice

Many commentators have highlighted the uneasy relationship that may exist between the government's emphasis on performance measurement and the complexity of day-to-day issues affecting the provision of social care services (Pillinger, 2001; Adams, 2002; Healey, 2002; Felton, 2005). The measurement of outcomes for service users is an issue with which social workers are increasingly engaging due to a number of influences, both within and external to the profession. Social workers themselves have recognised and been active in promoting the view that service users are entitled to the best possible services (Everitt and Hardiker, 1996) and that quality enhancement is an integral aim of QA systems. This chapter will familiarise you with terminology associated with QA and examine how QA systems have evolved and been adapted by the public sector to support the increasing need to describe and evaluate social work practice. We will unpick terms such as 'standards', 'audits' and 'performance indicators', terms used to describe ways of measuring care. Adopting jargon within social care organisations without questioning or fully understanding it has been criticised for its potential effect in alienating and distancing practitioners from the complex issues being described. A growing commitment to evidence-based practice illustrates the profession's recognition of the need to develop rigorous studies and evaluation to further develop its knowledge base. Being informed about and involved in the systems used to measure practice using audit and inspection are therefore essential to your professional training and development.

Why measure effectiveness in social care? – The policy context

A number of reasons, social, economic and political, over time have combined to create a demand for greater accountability and transparency in public services (Munro, 2004b). Within the social work profession itself, the continuous development of specialist research knowledge has contributed to its disciplinary knowledge base and the encouragement to articulate and measure the outcomes of social work practice (Rosen, 1994, cited in Felton, 2005). I will outline two broad historical eras during which ambitious attempts were made to consider the way in which outcomes of social work practice could be conceptualised and measured. The first era extended from the 1940s until the late 1980s, during which commentators attempted to answer the question 'Does social work work?' (Felton, 2005). This period marks the beginning of contested epistemological debates around evidence-based practice. The second era, from 1987 onwards, coincided with the development of the market economy in the UK health and social care services. The introduction of more comprehensive QA systems to both sectors is largely a phenomenon emerging from the late 1990s, with the introduction of the government's modernisation agenda (DoH, 1998a). From this time onwards, national standards or **benchmarks** for the majority of health and social care services were set down as a framework to assess how they measure up, with clear, definite auditing and inspection procedures and processes. We refer to this as the performance assessment framework (PAF). PAF will be explored in more detail later on. However, prior to a more detailed look of these developments we will now return to examine the concept of QA.

Defining quality assurance

A frequently used definition of quality is 'Delighting the customer by fully meeting their needs and expectations' (www.dti.gov.uk). The term QA refers to a particular system in an organisation, which tries to embody or assure aspects of quality during the process of delivering a particular product. The product being discussed here is the delivery of care and support services. It also refers to social work activities in organisations responsible for providing protection or social control for particular groups in society as a result of social services legislative duties. So already you can see that 'quality' is an ambiguous concept subject to interpretation. QA can be used as a mechanism to empower, for example, creative social work practice that seeks to improve the involvement of service users in the way in which services are provided. It can also be perceived as a means of controlling, by strictly regulating the way services are delivered and professional activities within them. This can include the potential to influence resource allocation and practice development (Adams, 2002). The key to defining quality in health and social care is to incorporate the views of both service users and service providers. To be effective in this the organisation needs to have a system in which it can assess and understand the needs and expectations of its service users. This may involve developing internal processes (between departments, teams or colleagues) and external processes (involving other agencies, providers or suppliers) to make

39

this happen effectively. This is sometimes referred to as the 'quality chain' (Martin and Henderson, 2001, p. 180).

In defining quality you may have included:

- the importance of providing services capable of meeting the exact needs of service users/carers;

- services easy to access or obtain, in the right place, at the right time, at the right level;

- equality in provision regardless of social, ethnic or cultural background;

- reliability, consistency and continuity;

- being clear in their purpose, with a statement of the aim and objectives of the service and description of the minimum standards or level that people could expect;

- services provided within the costs and resources available but which are efficient, effective and give value for money;

- being delivered by people who are committed and competent and who receive good quality training, supervision and support to do the best job possible.

I also asked you to consider the possible advantages or disadvantages of the different stakeholders in the process of measurement and evaluation of social care services, and you may wish to consult Table 3.1 opposite to compare and contrast your responses against my own list, which is by no means exhaustive.

As stated earlier, for an organisation to be really effective, quality must span all functions, people, departments and activities, and develop a common language for improvement. The quality delivered to the ultimate recipient of the service is dependent on requirements being met all along the quality chain including resource constraints. This can raise dilemmas when considering the different perspectives that might be held by users, providers and commissioners of services as well as the general public. Perhaps you drew this conclusion yourself in Activity 3.1?

Quality assurance as a system

Managing quality to achieve excellence in social care services requires a holistic approach to management in an organisation. Maximising the involvement of everybody through

Table 3.1

Stakeholder	Advantages	Disadvantages
Service Users/Carers	Being consulted Knowing someone is accountable Confidence in services Individual needs taken account of Can lead to change/improvement Fairness and equity	Feels tokenistic Doesn't always lead to change or improvement Tools to measure inaccessible No immediate benefits Doesn't consider my uniqueness
Staff	Clarity about expectations Accountability Feedback from both directions Evidence informing practice	Bureaucratic, administrative Misses important issues that can't be measured Information disappears with no results
Managers	Feedback helps review future planning Helps manage staff performance Local information on what's working Helps inform local changes to improve services	Bureaucracy Doesn't take into account resource limitations Not enough control on what's measured, valued
Organisations	Evidence to plan, target resources Meet legal/policy requirements Provides basis for dialogue with policy/ decision makers Reputation in community	Not a level playing field Hands tied nationally
Government	Establish consistency Identify inequalities in service delivery Monitor implementation legislation/policy Value for money Political support	Remote from actual service user/carer Information neither accurate nor provides reliable picture overall Doesn't help with unique or specific problems

leadership and innovation is crucial (Peters, 1995). Reputations of organisations are often built on the quality and excellence of the services they provide. We will look at the implication of this when we explore the concept of institutional discrimination in Chapter 6. The search for excellence is ideally driven from within the organisation rather than being imposed from the outside. This may incorporate a never-ending improvement cycle that ensures an organisation learns from its results, systematically standardises and documents what it does well and improves the way it operates and what it delivers from what it learns (www.dti.org.uk). This must be done in a planned, systematic and conscientious way to create a climate and culture of quality and excellence that permeates the whole organisation. Later on we will explore how these ideals and principles can become compromised or conflict with external social, economic and political pressures on the organisation's performance. The nature and complexity of social care services and the unpredictable and turbulent environments in which some social care services operate do not always enable them to fall in neatly with traditional models of QA systems. Similarly, systems that focus on more scientific or quantifiable measures as a means of evaluating the effectiveness of services can lack meaning where 'human services' are concerned. Meaning-based quality-of-life measurement may be more congruent with social work values and practice and plays an important part in measuring quality in any systems being designed and implemented (Felton, 2005).

The three basic principles of any QA system are:

- focus on the customer;

- understanding of the process;

- ensuring that all employees are committed to quality and excellence.

(www.dti.gov.uk/quality/)

The term 'Total Quality Management' (TQM) is a term now used in the public sector, having been adopted from management gurus in the 1960s, and describes a holistic framework for managing QA. It incorporates the principles above but stresses the importance of wider issues such as planning, organisation and management responsibility. TQM is a way of managing people and business processes to ensure customer satisfaction at every stage, internally and externally, and is achieved through effective leadership (www.dti.gov.uk). Later on in the chapter we will look at Donabedian's model, which utilises TQM approaches, to help us analyse ways of measuring quality of a service against one of the national standards in social care.

Now that we have a clearer idea of what we mean by the term 'quality' and how this may be achieved through the systems that organisations develop to improve their delivery of social care services, I will now go on to look at the development of QA systems within their social, economical, political and organisational context.

Scrutinising social care: a historical perspective

The development of a quality assurance culture within social work from 1940 to the late 1980s

The processes by which services have come to be subject to scrutiny can be understood by looking at the historical context and broader debates about the relationship between social policy, knowledge and practice. With the evolution of the social work profession, what social workers actually do has become an increasingly fragmented notion. Social work and social care have been affected both directly and indirectly by changes to public services from central and local government (see Horner, 2006, for a fuller account of the history of the social work profession itself).

In the late 1940s, during the emergence of UK welfare state, large-scale providers of social care developed, defining the type of care to be provided with little concern for the role of consumers. In the National Health Service, power, hierarchy and social status of the medical profession prevented the lay public from challenging how medicine and health care services were delivered. Likewise, in social care, the low social status and stigma attached to those on the receiving end of care had a similar disempowering effect (Malin et al., 2002). Social care originated in part from a moral response to control and contain certain marginal elements in society (Clarke, 1993). With the development of social sciences during the twentieth century, the possibility of applying measures and outcomes to aspects of social care arose. Models of care that had a more 'scientific' basis allowed 'treatments' and 'therapies' in certain areas of health and social care to be subject to discussion and scrutiny.

This is illustrated in the way models of mental health care have developed (see Golightley, 2008). During the 1960s and 1970s, a more radical political agenda emerged in which social work commentators primarily focused on ideology and activism in social work practice. The notion that results of social work input could be measured and evaluated was not only refuted, but found to be positively unacceptable (Corrigan and Leonard, 1978). As we saw in Chapter 1, the humanist tradition meant that social services were administered as a professional bureaucracy. Social workers were allowed high degrees of discretion, with minimum documentation of their activities, and styles of recording varied (Munroe, 2004b).

These factors, in the way social work practice developed, contributed to ideological underpinnings of the profession. They may have also contributed to the atmosphere of suspicion around current measurement of social work and its outcomes (Malin et al., 2002). Recent debates on 'managerialism' in public services have paid attention to the amount of time that social workers spent administrating and recording their work and whether this detracts from quality time spent with service users (Tsui and Cheung, 2004; Munroe, 2004b). This is a debate that arises from time to time in social work. The tradition of social work emphasises and prides itself on the importance of establishing good quality relationships, a factor which is constantly reiterated by service users themselves.

RESEARCH SUMMARY

A study by Weinberg et al. (2003) examined what care managers do in a specialist older people's services, through an analysis of their diary activities over a period of time. Analysis revealed that excluding travel, care managers spent 64% of their working week in direct and indirect user/carer-related activities, of which 32% was on administrative activities, 27% in assessment activities, compared with only 7% in monitoring and reviewing. Staggeringly, only 5% of time was directed to providing counselling and support. The study drew attention to the reduced opportunities to discuss emotional issues and options with older people and their families with appropriately qualified professionals. It questions the optimal balance between direct and indirect activities with service users. The researchers noted how the dynamics of not having sufficient resources affected the assessment. This had the potential to prevent care managers undertaking full assessments in the true spirit of the legislation and guidance around community care. (Weinberg et al., 2003)

To understand how we have come to such a position in social work practice means looking at the pivotal period during which interest began to focus on the actual effectiveness of social work practice. This was associated with debates about predicting and assessing risk (Beck, 1992). Child protection failures from the 1970s, 1980s and beyond led to large-scale public inquiries scrutinising the effectiveness of social work. These focused on its role in protecting or providing safeguards to children and vulnerable adults from neglect and abuse (Colwell, 1973; Beckford, 1985; Henry, 1986; Carlisle, 1987). First, social services became dominated by having to demonstrate their protective roles and duties. Second, certain models and methods in social work practice were developed which were at best preventative or, at worst, controlling.

Considerable difficulties became apparent in trying to monitor the effectiveness of social work. Questions were raised about the lack of consensus and ability to establish probability, cause and effect in social work intervention. The political environment of **neo-liberalism** encouraged the development of alternative approaches with a stronger theoretical basis with a need to diagnose and solve social problems (Walker, 2002; Munroe, 2004b). Evaluative research and the adoption of social work 'values' began to inform training and education of social workers around the 1980s. The government began to be explicitly interested in 'value for money' and increased the use of policies and procedures as a mechanism for prescribing how social workers should work with their clients.

The development of a market economy in social care and the drive for accountability

Developments in quality assurance from 1987 to the late 1990s

From 1987, the Conservative government gave considerable status to the 'value for money' principle and commitment to controlling public expenditure. Introducing the internal market via the National Health Service and Community Care Act 1990 developed these principles further. This provided a powerful incentive for introducing more sophisticated methods of quality measurement. To meet rising costs of care, it was felt that resources could be used more effectively by moving from a 'service-led' to a 'needs-led' provision (Means et al., 2003). The move to make Social Services a 'commissioner' of services from its traditional role as 'provider' had two consequences:

1. the quality and cost of care now being purchased from other agencies had to be demonstrated;

2. separate or arm's-length inspection units were established, whose specific role it was to scrutinise social services.

Both developments strongly underpin the current focus on quality in social care, giving birth to institutions whose role it is to audit and inspect services on behalf of the government.

One further boost to ideas that social care could formulate clear goals and evaluate itself against these came about by explicit debates on anti-discriminatory practice (Dominelli, 1988, 1989, 2002; Thompson, 2003). Although this was essentially driven by moral and political interests, a commitment to achieving measurable practical outcomes was expressed. The earnest attention given to equality issues in both practice and theory in social work, and demonstration of equality, contributed significantly to the culture of quality assurance in social care at all levels, e.g. individual, group and organisational level (Adams, 2002).

Centralisation of power and decision-making by successive governments in the late 1990s had major consequences for the way in which practice is now managed. Organisations delivering social care are expected by government not only to manage services efficiently and effectively but simultaneously to manage quality and effectiveness of direct work with service users and carers. This has caused tensions and dilemmas for both managers and practitioners. Organisational frameworks designed to give clarity and increase the effectiveness of the way in which services are assessed and provided for were criticised for having subtly taken over the exercise of professional skill and decision-making. Increasing expectations of service users conflicting with the demands and constraints of the social care system meant that large bureaucracies, for example in statutory settings, could no longer respond flexibly (Kearney, 2004, p. 104).

RESEARCH SUMMARY

Following the publication of policy documents such as the NHS Plan (DoH, 2000a) and *National Service Framework for Older People* (DoH, 2001), health and social care agencies in the UK were expected to devise and implement a single assessment process (SAP) by April 2004. This was designed to ensure that older people receive appropriate, effective, timely responses to their health and social care needs, and that professional resources are used effectively without duplication (DoH, 2002a). Putting this into practice has been difficult. In some areas, development and use of dependency measures to determine eligibility for services has potential to become so mechanistic and standardised that a more in-depth social work assessment and professional discretion has been bypassed. Unintentionally, the result may be that service users lose out even more if the assessment does not value their abilities, mental status, social well-being and positive contributions of communities they are part of.

(Glasby, 2004)

Outcomes-based cultures

Development of regulation and performance measurement from 1997 to the 21st century

Partial withdrawal of the state from direct provision of welfare services and giving more responsibilities to the independent sector to provide care on their behalf has given rise to a substantial growth in regulation and control. The implications have been far reaching. Regulation through contracting, monitoring and inspection is symptomatic of wider cultural changes and development of what is referred to as an **'audit'** society (Means et al., 2003). The incoming Labour government of 1997 brought a complex and interlocking set of reforms intended to transform the regulatory framework for social care and improve performance in every area. These initiatives formed part of New Labour's agenda for local government in 'modernising' public services and represented a significant increase in the involvement of central government in direct management and delivery of services. We saw in Chapter 1 how the modernising social services framework stressed the importance of raising service quality and consistency, highlighting differences between the objectives of social care and the actual standards achieved (DoH, 1998a). This meant that there was a significant increase in the mechanisms for controlling social services at a national level which focused on the quality of services and outcomes for users and carers. Examples of policy initiatives which have reinforced the quality assurance approach and with which you may already be familiar include the following:

- **Best Value:** a method of reviewing and evaluating services founded on the 'four Cs': **Challenge**, why the service is needed; **Compare** cost and quality with other 'like' services; **Consult** with public and service users to test the validity of conclusions; and **Compete** to ensure the best way of providing the service.

- **Fair Access to Services** (2002) to address geographical variations or the 'postcode lottery' of service provision by setting four categories for eligibility for services: **critical, substantial, moderate** and **low**. Individuals' needs and risks to independence are subsequently assessed in these key areas.

- **National Service Frameworks** in adult and children's services, aimed at providing a coherent set of national standards and objectives for social care. These are holistic. Collaboration between relevant agencies is essential to provide quality services that promote health and well-being. Structural and organisational changes to achieve these alongside changes in practice are included.

- **The National Care Standards Act 2000** legislation set out national minimum standards for social care determined by government. The Commission for Social Care Inspection (CSCI) until 2006 was responsible for regulating all residential, nursing homes, adult placements, domiciliary care providers, children's residential, including special education, fostering and adoption agencies, and some local authority services. Structural change in the regulation of social care and health services initially as a result of Every Child Matters and the White Paper, 2006 has since led to proposals and the implementation of a new regulatory framework in which adult and children's services are now subject to different inspection regimes.

- **The Health and Social Care Bill 2008** created a new social care and health regulator for adult services, the Care Quality Commission, which brings together the Commission for Social Care Inspection, the Healthcare Commission and the Mental Health Act Commission. As a result of Every Child Matters, Ofsted also took over inspection of children's services in April 2007 using the same judgement criteria as CSCI pending the revised National Minimum Standards for children's services in 2009.

- **Workforce development** aims to raise standards of training and skills development of the social care workforce. A number of organisations currently work together to achieve this; the GSCC sets national benchmarks for training and education as well as holding responsibility for registering and regulating different strands of the workforce. This has been an incremental process since 2003. The Children's Workforce Development Council (CWDC) was established in 2006. It is an employer-led organisation representing many different types of worker and aims to address workforce issues needed for the workforce to achieve the five outcomes of Every Child Matters and to strengthen integrated working across all services. Skills for Care is the equivalent employer-led organisation for developing the Adult Social Care Workforce. A fuller discussion on the work of these organisations will be covered in Chapter 8 in the context of our examination of learning organisations.

In the previous section, I provided an outline of the history of how QA systems have been established in social care. I have also identified some of the key initiatives and policies that successive governments have put in place as an attempt to ensure that standards of care improve and how social care is scrutinised and regulated. We are now going to look in more detail at how actual standards in care are set and inspected, by looking at national service standards and the various methods of evaluating practice against these.

National service standards

The introduction of national minimum standards over the last decade has established different sets of standards for different care services, including statutory, private, voluntary, hospitals and nurse agencies in England. National minimum standards involve extensive analysis of the quality of care that must be provided by specific services and define these in a way that enables them to be measured for quality or to identify shortfalls in provision.

The key characteristics of a service standard

- It can be measured, monitored and evaluated;
- It's realistic and attainable within available resources;
- It's expressed clearly and unambiguously and tells people what they can expect;
- It's consistent with service aims and values;
- It's set in conjunction with the people asked to achieve it;
- It reflects what people say they value most.

(Martin and Henderson, 2001, pp. 194–5)

One of the issues that we have been discussing throughout this chapter is the identification of appropriate measures of the effectiveness of social work. These may be quantitative, for example, using numerical measures. These might be the number of times a person is referred to a service, timescales telling us about how quickly services were accessed and delivered, information about any delays, the duration of a service or, finally, numerical comparisons between individuals or populations involved in using services. On the other hand, qualitative measures, sometimes seen as less neutral, use methods which attempt to analyse data presented in words or which are socially constructed through a narrative. An example of qualitative data might be the documentation of the actual experiences of service users, including their subjective views and feelings, or a comparison of the effect of services on certain populations, expressed in words.

ACTIVITY **3.2**

Building on the above information, let us consider Standard 5 from the Children's Assessment Framework on Safeguarding and Promoting the Welfare of Children and Young People. This says:

All agencies should work together to prevent children suffering harm and to promote their welfare, provide them with the services they require to address their identified needs and safeguard children who are being or who are likely to be harmed.

(DoH, 2007a)

CONTINUED

Imagine you are a social worker working for the National Society for the Prevention of Cruelty to Children (NSPCC) which takes referrals about children who are reported to be 'at risk'. The NSPCC might be one of the agencies referred to in Standard 5 and be required to provide evidence of how well they might be performing against this standard as a way of maintaining their contract with the Children's Trust.

You have been asked to design some appropriate measures of the NSPCC's performance. You could start by identifying exactly what it is you need to measure; for example, this could be how long it takes for a social worker to assess a family from the time of referral, the outcomes of assessments in terms of the actions taken, the experiences of children, their parents and carers of the assessment, or the views and experiences of other agencies you work with.

Make a list of exactly what you intend to measure and your methods for doing this. State whether your measures or tools to evaluate the service are quantitative or qualitative.

If you found this activity difficult, don't worry. No doubt, in working through the above questions you would have begun to realise that setting a standard was probably a much easier task than identifying effective and reliable ways of measuring whether or not it has been met. Fundamental questions in trying to assure quality in a service such as safeguarding children are influenced by policy process as well as political and economic contexts in which measurements or indicators of quality are developed. For example, how do we distinguish between shorter- and longer-term outcomes for children we want to protect from further harm? How will we know if their needs had been met during the time they received services as well as in the outcomes? (Tilbury, 2004). Assumptions and values that we place on certain social work activities are pertinent here. We have to consider the need for accountability. Everybody involved in child care – professionals, managers, politicians, the general public and most importantly, children, young people themselves, their parents and carers – will hold very different and diverse views about what's most important. As you will see from the above activity, the best standards are also those which enable the person doing the job to see fairly easily when their performance is satisfactory and recipients of the service are satisfied. In safeguarding children, satisfaction with a service which the parties may not have wanted or even resisted altogether is another issue. How do we make sense of this when talking about quality assurance and satisfactory performance?

In a climate of targets and outcome measures, it is wise to keep in mind that good child welfare outcomes are inextricably tied to the quality of relationships between workers and families. If we fail to maintain the responsiveness, empathy, creativity, tenaciousness, knowledge, skills and motivation of our front line staff, then at the end of it all, new policies may have little or no impact in improving responses to vulnerable children and their families.

(Morrison, 2000, p. 373)

The use of quality groups to set standards and measure quality

Pillinger (2001) advocates the importance of what he terms 'quality groups', meaning teams of users, parents, staff and managers who work together to develop appropriate standards. His European study highlighted that national standards may prioritise efficiency and cost effectiveness at the expense of relevant standards that are locally based. To measure effectiveness we need appropriate and reliable measures of outcomes. Indicators used to measure quality of services can pay limited attention to service users' own, subjective perceptions. Focusing on service users'/carers' experiences and their priorities as an indicator of quality is more helpful. At an organisational level, core indicators may include the level of staff knowledge, whether services are meeting needs, the quality and attention given to listening and respecting service users (Mitchell and Sloper, 2002).

Quality assurance systems – Donabedian's model

At the beginning of this chapter we tried to define quality and referred to the need for a QA system to help implement quality management. Donabedian's model is one which picks up on the interrelated 'quality' elements referred to in the previous section. Donabedian identifies these as: structural inputs, process relationships and service outcomes. Each one is essential to the other in order to achieve quality in the final outcome. The process of achieving this is equally important. He explains it as follows:

- **Structure** – the stable characteristics of providers of care such as organisational frameworks referring to staffing, financial resources, management and structure. In Chapter 1 we saw that structure can increase or decrease the probability of good organisational performance, in the way it helps planning, or design and implementation of systems. Stable structures and organisations provide stable bases for continuous monitoring and evaluation of service delivery. Obviously, with the fluid nature of care organisations, this is probably the most challenging element.

- **Process** – the interaction between practitioners and service users referred to earlier, incorporating values and ethical principles in delivery of care. Autonomy would be one example. These factors are important to design, delivery and evaluation of care and are embedded in organisational procedures and practice to which these principles are key.

- **Outcome** – defined as the changes resulting from, or attributed to, the service provided. These include social and psychological as well as physical aspects of performance (Donabedian, 1980).

Legislation and policy guidelines in social care prioritise philosophy and practice of listening to service users. Despite theories and research findings, there is still a gulf between theoretical ideas and actually achieving these quality indicators in service users' and their families' everyday service experience and finding ways to express these in quality assurance systems. The need to be able to formulate and apply standards of quality is not only internal to particular organisations but is universal to systems of care. This explains one rationale behind national service frameworks which attempt to spell out basic standards for all different service user groups based on research.

We are going to look at how Donabedian's model can help us utilise one of the national objectives for children's services, but first a few words to clarify how governments go about inspecting, measuring, recording and publishing performance at a national level through the use of performance indicators (PIs) and the performance assessment framework (PAF).

National star ratings and league tables

Star ratings for social service were announced in 2001 as a means of summarising an inspection body such as CSCI, independent judgements of performance across all social services on a scale of zero to three stars. This was part of the government's comprehensive performance assessment framework (PAF) where the allocation of ratings is aimed at improving public information about current performance of services and capacity for improvement at local, regional and national levels. The ratings are supposed to provide an objective starting point for reviewing and planning improvements to services and are contingent on good services inspections. Organisations demonstrating substantial improvement and scoring three stars have more freedom in the way they use their centrally provided grant funds with reduced programmes of inspection and monitoring. Those with zero stars are subject to more frequent monitoring and have special monitoring arrangements and additional support put in place. Examples of personal social services (PSS) and PAF indicators you might come across in your local councils are:

- indicators to demonstrate that people from minority ethnic groups are treated fairly;

- providing services at a reasonable cost;

- investing now to prevent people needing more services later;

- helping to promote older people's independence.

Star ratings are designed to be compatible with performance information and independent ratings of organisations delivering care services. They are based on amalgamation of all performance indicators in a care trust, council or in a specific service area. A PI is one of the ways in which government measures how social care is integrated with other services. Judgements about the delivery of outcomes are focused firmly on the outcomes from the two key policy documents referred to at the end of Chapter 1 as well as judgements about the organisation's leadership, commissioning and use of resources. These performance ratings are summarised on a scale from zero to three stars and contribute to the Audit Commission's overall Comprehensive Performance Assessment of each council.

In order to reduce the burden of regulation and the extent of duplication of assessment of corporate governance within councils, corporate assessment (CA) is now delivered at the same time as the joint area review (known as the JAR) in children's services. This corporate assessment measures how effectively a council is working corporately, and with its partners, to improve services and deliver improved outcomes for local people. The JAR, for example, aims to judge the contribution that a council and its partners in the local area are making to improve outcomes for children and young people by gathering evidence during on-site fieldwork investigations. These focus on the contributions local services make to improving outcomes for more vulnerable groups of children and young people, and those groups not doing well enough or at risk of underachieving. They also follow up areas of weakness identified in the annual performance assessment. Such on-site fieldwork investigations include gathering evidence directly from children, young people, their parents and carers, front-line workers, senior managers, elected council members and the council's partner agencies and organisations. Inspectors also scrutinise a number of randomly selected case files to examine how far services work together to address the specific needs of these children and young people and promote their well-being. JARs seek to undertake reviews proportionate to risk, so higher-performing areas receive fewer on-site fieldwork investigations and a smaller inspection team than poorer performing areas which have a greater number of on-site fieldwork investigations and a larger inspection team. The JAR is also aligned with the inspection of youth offending teams undertaken by HMI of Probation and an enhanced youth inspection is also carried out at the same time.

The PAF requires authorities to translate their labours into numbers, such as the unit cost of each resource, the percentage of looked-after children who are adopted, the number of older and disabled people helped to stay in their own homes (DoH, 1999). Individual caseloads are not enough to make quantitative judgements about whether particular Children's Trusts are getting enough children in or out of care or the child safeguarding system. These have to be benchmarked against what others have achieved in similar circumstances and within standards expected. You may identify difficulties with this approach, which is not as straightforward as laid out in the guidance. To illustrate this we are going to examine one of the standards from the Children's Plan, 2007 and what's involved in measuring and assessing its success or achievement in achieving quality services.

RESEARCH SUMMARY

Outcomes for children looked after – education and life-chances

Following extensive research, it's widely acknowledged that children looked after (LAC) are substantially disadvantaged in their life chances (DfES, 2006). Raising the educational attainment of the looked after children is a central responsibility of local authorities and their partners. Under section 22(3)(a) of the Children Act 1989 amended by section 52 of the Children Act 2004, in England, there is a duty to give particular attention to the educational implications of any decision about young persons' welfare. A report by the Social Exclusion Unit's report A better education for children in care *(2003) identified five key reasons why looked after children underachieve in education. These were instability in placements; too much time out of school; insufficient help with education if they fall behind; poor expectation or preparation of primary carers to provide sufficient support and encouragement for learning and development; and unmet emotional, mental and physical health needs impacting on children's education.*

Statistics about the attainment of children in care

In 2006, just 12% of children in care achieved five good GCSEs compared with 59% of all children.

37% of children in care do not achieve any passes at GCSE, compared with 2% of all children.

Care leavers were also found more than twice as likely not to be in education, employment or training and only a fifth as likely to be in higher education at age 19 as other young people.

CONTINUED

Table 3.2

National indicator: PSA 11/DSO4 – Increase the educational qualifications of children looked after.

Rationale: Based on one of the *Every Child Matters five strategic outcomes* – 'Enjoy and Achieve'. This outcome spells out the DfES's strategic objective to close the gap in educational achievement for children from disadvantaged backgrounds

This indicator measures:
- Percentage of the numbers of LAC that reach level 4 in each of English and maths at Key Stage 2
- Percentage of LAC that achieve 5 A*–C GCSEs (or equivalent) at Key Stage 4 (including English and maths)

Aims: To narrow the gap in educational achievement between LAC and their peers; improve educational support and stability. By 2008, 80 per cent of children under 16 looked after for 2.5 years or more to be in the same placement for at least 2 years.

Other sources of evidence required: Each JAR will look for:
— The presence of an effective personal education plan (PEP) for LAC and its implementation. Level of support given to ensure participation in education to achieve potential.
— Action taken to maximise school attendance, and in avoiding exclusion from school of LAC.
— How educational achievement, school attendance and cultural experiences of LAC are monitored on an individual basis, and collectively in reports to senior officers and elected members, and any action taken to address the findings.

JARs also make judgements on how LAC are helped to achieve economic well-being, through preparation for leaving care and after-care support. Evidence would include Personal Pathway Plans (PPPs); personal and welfare support; encouragement and support to engage in further and higher education and employment and training. Ofsted now considers how far education provided meets the needs of a range of pupils at those schools, including giving specific attention to how far the needs of LAC on a school's roll are met.

(*Source: Every Child Matters Outcomes Framework* from *The Children's Plan*, 2007. DfES
www.dfes.gov.uk/publications/childrensplan/implement.shtml)

ACTIVITY 3.3

Thinking about quality and the need for in-depth investigation, you are asked to look at the government standard for LAC education using Donabedian's model. This is set out in Table 3.3. I have put some of the elements in, to help you get started. You are asked to think about what's involved in evaluating whether LAC are getting a better or equal education by describing each element required.

Hopefully, during this exercise you established that any measure of how LAC are doing in education involves identifying for each unique child, numerous organisational issues relating to staffing, resources, management, multi-agency working as well as the process embodied in social work practice. This attends to how it might improve the physical, emotional, sexual health, family contact, community involvement and preparation for independence of LAC (HM Govt, 2005). It is not merely a matter of each stakeholder reporting back to government performance in this area.

Table 3.3

Using Donabedian's model to evaluate whether LAC are getting a better or equal education

Objective: To ensure that children looked after gain maximum life chance benefits from educational opportunities, health care and social care.
Sub-objective: To bring the overall performance of children looked after, for a year or more, in National Curriculum Tests closer into line with local children generally.

Structure	Process	Outcome
Children's Trusts establish systems for identifying LAC	Social workers will discuss child's needs and abilities with the school staff and be involved with planning and ensuring support is in place for children to do their homework, learn as best they can Social workers will work with the carers/parents to encourage them to prioritise school work and focusing on issues to do with school	Every looked-after child will take national curriculum tests and have a record of their achievement Every looked-after child will achieve one or more GSCE Grade A* – G in Year 11
Ensure every tier of the authority management structure has an endorsed policy signalling ownership of how it will meet this objective	Written plans are drawn up for each child in accordance with the national local guidance	Every looked-after child has been assessed and received support services from the multi-disciplinary team and has an educational pathway plan
Ensure a suitable range of care and education placement options are commissioned and available to meet the needs of LAC	Nominated persons will discuss and assess suitability of educational arrangements for the child and make recommendations to the multi-disciplinary team about what is needed	Looked-after children have been involved in plans for their own education and have a personal education plan
Ensure there are agreed procedures and protocols in place to support a shared understanding of the LA's role as corporate parent in meeting the best educational interests of LAC, wherever they are placed	Independent Reviewing Officers responsible for monitoring the local authority's function as a corporate parent in respect of the statutory review of a child's Care Plan, ensure educational needs are considered, decided upon, implemented and monitored	
Ensure that the wider services developed for LAC through the Children's Trust take full account of the duty to promote their educational achievement as an integral part of their well-being.	Train carers and those involved in how to support LAC and how to actively promote their needs. Provide those supporting children with good information and knowledge of local arrangements and services Use the PEP tool to personalise and involve the child or young person in identifying their own ambitions	

Source: Donabedian (1980) using table adapted from Martin and Henderson (2001, 205). Used with permission from *The Definition of Quality and Approaches to its Assessment, Exploration in Quality Assessment and Monitoring,* Donabedian, A. (Chicago: Health Administration Press, 1980) pp 79–92 and with permission from Thompson Publishing Service: *Managing in Health and Social Care*, Martin, V and Henderson, E (2001) London: Routledge, Open University Press p 205

RESEARCH SUMMARY

An evaluation of educational needs and performance of children living in a private residential care setting searched for other factors that might be influential. In the context of prescribed educational frameworks for assessing children's success at school, it found of equal importance other areas in children's lives. Attendance, peer relationships, involvement in extracurricular activities highlighted that it is not just academic attainment but vocational skills and practical abilities which are significant. Recommendations reinforced the importance of talking to children and young people about their aspirations and motivation and the supportive role of social work in boosting children's emotional competencies in areas such as self-esteem, confidence and assertiveness.

(Gallagher et al., 2004)

Messages from research studies tell us that focusing on success rather than weaknesses or failures is an area that needs development in policy-making. Any measure of how LAC are doing in education must not underestimate the challenges and must pay attention to the level of educational disadvantage many children will have experienced before being looked after; for example, their feelings of ambiguity, if not hostility, towards education. The importance of agencies working together is stressed. This is reinforced in the Children Act 2004 as an instrument for overhauling the organisational arrangements for delivering seamless services to children.

Service user's comment

> Moving around a lot is one of the real issues for young people in care, especially as it can affect your education ... you need someone who encourages you with your school work or even leisure activities. You need someone who cares for you – a social worker, foster carer, support worker – someone who is also your best friend.

(Ruth Hayman giving a first-hand account of her experiences of being in care, 2001, p. 27)

When the inspector calls – regulation and inspection regimes

On a national level, social care services are inspected in a number of ways within integrated inspection regimes in order to reflect the joined-up way in which they are delivered. We have established during this chapter a degree of consensus between government, organisations, staff and service users that setting standards for services is necessary and important and a process, of inspection, measurement or evaluation is essential to enable quality to be maintained. However, there is still a psychology of anxiety which pervades the regulatory process particularly in connection with the inspection process. Why is this?

Humphrey (2003a, b), in a series of articles on government inspection of social services, identified interesting dynamics and issues that can emerge during inspection processes. She highlighted the following benefits and difficulties from the organisational perspective.

Benefits of external formal inspection:

- Role modelling by inspectors in the process of reviewing, collating, interpreting and utilising a wide range of qualitative and quantitative data about social care.

- Emphasising democracy in social care by talking directly with service users/carers, junior staff and professionals from other agencies in areas where dialogues have been neglected by senior staff and politicians.

- Forcing senior managers to gaze beyond their immediate work tasks and to network with other colleagues and agencies.

- Giving immediate attention to issues that need putting right before they are judged or the inspection team arrive.

- The political value that forces key people to take responsibilities or listen to people either receiving or delivering services.

Difficulties

- Ambivalence of staff in statutory organisations and the impact of public labelling that causes key actors to be at loggerheads with each other rather than concentrating on more supportive aspects of inspection.

- The actual cost of reviews and inspections, for governments and by diverting staff away from their 'day job'. Unless outcomes lead to improvement in efficiency, quality and allocation of resources to problem areas, the cost is not legitimised.

- Recognition that regulatory regimes alone will not shift fundamental problems like culture in public authorities, material inequalities between communities or inadequate resources for social care.

- The use of managerialist language alien to professional practice and everyday life.

- The lack of direct observation of social work, supervision or management practice in the inspection methodology.

In summary, using audits as a tool to measure outcomes in social care can end up merely as a ritual to ensure compliance with procedures rather than as a signpost to the vitality of practice (Nocon and Qureshi, 1996; Humphrey, 2003b). This is illustrated in the case study below.

Involvement of service users in inspection – experts by experience

More recently, inspection and regulation work has involved people who use services in order to add value to the process. The phrase 'experts by experience' is used to describe people whose knowledge about social care services comes directly from their experience of using them and who have chosen to become more closely involved with regulatory bodies by developing their skills, knowledge and expertise. Some evaluations of using experts by experience during inspections have demonstrated that their involvement enabled the inspection to pick up on and note details such as care practices, accessibility within care, particularly in residential homes, and on the interaction and non-verbal communication between staff and people who use the services (CSCI, 2007). The use of different tools, such as picture cards, easy questions with pictures and direct observation techniques has contributed much-needed evidence to the inspection reporting process. Partnerships and relationships between the stakeholders involved have been developing from this work and can provide mutual recognition of the benefits of working together with service users for a common purpose. In children's services, the Lilac (Lifelong Improvement for Looked-After Children) project has trained young people who have been in care to become inspectors focusing on how well looked-after children are involved in their own care and how effectively complaints are dealt with. This scheme has enabled young people to develop their own standards and has paid them to train in inspection work, giving it professional status and the ability to award a kite mark to services considered excellent (Conn, 2007).

CASE STUDY

Inspectors from joint review teams inspected a fostering and adoption team where there was agreement that too many young people were in 'out of area' placements because of a shortage of foster carers. During the interview, the team explained how they had invested in training, support packages to retain existing carers, lobbied councillors for improved payments, been working out of hours to recruit at local festivals, etc. The reviewer repeatedly asked for evidence of outcomes in terms of numbers of new carers recruited. As these were in the preparation rather than the availability stage, the team failed to meet the regulatory test, highlighting the hazardous journey from process to outcomes.

(Nocon and Qureshi, 1996)

Now that we have examined the pros and cons of measuring performance, in this final section, I will invite you to focus inwards on your own practice by examining ways in which teams and professional practitioners within organisational settings can redress this balance to develop quality in their own services.

Creating a framework of continuous quality improvement in your own practice

Without a doubt, whether you are working in an integrated or inter-agency service in the public sector or within the third sector, your service will be subject to quality assurance, performance assessment and measurement. This affects everyone involved in service delivery, especially our relationships with managers at all levels in the organisations we work in. Emphasis on evidence-based practice means constantly examining and questioning what is being learnt about the effectiveness of services, targeting and improvement. To achieve outcomes consistent with social work values, the GSCC codes of practice and professional aspirations, we must be conversant with these issues.

In previous chapters we emphasised the importance of relationships and trust in social work practice when working alongside individuals and communities to enhance the capacity of people we are working with. Pragmatism by recognising the limited capacity of service organisations to meet everybody's needs is required. Management processes which maximise opportunities for collaboration with service users and service providers are vital. This ensures effective information sharing and feedback between management and stakeholders (Healy, 2002, p. 528). Collaboration is preferred over more hierarchical approaches to management. Structures should be developed to allow for information flow and exchange about what can be changed and how it can inform decision-making. This does not necessarily mean everybody having equal input but indicates the need for appropriate input at key points in the process.

ACTIVITY **3.4**

If you are working towards a degree in social work or another award, you will very likely be asked to produce evidence in one way or another that your own practice is delivered to a high standard, and this will require the involvement of service users/carers in assessing your practice.

Spend a few minutes considering how you might demonstrate 'quality' in your own practice and appropriate methods of obtaining the evidence for this.

Some of the approaches to the above task would have included two very important aspects in day-to-day practice. Firstly, your direct work with service users, which is probably the most natural vehicle for ensuring accountability and quality of practice by asking service users regularly and sensitively what they think of the service and finding ways of documenting this as objectively as possible. Secondly, your relationship with your first line manager, who acts as a key watchdog for social work practice and as your supervisor would be expected to give and receive feedback on a regular basis to ensure the standards of service that you provide are high.

As professionals we need to go beyond what is handed down in our organisations, for example more formal inspections and reporting, and take responsibility for setting our own standards, by enhancing professional practice and moving beyond procedurally driven analyses of problems and solutions. In addition, you should look out for and contribute to local policies and procedures within the organisation that can help us improve the quality of day-to-day practice. These may include:

- establishing learning cultures in your team and service area supported by effective information sharing and communication;

- supporting and applying evidence-based practice, identifying the right models of intervention to presenting situations;

- accountability and performance monitoring which is evaluated through regular supervision;

- risk management, achieving the balance between assessment and management of risk which is rights-based and clearly addresses issues of users' vulnerability and need for protection;

- quality improvement systems that include checking and auditing case files and recording systems, directly observing practice, training programmes, setting local standards as well as national ones against which evaluation is discussed and published;

- establishing research and development cultures, which can be in areas where there are minimal legislative frameworks to guide staff, such as domestic violence, vulnerable adults, community development, or by sharing ideas and good practice locally in your teams;

- involvement of service users and the public, in all areas of service delivery, in assessments, individual planning, new service developments, policy development, complaints, working groups to solve problems, mentoring and role modelling for other service users.

(McCullagh, 2001, cited in Statham, 2004, p. 88)

Creating a culture of quality and performance – collaboration or conflict?

Some commentators argue that the measurement of quality and performance in organisations can be a potential battleground between managerial and professional interest (Dominelli, 1997; Tsui and Cheung, 2004). Personal experiences of audits, inspections, or involvement in change management will also determine how responsible you feel towards these issues. Perception of how we value performance measurement is determined by the approach used, especially in the way in which our organisations and management involve staff and other stakeholders in the process.

A culture of quality assurance can only evolve over time and in a way where it is seen less as an instrument of external control. This is an even greater challenge in highly diverse workforces. Monitoring and inspection procedures must be instituted alongside other incentives for professionals to have a positive effect on the culture of quality assurance and their closer involvement with organisational priorities. Developing critical reflective practice acts as an alternative to blaming the organisation for poor quality services and being accountable for this (Fook, 2004).

Taking a team approach

The work of Smyth et al. (1999) engaged social workers, managers and service users to define standards, which represented their day-to-day work. This was then developed into a practice-based tool to provide social workers themselves and their line managers with a mechanism for reflection and feedback. Embedding this model into a supervisory framework can help social workers move away from a mechanistic task-centred focus prescribed through legislation and policy. In a stable and experienced workforce, custom and practice can even work better over policies, procedures or written guidance.

The future of quality assurance and performance management

Quality assurance, its management and regulation are here to stay and are integral to our organisations and our professional development. As we have seen, these are also firmly enshrined in legislation and policy. The future of social care regulation is changing, starting with the Better Regulation Task Force Report *Bridging the Gap* (2004) which emphasises the increasing participation and contribution of service users of care services in the process of inspection and regulation. With the development of separate bodies for regulating and inspecting adult and children's services (CSCI, 2008c) and the integration of these with other disciplines, there is a concern about the rise of 'super-inspectorates' following the merger of service provision and which are accountable directly to Parliament. This has led to criticism that these new bodies will no longer remain as independent regulators but become arm's length from the government by other indirect means. It is asserted that any regulator should carry out its duties using best evidence *in a fearless manner on behalf of the people who use services* (CSCI, 2008c, p. 7). Within adult services in particular, where health issues tend to attract more political attention, and where individual social care purchasers are not generally in a strong position, they may subsequently lack good sources of information and advice needing regulatory protection. Further, there is concern that the experts-by-experience programme may be subsumed into an advisory committee which undermines a more consultative approach. On a more positive note, there are expectations that inspections focus much more on outcomes, which means looking at how services deliver for their users and take user perspectives as central to judging effectiveness. At a local level, motivation to co-operate with this approach needs to be sustained by good inter-organisational and external relationships and obligations which take on board moral and ethical values as well as regulatory ones. This is the role of professionals, government and their organisations.

C H A P T E R   S U M M A R Y

This chapter has looked at the development of quality assurance and performance management within social care and other organisations we work with. We looked at the complexities and difficulties of measuring effectiveness of social work and social care services in an historical context. We concluded that we cannot maximise quality and performance through measurement alone and looked at some of the ways that you as a practitioner can contribute to quality services and the reputation and effectiveness of these.

FURTHER READING

Hafford-Letchfield, T (2007) *Practising quality assurance in social care*. Exeter: Learning Matters.

This book takes a more in-depth look at the challenging topic of quality assurance and performance management in such a way that it enables readers to apply this knowledge to their own settings and roles.

Martin, S and Davis, H (2008) (eds) *Public services inspection in the UK: Recent changes and future challenges*. London: Jessica Kingsley.

This book provides a detailed account of the changing role of inspection in public services management. It outlines the continuing debates about providing inspection that encourages accountability and provides insights into the different methods and the underlying issues and tension involved.

If you are interested in reading more about the education of children looked after, there are a number of good quality resources and publications on the Who Cares? Trust website. These offer practical tools to improve literacy, promote the enjoyment of reading and writing, and develop self-esteem and decision-making skills.

www.thewhocarestrust.org.uk/publications/htm

WEBSITES

www.rip.org.uk/
Research in Practice provides support and up-to-date reports on evidence-based practice for children and families.

www.uea.ac.uk/swk/research/mrc/welcome.htm
Making Research Count is a national initiative where collaboration between academic and operational staff in social care aims to develop evidence-based social work and social care practice, and to improve the dissemination of research.

www.scie.org.uk
The Social Care Institute for Excellence, a body which develops and disseminates the knowledge base for social care as a means of improving quality through best practice.

www.csci.org.uk
The Commission for Social Care Inspection. Here you can find a range of information about the inspection process, public inspection reports, the national standards and performance indicators for adult social care.

www.everychildmatters.gov.uk
Here you will find the outcomes framework which supports the five outcomes and underpinning aims for children's services. It links to national targets and other key indicators on which services are judged.

Chapter 4
Service user involvement and customer care

This chapter will help you achieve the following National Occupational Standards and General Social Care Council's Code of Practice.

Key Role 1: Work with individuals, families, carers, groups and communities to help them make informed decisions.

- Enable individuals, families, carers, groups and communities to identify, clarify and express their strengths, expectations and limitations.
- Enable individuals, families, carers, groups and communities to assess and make informed decisions about their needs and circumstances, risks, preferred options and resources.

Key Role 3: Support individuals to represent their needs, views and circumstances.

- Advocate with, and on behalf of, individuals, families, carers, groups and communities including accessing independent advocacy.
- Work with individuals, families, carers, groups and communities to select the best form of representation for decision-making forums and to be involved in or understand the procedures and outcomes from decision-making forums.

General Social Care Code of Practice

Code 1: Protect the rights and promote the interests of service users and carers

- Respecting and where appropriate promoting individual views and wishes.
- Supporting service users' rights to control their lives and make informed choices about services they receive.

Code 3: Promote independence of service users while protecting them as far as possible from harm

- Promoting the independence of service users and assisting them to understand and exercise their rights.
- Helping service users and carers to make complaints, take them seriously and respond appropriately.

Code 4: Respect the rights of service users while seeking to ensure that their behaviour does not harm themselves or other people

It will also introduce you to the following academic standards as set out in the social work subject benchmark statements:

2.4 and 5 Defining principles

- Understand the impact of injustice, social inequalities and oppressive social relations.
- Work in a transparent and responsible way, balancing autonomy with complex, multiple and sometimes contradictory accountabilities.

3.2.3 Communication skills

- Listen actively to others, engage appropriately with the life experiences of service users, and understand accurately their viewpoint. Identify and use opportunities for purposeful and supportive communication with service users within their everyday situations.

3.2.4 Skills in working with others

- Involve users of social work services in ways that increase their resources, capacity and power to influence factors affecting their lives.
- Consult actively with others, including service users who hold relevant information or expertise.

Introduction

This chapter will focus specifically on frameworks used by organisations to involve service users in the design, delivery and evaluation of social care services. This forms the cornerstone of any effective quality assurance system and is essential to the provision of high quality care and support. We will start by looking at service user involvement from a theoretical perspective by looking at a model which describes the different levels of participation possible within social care organisations. There will be reference to the relevant legislative and policy frameworks which make service user involvement not only desirable, but a statutory requirement. By identifying specific issues and challenges arising from implementation of service user participation strategies, we will then go on to consider specific features of organisational structures and cultures necessary for its success. This chapter is particularly concerned with service user perspectives on their involvement in social care. There will be an overview of how the service user movement has provided alternatives to traditional social care services through the development of user-controlled services and self-advocacy. Towards the end of the chapter, we will look briefly at the role of organisational customer care policies, specifically statutory customer complaints and representation procedures. Whilst these provide just one mechanism for organisations to get feedback from service users, they are an important tool for ensuring service users' rights to representation and redress. We will conclude by looking at the role of **advocacy** as a tool to support service users' and carers' participation.

Service user participation

Service user and carer involvement has become a guiding principle in social care planning, development, provision and arrangements of services so that they can improve and become more effective in meeting complex or diverse needs. There is plenty of evidence of the vision and leadership provided by service users at both a national and local level in the social care system (Manthorpe, 2004; Barnes and Mercer, 2004). Service users not only bring expertise but can help professionals define the roles and support needed to be accountable and responsive to change and improvement. Opportunities for service users and carers to take on leadership roles are equally dependent on the cultures of organisations providing social care and the presence of structures to facilitate meaningful working relationships between them. That users should have to adapt to the existing organisational culture, rather than the other way around by providing user-friendly practices, is the subject of much criticism. Both Bailey (2004) and Carr (2004) have identified organisational responsiveness as a common issue in their reviews of service user participation. In Chapter 1, we saw that some services now provided by statutory organisations originated from small charitable and voluntary organisations, the development of which has since been influenced by constant change in various governments' economic, political and social policies. Traditional divisions between services users and professionals have their roots in the history of this development of 'welfare' in the UK affecting decision-making about 'care' through the development of exclusionary structures and institutional practices and attitudes (Carr, 2004). These structural factors continue to play a major role in determining not only the required outcomes of services in the public sector but in the way they are designed and delivered. On the other hand, significant pieces of legislation have marked a theoretical movement away from paternalistic to partnership-based approaches. Legislation and policy statements now explicitly state the importance of enabling those who are in receipt of services to have their say in how those services are run (Beresford and Campbell, 1994). Examples of these are the NHSCCA 1990, Children Acts 1989 and 2005, National Care Standards Act 2000, Best Value guidance, the White Paper *Valuing People*, 2001. The principles of personalisation and self-care in public services have further challenged the capacity of the care system to empower service users and to increase the autonomy of practitioners in empowering service users. Recent government guidance (HM Govt, 2007a; DoH, 2007d) has promoted the concept of 'co-production' in which support is directed towards working in partnership through a process of two-way communication, negotiation and decision making between individuals and professionals to achieve the best possible outcomes (SfC, 2008b). These documents refer to:

> *The actions people take for themselves, their children and their families to stay fit and maintain good physical and mental health; meet social and psychological needs, prevent illness or accidents; care for minor ailments and long-term conditions; and maintain health and well-being after an acute illness or discharge from hospital.*

> (DoH, 2005e)

During the 1990s, consultation exercises and responding to campaigning user-led groups became an increasingly common element of government policy reviews. The Direct Payments Act 1995 is an explicit example of the direct impact of service user-led organisations on national and local government decision-making. Through working together, the government was able to capitalise on the expertise, knowledge and experience of disabled people in employment and personal assistant issues lending credibility to decisions made as a result of involving service users at all levels in public services. Many of the pilots introducing individual budgets have been informed by users' experience of what has worked and what hasn't in attempting to implement direct payments. In essence, user involvement has become the process whereby service users can contribute in some way to the decisions made within the statutory and third sectors to services that may have a profound effect on their lives (Carmichael, 2004, p. 195).

The user involvement process

In the previous chapter we looked at quality assurance and performance measurements and the potential impact of service user involvement on the evaluation of service outcomes. We are now moving on to concentrate more on the process of involvement. As stated earlier, doubts still persist about how well organisations are tackling service user participation within established mainstream structures which on the surface seem to be commonplace. However, power dynamics continue to underline effective user-led change and power issues are still inadequately acknowledged or addressed even within well established consultation mechanisms at various levels within organisations. According to Carr (2004), these power relations may be present at a strategic level, right through to how managers and professionals interact on a day-to-day level in practice with users, carers, their families and networks.

The social model of disability and theoretical models

The acceptance of the **social model of disability** has been a key achievement of the service user movement and its allies in the wider development of consumer and citizens' rights and the right to independent living (Oliver, 1990). The social model has implications for the way in which services have been organised and participation initiatives conceived. People using social care services for support and assistance to live independently understand participation to mean more than just being a consumer of services and are interested in how services can help them become active citizens to whom such services are accountable (Carr, 2004). For example, when asked, older people have strong views about the factors that make a difference to their lives. These include good quality housing, safe neighbourhoods, getting out and about and having useful, enjoyable ways of contributing to the community (Audit Commission and BGOP, 2004b). However, because we often see older people as dependent and frail, rather than as citizens with a broad range of concerns and a contribution to make, services for older people focus on a narrow range of intensive services that support only the most vulnerable in times of crisis. Listening to older people beyond health and social care issues and engaging with them as a valuable resource entails a fundamental shift in the way services are delivered away from dependence to interdependence.

Models of service user involvement

Models of service user involvement are related to theories of empowerment and advocacy which incorporate critical, feminist and anti-discrimination theories but originate from social democratic practice. **Social democracy** is aimed at enabling people to overcome barriers in achieving life objectives and gain access to services (Payne, 2005, p. 295). The management view of empowerment is concerned with motivating individuals and teams to achieve more towards organisational objectives by granting them greater independence from managerial control. This is not an easy concept to address within public sector organisations that hold legislative and regulatory responsibilities. Hasler (2003) notes that democratic and inclusive practices can sit uneasily with a target-driven public body where participation and other aspects of service delivery are affected by managerialist approaches (p. 47). However, whilst the use of statutory powers raises obstacles to trust and respect necessary to successful partnerships, this is not impossible to attain (Thompson, 2003). Parsloe (1996) agrees that the term 'empowerment' is used to mean giving people a greater say in how services are organised by allowing people to take part in planning, through representative consultations and mutual self-help. The use of empowerment as a fashionable concept creates an idealistic and perhaps misleading objective for practice in a period when the role of social work agencies is increasingly limited to protection or in rationing service provision within a restricted financial environment. We should not mistake empowerment for enablement (Payne, 2005, p. 302) and advocates of the social model of disability frequently challenge these concepts:

> *it [the social model] is nothing more complicated than a clear focus on the economic, environmental and cultural barriers disabled people encounter including inaccessible education systems, working environments, inadequate disability benefits, discriminatory health and social support services, inaccessible transport, houses and public buildings and amenities, and the devaluing of disabled people through negative images in the media.*

(Oliver, 2004, p. 21)

The social model has led to a growth in alternative organisations within the sector led by disabled people themselves and disability activists. Taking off in the 1980s, the social model has been seen as a primary means of achieving disability equality across the whole range of organisations. Further, by incorporating this model into state provision, activists concur that this approach counters individualised casework and moves towards targeting the disabling society to meet disabled people's self-articulated needs. It is this structural change to which partnerships, alliances and opportunities that are community orientated are necessary (Oliver, 2004). You may be wondering how social work practitioners and public sector organisations are able to influence external barriers to independent living which may often feel beyond their control, for example with issues such as inaccessible transport and lack of employment opportunities. Activists argue, however, that social care organisations through proactive user involvement and participation do have a role to play in supporting service users to campaign for themselves. They can do this by listening and consulting with them about their issues and support needs, by funding their organisations, and actively supporting them through planning mechanisms with other public sector structures using the social model (Barnes and Mercer, 2004).

The service user participation continuum

As you can see from the above discussion, the extent to which service users participate or are involved in social care services is more usefully described as a continuum where different levels or stages of relationships occur. These range from the sharing of information through to increasing levels of partnership between service users and providers and ultimately full delegated control to service users. This model was originally developed through work done by the King's Fund (2002) and is illustrated in Figure 4.1.

This continuum does not have any right or wrong levels as service users need to proceed at their own pace and determine the level of involvement that they desire, or are comfortable with, or is appropriate to their situation. This model is helpful but makes assumptions that the status of people who are involved are consumers or users of services. Further distinctions can be made between 'consumerist' perspectives which accompanied the introduction of the market economy into social care from the 1980s and which considers service users as consumers of services; and democratic approaches which are more democratic in origin and based on the achievement of full and equal citizenship for users (Oliver, 1990; Beresford and Campbell, 1994). This latter approach is one adopted by service user-led organisations and campaigners such as People First and Shaping Our Lives. The debates around levels of participation and involvement are even more complex, according to Pollitt (2003) and Martin and Boaz (2000), who incorporate two further dimensions in their analysis. The first dimension is that of the 'identity' of those engaging in participative activities and whether we are talking about 'service users', 'citizens' or 'communities'. This is in part determined by the forum through which they play a part in discussing how the authority and resources of the state should be deployed. It is also determined by the status attributed to those participating. The second dimension is the 'intensity' of interaction with the state through the four levels of involvement as outlined in Figure 4.1. Therefore people participating as members of communities would be involved in public relations exercises at the information level but at the participation level would be exercising active community leadership (Pollitt, 2003, p. 99).

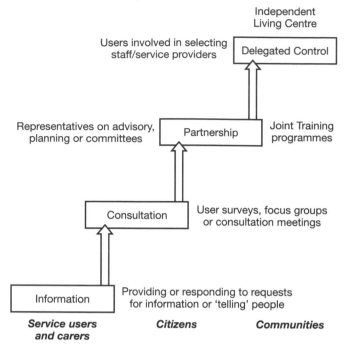

Figure 4.1 The service user involvement continuum.

Reproduced with permission from the King's Fund from *Living Options in Practice* (1992) *Achieving User Partication: Planning Services for people with Severe Physical and Sensory Disabilities,* Barrie Fiedler with Diana Twitchin

---

ACTIVITY **4.1**

Think about an organisation that you are familiar with and provide examples of how it consults its stakeholders, service users or customers. Using the model of Figure 4.1, decide at which level the organisation mostly operates on the service user continuum.

User participation – messages from the literature

The extensive literature on service user involvement comes mainly from the service user movement itself (HCIL, 1990; Beresford and Campbell, 1994). Attention to developing knowledge about participation techniques has been said to have been at the expense of critical reflection on the outcomes of participation. This has led to neglect in the research and evaluation on the relationship between the process of participation and the achievement of tangible user-led change (Carr, 2004; Bailey, 2004). The challenge remains for social care organisations to achieve meaningful and genuine service user involvement in practice and to make links between experience, research and participation. Whilst the social model provides a tool to communicate ideas, its language has penetrated into institutional and organisational literature often concurrently with continuing oppressive practice (Bailey, 2004).

> *It is only the disabled person who can satisfactorily define his or her needs in terms of the enabling of equal opportunity. This is the basis of demanding consultation, and it is the purpose of consultation.*

> (Hampshire Centre for Integrated Living, 1990)

Developing successful strategies involves recognition of factors which impinge on the process including necessary support from managers, colleagues and resource allocation. According to Harding and Beresford (1993), organisations must take a closer look at the ways in which they can easily exclude people, for example in the way in which they conduct formal and sometimes daunting meetings, the use of incomprehensible language and pre-ordained objectives and timescales.

Service user involvement in social work practice

So far, we have been discussing service user involvement from a collective perspective. At the individual level, the way in which service users and carers are involved in constructing their own care or support packages in direct social work practice is based on ideas around promoting greater choice and control. This depends on power sharing at the practice level and the way in which, on a day-to-day basis, professional perspectives and attitudes towards service user decision-making capability is encouraged and maximised. This can sometimes mean finding the right balance between protection and self-determination. Self-determination is a problematic principle because it presupposes the existence of a neutral environment. However, the environment can be heavily constrained by legal mandates, the range of services and resources available including information about options, appropriate and flexible provision and the presence of good communication skills and assessment (Preston-Shoot, 2001). For children and young people, constructive and ongoing involvement in decision-making is more likely in organisations which have developed a participatory culture: one in which children are encouraged to participate in small as well as big decisions. Service users of all ages, their parents and carers highlight the importance of good communication. Many understand issues about accountability and resources but want to be kept informed about things that affect them as well as knowing that social services departments are working together with other agencies in their interests particularly at transition points (DoH, 2004c).

RESEARCH SUMMARY

The National Children's Society made 35 consultation visits to children's homes and held two national children's conferences and six special workshops with children and young people. The following key messages emerged:

- Treat us individually, not just as children as a whole;

- When we make a complaint – sort it, not just report it;

- Ask us what we think on our own and listen to what we say;

- We want to be looked after by adults we can trust, don't always believe an adult over a child, ask for evidence and decide for yourself;

- Don't patronise us – but explain so we can understand. Don't talk complex;

- Children have a right to privacy;

- Treat our private worries confidentially – they're not for chatting and joking about.

(DoH, 2004b, p. 9)

Evidence on the participation of children and young people in their individual care planning emphasises that children continue to feel that they are not listened to despite having a statutory framework that supports participation. Children perceive formal processes as boring, repetitive, intrusive and also frightening and these are not working well for young people from a minority ethnic background and who are disabled or looked after (Carr, 2004). At the level of direct service delivery, there can be a conflict between staff and managers' desire to involve service users which can compromise any meaningful engagement in organisational processes. Organisations and their managers need to be supportive of front-line practitioners in their focus on user concerns and create space for users and staff to debate issues that can be compromised by organisational structures and **audit** cultures.

ACTIVITY **4.2**

What do you envisage to be the main barriers to participation and service user involvement in social care organisations?

First and foremost, a genuine shift in attitudes to facilitate participation is fundamental. Effective user involvement has two preconditions. It requires, first, the commitment of managers in the service and, second, a readiness to invest time and resources to ensure service users and carers can play a full part in the process (Bamford, 2001). The latter needs commitment to planning time and giving consideration to people's needs. This means being proactive in offering support to service users, for example in providing suitable transport, meeting support needs, and giving training so that unnecessary barriers are not created. These barriers can be physical or cultural. Physical barriers may be easier to resolve although these may be affected by financial constraints and unrealistic timescales. When working with service user groups such as young people, people with learning disabilities or mental health problems, difficulties with professional ideas about their 'competency' or 'decision-making' can also get in the way. Research shows that generally, levels of involvement with these groups do not often progress from information giving and consultation levels as opposed to the level of sharing or giving full decision-making power (Carr, 2004).

Sensitivity is a particular requirement when engaging people from minority communities, not just in relation to attention needed to the process through the use of interpreters or respect for the cultural issues involved but also acknowledgment of more experiential and political understanding of their experiences. When working with the black community, for example, the basis for achieving a detailed analysis and understanding of the views and experiences of oppressed groups through their direct involvement can often conflict with institutionalised approaches to consultation or participation (Ejo, 2004; Butt et al., 2005). The way in which black service users and their community organisations have been marginalised and made invisible when it comes to engaging them in commissioning and contracting for social care services is well documented (www.cemvo.org.uk; DoH, 2005c). Barnes et al. (2000) found that where small, often user-led community-based organisations have difficulties in securing funding beyond the current financial year, this can make planning difficult and service user involvement unrealistic. Diversity in user involvement should ensure that some groups are not less represented than others and that there is a balance in terms of gender, sexual orientation, race, age and disability, amongst other diversity factors.

The Bibini Centre for Young People is a wholly independent and registered charity. Bibini is managed by and for people from black and minority ethnic communities. In response to considerable dissatisfaction with the lack of appropriate practice and disproportionate level of control of support services for young black people and their families, adults and young people combined their skills to develop a culturally competent resource that has been successful in:

- providing high-quality residential and community-based services for black young people in or leaving care and at risk of family break-up;

- developing a range of innovative projects offering practical solutions to the support needs of black young people;

- highlighting and challenging discrimination and disadvantage within social care and wider society.

As innovators, the Bibini Centre shares several difficulties with black-run organisations such as insecure funding, suspicion and insensitivity from the statutory sector and wider voluntary sector. The role of managers in reconciling demands of service users and the impact of discrimination on the organisation and individuals within it, whilst still trying to successfully deliver services from a community based perspective, has been difficult. However, Bibini's strength lies in its success in reclaiming research into black communities by consistently drawing on the expertise of young people, their families and communities.

(Ejo, 2004)

Making service user involvement happen – the issues

We have already identified that organisations need to ensure that the appropriate structures are in place so that they can use these to communicate with service users. Clarity of purpose should specify rights, powers and responsibilities within any consultation process. In her research into the outcomes from evaluation of service user involvement, Carmichael (2004) found that satisfaction with the process and outcomes was greater among professionals than users themselves. 'Consultation fatigue' is an issue, especially if few improvements are made as a result of a lengthy bureaucratic consultation process. In her own research with disabled people, Carmichael found that accountability and control of projects were the key determinants of service users' satisfaction levels; they gave noticeably higher rating to exercises in which they had taken a leading role, or when they had been the initiators (Robson et al., 2003; Carmichael, 2004).

The challenging agenda of personalising public services represents a much greater wholesale strategic shift towards user involvement which aims to give every person across the spectrum of need greater choice and control over the shape of his or her support, in the most appropriate setting. For some, exercising such choice and control will require a significant level of assistance either through professionals or through independent advocates (DoH, 2008b). Your organisation will be thinking about its local philosophy alongside issues such as demography and how to engage its workforce in a considerable programme of change. Some predict that as service users gain more control over their services and support, there will be a struggle for power. Management will need to energise its workforce by bringing it along to ensure that it signs up to this new agenda and works collaboratively with people who use services, particularly in supporting diversity in communities and meeting the high expectations of people including the risks they wish to take. Personalisation further stresses the importance of the principles of self-assessment in which social workers may become more focused on advocacy and brokerage rather than on assessment and gatekeeping. This should move us away from a model of care where individuals receive care determined by the professional, to one that is determined by individuals themselves. While these ideals are not new to social work and their organisations, putting these into practice certainly is, as we saw in earlier chapters in the discussion about managerialism and increased market involvement in care. These concepts merit critical scrutiny as Ferguson (2007, p. 410) reminds us:

> *Uncritical acceptance of the marketisation of social work and social care, in its neglect of issues of poverty and inequality; in its flawed conception of the people who use social work services; in its potentially stigmatising view of welfare dependency; and in its potential for promoting, rather than challenging the deprofessionalisation of social work, the philosophy of personalisation is not one that social workers should accept uncritically. At the very least we should be questioning the claim that the principle of personalisation needs increasingly to be the philosophy on which social services are founded.*

Developing user involvement and user-centred practice in voluntary organisations

RESEARCH SUMMARY

A project involving disabled and non-disabled researchers looked at what is meant by 'user involvement' in two provider organisations in the voluntary sector, national and regional. They found a wide range of interpretations. A distinction was made between 'management-centred user involvement', where users participated in a mainly predetermined agenda defined by the organisation, and 'user-centred user involvement', where it was users who set the agenda. The report highlighted factors which promoted user involvement including a clear focus on users' own priorities, good communication, the important role of leadership and a strong sense of direction and vision whilst allowing sufficient opportunity for change. A key dimension to vision and commitment was clarity about who the organisation was for and therefore how and why it was trying to involve users. What hindered progress in user involvement were fragmented structures, problematic leadership styles, and 'glass ceilings' which prevented users from reaching real centres of power in organisations. Staff turnover leading to loss of momentum and continuity were also barriers to implementing successful change.

(Robson et al., 2003)

Designing a framework for participation

We will conclude this section by summarising key messages for policy and practice which will enhance planning and implementation of service user participation to achieve service enhancement and change.

- Clarity about the aims and scope of participation and the identification and engagement with any existing local or regional initiatives that cut across the sector or relate to aims and visions of other key partners or stakeholders (Carr, 2004).

- Clear communication about the aims and scope to potential participants from the outset and attention to resources needed to assist the process and make it accessible. Ensuring that participation is responsive to the perspectives, priorities and needs of local service users and that these are fully representative (Hasler, 2003).

- Awareness of power relationships between service users, managers and professionals and clarity of the extent and potential of information sharing and decision-making power.

- Valuing of knowledge, expertise and experience of people using services and flexibility in the methods used to communicate with them to ensure these are diverse, flexible and responsive to their needs.

- Planning frameworks for monitoring and evaluating both the process and outcomes of service user participation and giving feedback.

- Ensuring that certain groups or individuals are not marginalised by being creative and consulting them on the best way of working together.

- Ensuring all staff in the organisation are involved and understand the expectations, principles and practice of service user participation. Provision of training and management support to ensure it is valued (Carr, 2004; p. 27).

- Making space for the expression of emotion and feeling that can arise in the process (Beresford, 2004).

- Embedding the common core principles to support self-care in all organisational processes so that individual choice and control through individual budgets and direct payments are promoted (SfC, 2008b).

- Supporting and ensuring that services commissioned are delivered in the most personalised and practical way that requires quality and outcomes for service provision.

- Evaluating the effects of service user participation by designing methods that involve service users in defining what difference it makes.

Other standards used as a measure of the success of user involvement include raising consciousness and supporting the empowerment of service users and the sensitive politicisation and promotion of their needs as a civil and human rights issue (Campbell and Oliver, 1996; Thompson, 2003).

Organisational customer complaints and representation procedures

We will now look at statutory customer complaints and representation procedures which are an important aspect of QA within health and social care. Emphasis on service users' rights to a specified standard of service, which is accessible and responsive to their needs, and promotion of 'consumer power' led to the development of representation procedures enshrined within social policy developments and specific pieces of legislation since the 1990s. The translation of these requirements into complaints and representation systems is evident within all statutory organisations in both health and social care as well as provider organisations in the independent sector subject to regulation and inspection.

Foster and Wilding (2003) found that promotion of consumer power without careful assessment of the consequences entails losses as well as gains. One such cost is the development of more adversarial relations between professionals and service users. Whilst increase in complaints and litigation against professionals and social care staff has led to more attention to professionalism, for example in the creation of the General Social Care Council and its code of practice, it has also had the effect of moving away from potentially building on the positive elements of the service ethic and commitment to high-quality work into greater use of control through legislation, regulation, inspection and audit roles within the sector, as we saw in Chapter 3.

Complaints and representations – legislative framework

A complaint is defined as an expression of dissatisfaction or disquiet which requires a response (DoH, 2004c). This open definition intends to encourage open and transparent exchanges between service users and staff where the resolution of issues and problems is dealt with as quickly and informally as possible.

A complaint may arise from:

- an unwelcome or disputed decision;
- concern about the quality or appropriateness of a service;
- delay in decision-making about services;
- delivery or non-delivery of services;
- aftercare and decisions relating to placement or the handling of a case;
- quantity, frequency or cost of a service;
- attitude or behaviour of staff;
- application of eligibility and assessment criteria.

(DoH, 2004c)

Key legislation and guidance underpinning complaints procedures were initially introduced via the Children Act 1989, the NHSCCA 1990 and the Care Standards Act 2000. These pieces of legislation and their associated guidance set out the specific requirements for LAs and providers of services in the private and third sector in order to establish and publicise formal representations procedures stating exactly how people's complaints would be responded to. Legislation in this area inevitably interacts with a number of other Acts and policy guidance which serve to protect the interests of the public, for example Human Rights and Data Protection Acts, 1998. Practice guidance was also set out in *Learning from complaints* (DoH, 2004c) and changes as a result of the Children (Leaving Care) Act 2000, Adoption and Children Act 2002 and the Health and the Social Care (Community Health and Standards) Act 2003, all of which have resulted in new regulations coming into effect in 2006 and specific guidance in responding to complaints involving children. Complaints procedures should be accessible and active in providing support to people to make representations, for example through more extensive use of advocacy. All LAs are required to appoint a manager specifically responsible for responding to and coordinating complaints and this person is directly responsible to senior managers or chief officers as well as being independent of the service operational management and direct service provider. This does not mean that a complaints manager is responsible for resolving all complaints but has an active role in facilitating resolution of complaints by identifying appropriate colleagues and external people (including investigating officers and advocates) to contribute to complaints work. The complaints officer also has a role in fostering and developing good working relationships with key bodies and partner agencies so that a common approach and understanding are reached. All LAs are also required to monitor their performance in handling complaints, deliver what they have promised, and demonstrate how they have learnt from complaints in a way that leads to improvement of services.

In 2008, following government consultation with a number of bodies, further major review was undertaken of the way in which complaints and representations are dealt with (DoH, 2008a). This was to reflect the broader reforms of health and social care and its emphasis on person-centred care. It has been noted that there are also some anomalies arising in the system given the rising number of people arranging and financing their own care services who are currently excluded from statutory complaints procedures and access to support and independent resolution.

Guidance as to who may make a complaint is also very broad and covers any person eligible for a service or determined to be in need. Users can make complaints through appointed representatives should they not be able to represent themselves for whatever reason and independent advocacy may be appropriate. The complaints procedure does not supersede other procedures such as those for safeguarding children or vulnerable adults. Their interests must be paramount and complaints procedures should therefore not be used to prevent social workers from intervening in those situations. The LA does have discretion in deciding whether to consider complaints which may prejudice concurrent investigations such as court proceedings, tribunals, disciplinary or criminal proceedings as long as they are transparent in dealing with the complainant and explain clearly the reasons for such decisions. Likewise, a complaint highlighting poor or dangerous practice takes these issues into the staff disciplinary arena. Research into outcomes of complaints has demonstrated that powerlessness of service users, lack of knowledge about complaints procedures and the absence of dedicated support systems prevents them from fulfilling their function (DoH, 2000c; DfEE, 2004). Social workers have a key role in promoting this vehicle for service user participation. The following activity is designed to help you to consider what other factors may conflict with these principles.

ACTIVITY **4.3**

Spend about five minutes thinking about your own personal experiences of making a complaint or a situation where you perhaps you wanted to make a complaint but didn't. How did it make you feel? How was your complaint received? What specific factors were present that made your representation either successful or unsuccessful and how were you left feeling about the outcome?

By doing this exercise you will hopefully become aware that complaining takes skills, energy and perseverance as well as the ability to overcome insensitive or inaccessible bureaucratic procedures which do not actively encourage people to express their views. Fear of repercussion and consequences of promoting this atmosphere is a real concern for both parties:

> *If staff do not feel that their concerns are being addressed, there is little chance that users will be treated positively and sympathetically when they complain or question the system.*

(Audit Commission, 1993)

The attitudes of professionals to complaints is often more complex than might be expected. Research done by Simon (1995) indicates that motives for actively supporting service users in making complaints include a sense of justice, a way of pursuing their own concerns and a way of forcing managers to face up to an issue. It has also shown that relatively few frontline staff have received any specific training on their procedures and assumptions about complaints run the risk of distorting the process. These assumptions include: the equation of 'complaints' with 'disputes'; belief that complaints involve something 'formal'; a reluctance to be seen to push people into complaining; and a belief that it is only worth complaining about things that can be changed (p. 87). It is important that any complaints procedure places greater emphasis on seeking to prevent a complaint escalating unnecessarily and that procedures are flexible to allow alternative ways of resolving problems such as through mediation or conciliation.

The complaints procedure

Complaints procedures can vary in their structure and features but generally any complaints procedure follows three key stages to ensure that it is accessible and fair to everyone involved. Within the procedures for both adults' and children's services, there may be several steps or stages within the stages below although the principles are the same and you should refer to your local procedures for exact guidance.

Stage one

The LA handles and considers the complaint and seeks a local resolution. Initially this will be from within the service involved with local managers and staff trying to find a quick and informal solution. If the person remains unsatisfied then a formal investigation should be provided by appointing an independent person outside the service area. This should result in a report with findings, conclusions and recommendations for the LA to make an adjudication (decision) concerning the outcome of the complaint. During this process, the service user and their representatives must be kept informed throughout according to strict timescales and in writing.

Stage two

If the person is still dissatisfied then the complaint will be assessed by the relevant adjudication officer to assess eligibility for a review and where appropriate it will take one of the following actions to consider the complaint further.

Set up an independent panel to review the complaint. Review panels are designed to listen to all parties; consider the adequacy of the previous investigations and generally assist to achieve a resolution. Members of a review panel will be independent of the LA and be able to demonstrate independence and specialist skills, knowledge or awareness in the area of the complaint itself.

Investigation by the relevant registration or inspection body particularly where there are complaints involving regulated services and covered by the National Minimum Standards under the Care Standards Act 2000. This may involve using powers of inspection or taking other enforcement action.

Referral to the Local Government Ombudsman.

Decide that there is no further action required.

Stage three

If the above process does not resolve the complaint then there may be recourse to the Local Government Ombudsman or Parliamentary Ombudsman. In the current multi-disciplinary environment, there can be complications in relation to boundary issues or (un)seamless services where the journey through complaints procedures are not sufficiently integrated. The Ombudsman has the power to investigate complaints by members of the public made to them direct and will then apply a test of reasonableness in respect of any decision that has been taken. Both the LA and the Ombudsman are empowered through legislation to remedy any injustice arising from maladministration following a complaint and remedies are not just restricted to financial redress.

Where a complaint involves an independent provider, a similar process is followed in relation to the local procedure and if this involves a dual complaint with LA, the LA will have responsibility for co-ordinating and ensuring that one overall response is provided. Throughout any procedure, the importance of keeping records and recording complaints is essential not only from an accountability perspective but also effective monitoring and evaluating outcomes from complaints can help identify issues in service delivery that require more radical change and service improvement.

In summary, recent reform points towards the need for a more locally led and person-centred social care system where arrangements for complaints handling should be in keeping with a more personal and comprehensive approach (DoH, 2008a). As discussed earlier in this chapter, it is vitally important that we use people's experiences to help improve services. These can be further facilitated by having a more flexible approach towards the way in which complaints are handled and to help the organisations concerned to respond in a more fair and transparent way. Social workers have a specific role in helping service users have their complaints handled quickly and decisively and by being particularly responsive to the needs of vulnerable people using services. Being familiar with your local procedure and proactive through early acknowledgement of any difficulties is more likely to contribute to an open culture which assists learning from complaints rather than apportioning blame and promotes a user-centred approach.

Advocacy and service user involvement

For vulnerable people, independent advocacy can be a vital means of representation and the advocate's job is to ensure that their client's rights and opinions are seriously considered. Advocacy has been given a prominent role in government policy, for example the Mental Incapacity Act 2005, *Valuing People*, 2001 and Section 26A of the Children Act 1989 (as amended by the Adoption and Children Act 2002). The latter introduced new requirements for LAs to make arrangements for advocacy services for children in need, looked after and care leavers or any young person making or intending to make a complaint under the Children Act 1989. The availability of advocacy for children has been shown to be directly related to their level of satisfaction with complaint handling (Ball and Connolly, 2004). Research shows that a relatively high level of complaints made by children in residential care endorse perceptions that they are more aware of the procedures and more easily able to use them. Where LAs appoint children's rights officers or provide advocacy services as a matter of course, the outcomes are resolved much more quickly.

Historically the provision of advocacy has been associated with people with learning difficulties but it has also informed widespread use with other groups of service users. The provision of advocacy services is a frequent feature of service user-led organisations. Changes in legislation such as the Mental Capacity Act 2005 have introduced a requirement to appoint an advocate in order to safeguard the rights of service users who are unable to participate fully with decisions about their care. Section 4 of the Mental Capacity Act has also introduced the role of the Best Interests Assessor. From April 2009 in situations where it has been identified that a service user may be deprived of their liberty or that this is likely to occur as a result of an intervention or decision, the organisation must appoint a Best Interests Assessor who will follow a number of steps to ensure that any decisions made about an individual who lacks capacity are made in their best interests. From a professional perspective, when working with service users on an individual level, we should proactively ask them about their views on the services being provided and take time to explain the complaints procedures and advocacy service before they ever need to use it. Inviting service users and carers to seek support from an advocate and working co-operatively with their advocates is an essential requirement and skill in promoting user particpation.

C H A P T E R   S U M M A R Y

This chapter has looked at service user involvement in social care organisations and the role of the complaints and representations procedure in getting feedback from service users and asserting their rights. It is natural for both professionals and service users to be anxious about user involvement in social care services. Users may challenge current approaches and raise issues which you feel are difficult to respond to because of the pressures faced by social care organisations and constraints beyond your or your managers' control. Service users and carers, however, are often themselves aware of these issues and are key partners for support in helping to resolve and improve services. The development of the service user movement has demonstrated that they are often able to provide alternatives and a different perspective. As social workers we are reminded about the basic principles which should underpin all service user involvement as stated by service users themselves. Service users want professionals to be:

- physically and emotionally available;

- supportive, encouraging and reassuring;

- respectful, empathic and warm;

- patient and attentive to the service users' problems;

- committed to the independence of the individual;

- punctual, trustworthy, reliable;

- friendly but not afraid to tell people how they see things;

- knowledgeable and practical especially about law and rights, benefits and diverse cultures;

- able to find practical ways to help them;

- willing to stay working with them or have a good handover if they must change.

(Reform Focus Groups, 2002, www.gscc.org.uk)

You should endeavour to find out how your organisation values and implements these qualities in practice and the support available from management. You should familiarise yourself with the local policies, procedures and guidelines and how they are publicised, monitored, evaluated and the outcomes shared with all those involved.

FURTHER READING

Further recommended reading using relevant websites

Carr, S (2004) *Has service user participation made a difference to social care services?*
SCIE have produced a comprehensive summary bringing together key themes and findings from six literature reviews on the impact of user participation on change and improvement in social care. It suggests ways forward and can be downloaded from **www.scie.org.uk**

Voice for the Child in Care – A national organisation offering advice, help and advocacy to young people and care leavers – **www.vcc-uk.org**

Central England People First who are run and controlled by people with learning difficulties. An accessible guide to social services complaints procedures and other advocacy organisations is obtainable from the website **www.peoplefirst.org.uk**

Opaal is an older persons' advocacy alliance, **www.opaal.org.uk** which seeks to work with advocacy schemes across the UK to build the involvement of older people and develop links with minority ethnic communities. Opaal aims to promote independent advocacy with older people as a right and co-ordinates a number of advocacy projects and produces a regular newsletter on advocacy issues in different areas of concern.

DfES (2006a) Getting the best from complaints: Social care complaints and representations for children, young people and others provides detailed guidance for LAs on implementing the new procedures and builds on good practice that has been developed across services and can be downloaded from the Department of Education and Skills website **www.dfes.gov.uk**

Chapter 5
Resource management in social care organisations

A C H I E V I N G   A   S O C I A L   W O R K   D E G R E E

This chapter will help you achieve the following National Occupational Standards and General Social Care Council's Code of Practice.

Key Role 1: Prepare for, and work with, individuals, families, carers, groups and communities to assess their needs and circumstances.

- Assess and recommend an appropriate course of action for individuals, families, carers, groups and communities.

Key Role 2: Plan, carry out, review and evaluate social work practice, with individuals, families, carers, groups, communities and other professionals.

- Prepare, produce, implement and evaluate plans including negotiating provision and monitor, co-ordinate and support the actions of others involved in implementing them.

Key Role 5: Manage and be accountable, with supervision and support, for your own social work practice within your organisation.

- Contribute to the management of resources and services.
- Work within multi-disciplinary and multi-organisational teams, networks and systems.

General Social Care Code of Practice

Code 3: Promote independence of service users while protecting them as far as possible from harm

- Bringing to the attention of your employer or the appropriate authority resource any operational difficulties that might get in the way of the delivery of safe care.

Code 6: As a social care worker, you must be accountable for the quality of your work and take responsibility for maintaining and improving your knowledge and skills

- Meeting relevant standards of practice and working in a lawful and effective way.
- Maintaining clear and accurate records as required by procedures established for your work.

It will also introduce you to the following academic standards as set out in the social work subject benchmark statements:

2.5 Defining principles

- Think critically about the complex social, economic, political and cultural contexts which social work practice is located.

3.2.2.4 Knowledge, understanding and skills

- Intervention and evaluation – implement plans through a variety of systematic processes including contracting with others.

Introduction

This chapter looks at the contemporary context in which social care is resourced and delivered. In the public sector, organisations are required to manage resources effectively and efficiently to meet the priorities set down by its stakeholders. Social care organisations in particular face complex challenges in meeting ever-increasing demands to deliver higher-quality services within finite resources. This is characterised by a socio-economic and political environment which emphasises markets, the contracts culture and managerialism (Healy, 2002). It is made even more complex by the way in which services have been restructured and where social care has become integrated into services within a number of different partnerships. Social care organisations have also collaborated with a range of different agencies to agree both national and local priorities and to establish an appropriate source of funding. You may wonder why social workers need to be concerned with these issues. The realities of practising in an environment where there are constraints and competing claims on resources will inevitably involve you on both an individual and team level in contributing to decision-making about resource allocation. This may be through the process of assessing, arranging or providing services and in your role of advocating or making recommendations for service users to access the services they need. This can give rise to different challenges and dilemmas to those traditionally embraced by the social work profession.

This chapter will help you develop an awareness of resource issues by outlining the relevance of government policy, demography and projected needs. There will be an exploration of how resources are allocated and the sources of funding for both statutory and independent sectors. We will touch on relevant legislative and policy mechanisms designed to encourage joined-up approaches to deliver services which meet needs within a whole-systems approach. This adds a further complicated layer in managing resources for the organisations involved. We will then go on to look at one aspect of managing resources, the specific role of commissioning and **contracting** as a process to secure social care services and the role that social workers play within this. We will conclude this chapter with an exercise which demonstrates the complexity of 'costing' a service. This will provide an opportunity to consider and weigh up issues concerning costs, quality, and value for money and the ethical principles behind this type of analysis.

Financing social care; where does the money come from?

In previous chapters we identified that, since the 1980s, the market economy and mixed economy of care have had a significant role to play in the provision of social care. In 2006–07, gross current expenditure by councils with social services responsibilities (CSSRs) in England on personal social services was £20.1 billion, having increased by around 70 per cent in real terms over the last 10 years (Information Centre, 2008). Local government finance has a well-deserved reputation for being complicated and there are three different separate systems for funding local authority expenditure. These are, first, spending on capital projects such as roads, school buildings or computers; second, revenue spending on council housing; and, third, revenue expenditure, mainly on pay and other costs of running services other than council housing. In its three-yearly public spending reviews, the government determines its total level of grants to local authorities. Councils also fund their spending through a number of local mechanisms such as by raising council tax, rates charged to local business and charging for local services such as rents and direct charges to service users for their services. For example, in 2006–07, councils recovered over 14 per cent of their expenditure on adult care through fees and charges to service users (CSCI, 2008b). Much of the remaining source of funding for councils comes from central government grants. These are the settlement grants where there are no restrictions on which local government can spend it on. It is based on a 'relative needs formula', which is a mathematical formula using information on the population, social structure and other characteristics of each authority to reflect the relative needs of local authorities in providing services (ODPM, 2006). These formulae are not intended to measure the actual amount needed by any authority to provide local services, but simply to recognise various factors which affect local authorities' costs locally. Assessment of these factors also does not relate to the actual monetary amount of grant that a council needs for providing services for its residents. The formula for each specific service area is built on the following characteristics:

- a basic allocation (per child or person);

- plus a top-up based on the level of deprivation in the area;

- plus a top-up for each LA area which is related to pay and recruitment difficulties reflected in the local labour market;

- plus other top-ups that reflect a range of local cost pressures such as rural sparsity, high density and a large visitor or commuting population.

(Glennester, 2003, p. 66)

In addition to this, central government distributes specific formula grants outside the main settlement. Some of these are known as ring-fenced grants which control council spending. These usually fund particular services or initiatives that are seen as a national priority. For example, funding for schools is paid through the Dedicated Schools Grant reflecting the priority the government places on education, and there is also one for mental health. Other specific formula grants are unfenced and are sometimes called targeted grants and these include resources for carers and children's services. They are distributed outside of the annual settlement, because general formulae are not appropriate. There are, however, no restrictions on what councils can spend the money on within these areas (ODPM, 2006).

Government policy and integrated provision

The government has identified that personalised care and systems that put people in control of their care are the cornerstone of policies in transforming care. Therefore future funding mechanisms are now far more integrated within a whole systems approach towards the promotion of health and well-being of local communities. In its comprehensive spending review of 2007, the government announced a social care reform grant worth £520 million over the next three years to take the personalised and responsive services agenda forward. This supports further both legislative and policy shifts to facilitate

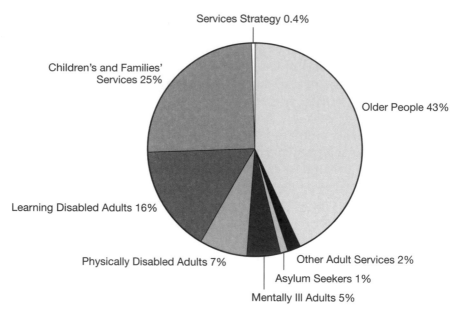

Figure 5.1 Expenditure on Personal Social Services, 2006–07
Source: Information Centre (2008)

the collaboration and incorporation of health and social care partners towards more seamless delivery of services and joined-up government underpinned by the following underlying goals.

• Joint strategic needs assessment undertaken by local authorities, relevant primary care trusts and NHS providers in conjunction with other local-needs assessments around preventative public health, hospital discharge, the management of long-term conditions, co-located services and universal information advice and advocacy.

• Commissioning which incentivises and stimulates quality provision particularly through the support of third- and private-sector innovation. Social enterprise is a priority undertaken jointly with the NHS and other statutory agencies such as the Learning and Skills Council, employment services and housing.

• A sustainable community strategy that utilises community resources to promote prevention, early intervention and supporting people to remain in their own homes for as long as possible.

• A uniform information advice and advocacy service for people needing services and their carers through one-stop shops and support to utilise the 'personal budget'.

• A common assessment process of individual social care needs with greater emphasis on self-assessment.

• Person-centred planning and self-directed support.

• Personal budgets for everyone eligible for publicly funded social care support, which may include NHS resources.

- Increasing numbers of direct payments.

- A transformed community equipment service consistent with the retail market.

(CSCI, 2008a, pp. 3–4)

As you will appreciate, this entails quite a radical shift in the use of resources in social care. Achieving this sort of joined-up approach, as we saw in Chapter 3, can create a trade-off between risks and rewards. The risks are not always financial but include less clear lines of accountability for policy and service delivery and greater difficulties in measuring effectiveness; and a need to develop and maintain more sophisticated performance measurement systems. There are also the direct and opportunity costs of management and staff time spent establishing and sustaining cross-cutting approaches and restructuring of organisations to accommodate these (Cabinet Office, 2000). These core changes have followed on from some prescriptive legislation and policy, for example the Single Assessment Process (DoH, 2002a), the Community Care (Delayed) Discharges Act 2003 and the various National Service Frameworks which have encouraged the pooling of resources and creation of organisational structures to support these. Section 31 of the Health (Flexibilities) Act 1999, section 10 of the Children Act 2004, and sections 28A and 28BB of the NHS Act 1997 and associated Partnership Regulations also provide a legal framework for managing the structure and resources to make partnership work more effectively. Additional challenges arise in the co-coordinating of multiple sources of funding and service provision, particularly for managers and commissioners of care services. The increasing fragmentation of responsibilities between purchasers and providers across different sectors will need to be carefully managed in order to maximise the coherence and comprehensiveness of service responses against the government's objectives and governance arrangements (Glendinning and Means, 2004).

The independent sector

So far we have established some of the main sources of funding for social care which may give you some idea as to how it reaches frontline services you may be working in. We will now turn our attention to the relationships between the statutory and the independent sectors in relation to resourcing services. The independent sector is made up of private 'for profit' and the third sector 'not for profit' organisations.

The private sector

Increasing emphasis on partnerships between public and private sectors besides those implied and implemented through the market economy are, according to Linder (2000), based on six government imperatives, as follows:

1. Management reform and modernisation. By working in partnership with the private sector, public managers can learn how to run programmes more flexibly and efficiently.

2. To allow the public sector to tap into private finance through the Private Finance Initiative (PFI) to pursue capital projects which cannot be afforded from the public purse alone. This has become quite a controversial area since the scale of PFI projects in

the health and education sectors since 1997 is now having a serious impact on public-sector budgets. PFI schemes can, for example, introduce dangerously long reporting and command lines between those who ought to be responsible for a service and those who deliver, and are inherently costly compared with the alternative, not least because the costs of finance are higher for private companies than the exchequer borrowing with all the taxing power of the state. Moreover, PFI schemes tie contracting authorities into long periods of particular patterns of provision. If health authorities or others then need to change the configuration of the services, they have often to renegotiate the contract at considerable costs to the taxpayer (Huhne, 2007). Since 2000 the government has introduced the term Public Private Partnerships (PPP). These are extensions of PFI partnership approaches to cover a wider range of business structures and partnership arrangements to bigger joint ventures and outsourcing of state-owned business. This is part of the government's intention to draw on business skills to develop an ever-widening range of public-sector activities, drawing on business skills to develop and implement policy by using the expertise of private-sector partners to make better use of public-sector assets. If privatisation represents a takeover of a publicly owned commodity, then PPP is more like a merger, with both sides sharing the risks and benefits.

3. Public legitimacy and the symbolic pooling of talents from government, the market and voluntary sector in a partnership which pursues worthy public purposes.

4. Risk shifting where private partners can assume part of all of the financial risk associated with particular projects.

5. Downsizing of the public sector by **contracting out** or privatisation to commercial or voluntary organisations who can do it better.

6. Power-sharing in partnerships that are seen to promote more co-operative 'horizontal', less authoritarian and hierarchical relationships.

PFIs in the UK are often used to develop large-scale capital projects in health and social care such as hospitals, schools and care homes. PFIs are promoted through the European Community Fund as a requirement to bid for particular types of finance such as those which support urban regeneration programmes (Pollitt, 2003).

The third sector

In relation to the third sector, about 40 per cent of its income comes from the state, with the remainder funded by grants from charitable trusts and voluntary gifts. Since the introduction of the market economy to social care, the third sector has become more dependent on **contracting** with the LA or through **service level agreements** attached to local grants in return for the direct provision of locally based community services. Some commentators, such as Paxton and Pearce (2005), have noted that the voluntary and community sector is now at a crossroads. In recent years it has expanded the role it plays in the direct delivery of public services and this shift has received sustained, continuing support across the political spectrum. Some organisations are more suited than others in providing social care services and entering into contractual relationships with the state. We will return to examine the implications of this dynamic later on when we look at the commissioning and contracting process.

In 2007, the government set out to review how its departments will take forward work with the third sector over its comprehensive spending review and developed a more robust framework to highlight its contribution to the delivery of key priority outcomes across government and to capitalise on its contribution. A White Paper (HM Govt, 2007a) sought to establish a clear expectation that the starting point for grant funding will be three years in all cases and that setting contracts alongside grants is crucial but they should be used where they are most appropriate, particularly in the case of small community groups. In order to increase the involvement of the third sector, there is a commitment to levelling the playing field by actively involving them in local strategic partnerships and reviewing the barriers and incentives to the transfer of assets and facilities to local community groups.

Other social care services such as residential and nursing care homes in both the voluntary and private sector can be funded directly by the people who use them, including those individuals who are required to make a financial contribution following an assessment by councils who have **commissioned** services to meet their needs. In relation to the independent sector as a whole, it is important to acknowledge that following the impact of tightening eligibility criteria by statutory services, the number of households receiving supported care has fallen and many older people, for example, now purchase care privately from these sectors. Around half of the expenditure on personal social care for older people now comes from private contributions, either from charges and top-ups for those receiving care with council financial support, or from spending on privately purchased care. This does not include the substantial contribution of resources from private individuals in the form of caring by families and friends.

Challenges in managing resources

Statutory organisations have to make difficult decisions about expenditure and decide eligibility for a service to enable them to target resources to people with greatest need. This includes deciding how much an individual will contribute towards their own care on the basis of a financial assessment and within government guidelines. Poor financial planning and management can adversely affect service users and can lead to personal distress and the loss of support and care to some of the most vulnerable people in the community. Effective long-term financial planning and good budget management ensure that users and carers are protected by avoiding poor short-term decision-making. This implies the need for very sophisticated financial systems and well developed skills of the people managing and administrating social care finance. In principle this may sound obvious, but the difficult and rapid change environments in which social care operates and the considerable spending pressures and responsibilities on social services budgets can make them especially volatile and difficult to control. These pressures include, amongst others:

- the rising costs in childcare placements which can easily cost over £100,000 per year;
- increased demand arising from the growing numbers of older people and the changing needs of the population;
- the increasing costs of supporting adults with complex needs in the community;

- the use of agency staff in places where it is difficult to recruit permanent staff (national vacancy rates of 11 per cent for social work staff with a 12.7 per cent turnover rate means more needs to be done to avoid additional financial burdens) (Skills for Care, 2005a);

- rising costs of domiciliary and residential care placements which can result from market pressures exceeding original budget assumptions as well as volatility in demand.

(www.joint-reviews.gov.uk/money/financialmgt/)

However much social services might like to expand to meet new demands and to address areas of unmet need, they cannot do so unless either additional resources are made available or existing services are withdrawn or cut back. Decisions which affect the type and cost of services to be purchased may be outside of the council's control; for example, as a result from a court decision or following over-reliance on informal care which is then no longer available. The challenge of managing the budget is a common issue for most public services but differs from the private sectors who sell their services at a profit (Beckett and Maynard, 2005, p. 90). For private companies, additional demand usually brings additional income which allows expansion to meet that demand. Public services with fixed income and budgets, however, have to respond to additional demand by spreading themselves more thinly. This causes conflicts and dilemmas when public services are encouraged to be more businesslike without acknowledging the challenges in prioritising one area of need over another or providing services in a way which may compromise quality (Beckett and Maynard, 2005, p. 90). Under the Local Government Act 1999, LAs have a duty to secure best value from the services they purchase, which means that, as well as looking carefully at the type and quality, councils have a duty to consider cost and develop commissioning strategies to specify which services will be provided and who will provide them. These local priorities and objectives are usually spelt out in the organisations' vision statements and in community care plans which state how the resources within each LA or Care Trust are allocated and the targets and measures expected. This latter task falls within the remit of managers and staff within the organisation, all of whom will have some input to these processes at different levels. This may be strategic or operational and you should be able to find out from your direct line manager the level to which your service budget is delegated and the specific role and responsibilities of the individual budget holders.

The key to successful management of **budgets** is the requirement of the managers or budget holders to act in partnership with those responsible for assessing and meeting needs and with the organisation's business support staff. A scheme of delegation within each organisation should make clear the range of budgets that the manager is directly responsible for in their service area with financial limits which provide boundaries to the extent of decision-making around expenditure. If a care management team is responsible for a specific budget, it is likely that there are agreed rates about how much can be spent on a package of care or individual service before needing to seek agreement from somebody in higher authority or taking it to a 'panel' for approval. The price of a particular service is likely to be pre-negotiated with the service provider by the organisation's commissioning and contracts department (in larger organisations).

In summary, while the agenda is firmly embedded in integrated funding, health and social care are two sides of the same coin in that if you under-invest in one, this will overstretch the other and this problem cannot be overestimated. A survey done by the Local Government Association of Local Authorities (LGA, 2006) revealed that the costs of contracts with the independent and voluntary sector are outstripping inflation with average increases of 4.2 per cent for nursing and residential care, and 4 per cent for home care.

The budget management process

As we have seen in previous chapters, performance should not always be judged solely by the ability to stay within budget but indicators should include the number and type of services purchased, their cost-effectiveness and quality. Responsibility for recording and inputting information about service-level activity is equally important to be able to project future budgets or resources based on needs as well as to achieve broader outcomes. This is often a direct responsibility of social workers and other frontline staff and it is important that you understand which budgets you are working to and how these are grouped for accounting purposes and reporting arrangements.

Budget control is the process which enables an organisation to assess the achievement of objectives on an ongoing basis. It will be governed by policies and procedures and open to scrutiny at a number of levels. With constrained resources, it helps to ensure that the level of overall expenditure is effectively managed and enables individual budget holders and managers to monitor management of resources to meet detailed objectives for each service area. Budgetary control is usually historical and provides financial and management information with the purpose of looking forward and putting into place preventative mechanisms to avoid crisis. A budget can be defined as a plan which sets out the financial details of the following: income – resources available to an organisation and the departments within it, and expenditure – uses to which these resources will be put, and these are almost always expressed in monetary terms.

ACTIVITY 5.1

Can you think of any examples from your current practice environment, previous experience of working in or using a public service where issues to do with finance, budgets or resources have arisen? If you have direct work experience in social care, try to identify the effect this had on your ability to carry out your duties. If you were using a public service, reflect on and identify what attitude you formed towards the issues and what effect this had on your motivation or feelings towards the service, either positive or negative.

You may have identified some of the following:

- being asked to make difficult decisions and to consider the costs more carefully before agreeing to provide a service;
- being asked to contribute to the process of setting or controlling the budget for your service or department;
- being expected by your managers including senior managers to be more efficient and to justify or account for any expenditure that you commit;

- frustration or lack of control in being able to achieve your goal or the goals of those you were working with.

The division of responsibility by which social workers at the front line assess needs but managers make decisions about how resources are allocated can contribute to the 'blame culture'. Staff can blame their managers for not making resources available to service users and managers can in turn disassociate themselves from the day-to-day contact with human distress, and blame practitioners for any casework that goes wrong. Too rigid a split between practice decisions and resource decisions ignores that these are closely inter-twined. Beckett and Maynard (2005) point out that at every level of a social work agency, from practitioner to director, staff have to think not only about what would be desirable in an ideal world but also about what the possibilities are in the real world. This involves eth-ical dilemmas and value-laden decisions about making choices about who gets a service at any given moment and clarity about responsibility. The role of accountability, reporting and supervision is very important here.

Informal care

Before we go on to look at how social workers can contribute more positively to the ways in which resources are managed via the commissioning and contracting process, it is important to acknowledge the role of informal and unpaid care within the context of our discussion about resource management. Informal or unpaid carers represent a huge share of the total social care workforce capacity and reflect the predominant reality of social care. In fact, the lack of, or breakdown in, informal care or stress on carers is the second most important reason leading to increased public funding for social care service users (King's Fund, 2005). The largest element in the costs of caring for children, older people and other service groups falls upon the family and disproportionately on women as carers (Dalley, 1996). Informal care forms a large element of provision, extending not just to direct care but to the emotional support given by those doing the caring. This 'support' function remains largely unmeasured although its eco-nomic importance is great (Glennester, 2003, p. 81). It has been argued that the supply of informal care will decline as the size of the adult population rises due to women working longer, a rise in divorce rates and changes in family structures. Recent trends and analysis tell us that the number of dependent older people with partners is expected to rise by 49 per cent (Wittenberg et al., 2001). Just over one in ten adults between 50 and the state pension age in Great Britain are not in work due to domestic responsibilities and over half of this group are carers (HM Govt, 2004). A survey of 1,000 people aged over 50 found that one in three look after elderly relatives or friends, one in six provided care for grandchildren and one in ten did both (Harkin and Huber, 2004). Older people also make up more than five million volunteers representing a sizeable share of the economy in value terms (Age Concern, 2005). Therefore the cost of social care is critically dependent on the effective functioning of family support and forms a plank in social policy. If this falls only by a small percentage, the demand could easily double or treble. In her research, Banks (1999) explains that:

> *frontline staff face very real pressures in interpreting policies to support carers. When budgets are tight, there may be little incentive to view carers as anything more than a 'resource' or 'co-worker'.*

(p. 10)

The Carers (Equal Opportunities) Act 2004 acknowledges that carers are entitled to the same life chances as others and should not be socially excluded because of their caring role. It seeks to ensure that carers are identified and informed of their rights; their needs for education, training, employment and leisure, and that public bodies recognise and support carers (Cass, 2005).

RESEARCH SUMMARY

It is estimated that one in ten people are carers and that there are 5.2 million carers in England and Wales, with almost 20% providing over 50 hours of care each week. In 2000, 40% of carers were 65 or over. Continuity of data collection from the next Census and Household Surveys are important in order to compare demographics about carers' specific and changing needs as well as more detail about their current issues and involvement with services. The right to request a carer's assessment was established in 1995 but the rights of carers to have their own needs assessed was strengthened by the Carers and Disabled Children Act 2000 supported by the Carers Grant to encourage the development of more flexible and responsive provision. The Carers (Equal Opportunities) Act 2004 made three further changes to the existing law around carers' services.

- It placed a duty on councils to inform carers, in certain circumstances, of their right to an assessment of their needs.

- It provided that when assessing a carer's needs, councils must take into account whether the carer works or wishes to work, undertakes or wishes to undertake education, training or leisure activities.

- It facilitated co-operation between authorities in relation to the provision of services that are relevant to carers.

As mentioned earlier, the Carers Grant is a ring-fenced fund within the local authority financial settlement, and has been used to provide information and support to carers in partnership with the third sector through the provision of one-stop carers' centres. Direct payments have been extended to carers and can be used for taking short breaks, sittings services and to purchase support in people's own homes in the evenings, overnight and weekends. The Carers Grant has been used to fund carers' provision of training for staff to try and to improving the quality of carers' assessments and on supporting joint working with health to prevent hospital admissions and to facilitate improved hospital discharge.

(DoH, 2004b)

In the preparation of the White Paper, *Our health, our care, our say*, the Department of Health (2006) conducted an extensive public consultation. This revealed considerable support for carers and the Department responded by announcing a New Deal for Carers in 2008. The New Deal for Carers is aimed at improving support for carers through a range of measures. The Department has been working on the following key commitments:

- updating and extending the Prime Minister's 1999 strategy for carers;

- establishing an information service/helpline for carers;

- ensuring that short-term, home-based breaks support to carers in crisis or emergency situations is established in each council area;

- allocating specific funding for the creation of an expert carers' programme, which will provide training for carers to develop the skills they need to take greater control over their own health, and the health of those in their care.

(DoH, 2008a).

Balancing prevention with meeting complex needs

Stated policy objectives of the 1990 community care reforms appear sympathetic to the notion of prevention and the promotion of independence and have been restated in the government's White Paper, *Independence, wellbeing and choice* (2005a and more recently *Putting people first* (2007b). The central message, consistent with those from other service user groups, is the need for support services that enable people to continue to exercise choice and control over their lives based on mutuality, community development, and capacity building (Tanner, 2003). However, resource concerns have continued to affect the actual successful implementation of these principles consistently despite prevention **grants** made by central government around key issues. Community care policy and practice have continued to prescribe mechanisms such as Single Assessment (2002) and Fair Access to Care Services in which LAs have used eligibility criteria as a key mechanism in the definition and management of need. This has served to regulate service provision within available resources, increasingly prioritising those most at risk or in crisis. By screening out those with medium or low-level needs, service users are precluded from accessing essential services to maintain their independence. The increasing take-up of direct payments and the piloting of individualised budgets in 2007 and 2008 have attempted to address this constant tension by enabling service users and their carers to design their support in such a way that it does not necessarily cost more and has contributed to service users' support networks and a move away from a life of segregation and exclusion by building new friendships and relationships in the community.

CASE STUDY

Escape from serviceland

Joe had complex disabilities as a result of meningitis when he was six and experienced life as a turmoil of assessments, meetings and reviews. His 'special education' cost over £60,000 per year. Joe was involved in the first pilot programme around self-directed support known as 'In Control'. The secret of success came about because of the partnership between his parents and professionals that was open, transparent and honest. Joe hired his own personal assistants who help him do ordinary things like go to college; support him with his micro-enterprise; go to the gym; have a bath and eat his meals. Having an individual budget has helped Joe buy his own car and buy his own home next door to his family. 'In Control' has persuaded many local authorities, organisations, families and individuals to reconsider the way we do things, demonstrating that using the resources already available and reorganising these within a clear ethos and value base contributes towards co-production in service provision.

(Tomlinson, 2008)

The above case study demonstrates two central components within the concept of prevention: firstly, preventing or delaying the need for more expensive services and, secondly, promoting quality of life and participation in the community. The Association of Directors of Social Services in their response to the government's emphasis on prevention and successful implementation in *Every child matters* (DoH, 2004a) and *Independence, well-being and choice* (DoH, 2005a) highlighted the need for these assertions to be based on evidence and research that sheds light on the value of different low-level interventions. Certain interventions may have important preventative value as well as the intrinsic value in promoting other objectives in terms of social inclusion, quality of life, health and well-being that cannot be evaluated in terms of cost alone (ADSS, 2005).

RESEARCH SUMMARY

Tanner (2003) undertook in-depth interviews with a small number of older people over a three-year period and highlighted the importance of attending to subjective factors related to the maintenance of a positive identity. Older people made concerted efforts to 'keep going' especially with tasks associated with maintaining their identity. Help from others, either formal or informal, was seen to support or undermine this process. Tanner concluded that greater attention to ensuring people's access to services that accorded with their own perception of need, support and own problem-solving efforts was most valued by them.

The commissioning and contracting process

In previous chapters, we saw that the development of the market or **quasi-market** in the 1990s gave statutory agencies the role of 'purchaser', 'enabler', 'collaborator' and 'commissioner' on the premise that these roles help to restrain costs, allocate resources efficiently and encourage innovation through the 'mixed economy of care' (Leece, 2004). New Labour's modernisation of public services sought to expand the role of the independent sector through **pluralism**, competition, variety, innovation and flexibility.

Commissioning is the process by which LAs plan to get the best possible services for the local community within its resources and should be an inclusive process which involves all stakeholders including service users and their representatives. Through specifying, securing and making arrangements to meet individuals' needs at a strategic level, commissioning is about enhancing the quality of service user/carer by:

- having the vision and commitment to improve services;

- connecting with the needs and aspirations of users and carers;

- making the best use of all available resources;

- understanding demand and supply;

- linking financial planning and service planning;

- making relationships and working together in partnership.

(www.joint-reviews.gov.uk/money/financialmgt/)

Rather than voluntary organisations bidding directly to LAs for funding, they are increasingly making applications directly to central government in partnership with LAs via Local Strategic Partnerships which provide an overarching framework in the public, private, voluntary and community sectors to meet community development needs. Alternatively, they may get funding via contracts with the LA for the direct provision of services. This partnership approach to service delivery brings both threats and opportunities for the third sector.

ACTIVITY 5.2

What are the benefits of the third sector organisations delivering social care services and what issues may arise in them doing so?

In having more expert knowledge and greater proximity to users, the voluntary and community sectors are more able to innovate and provide services flexibly. In Chapter 4, we learnt that they can also offer greater community and local engagement or control with potential for users to lead and manage services themselves. Voluntary organisations operate within a complex ecology of services and activities by strengthening the communities in which services operate using advocacy and scrutiny that holds public providers of services to account (Unwin and Molyneux, 2005). However, there are a number of concerns and risks for the voluntary sector through accepting significant increase in state funding in return for delivering services (Paxton and Pearce, 2005). Trust is crucial if the sector is seen as a vehicle for people's participation and this may be compromised where they develop closer relations with the state. Tensions may grow between 'doing good' in an ethical sense and 'doing well' in an organisational sense. Similarly, where the voluntary sector relies more on state funding and on its objective to deliver services, independence may be compromised through the political influence and regulation that reflect wider government objectives over the organisation's own mission and values. In summary, integration of the voluntary sector with the state is a key concern to ensure that their campaigning and lobbying role is maintained (Paxton and Pearce, 2005).

Finally, if voluntary sector organisations do not have established overheads, strategic capacity or business skills to engage in the contracting process, then some groups may not be able to participate. The exclusion of disadvantaged and marginalised groups in particular can lead to structural inequalities (Badham and Eadie, 2004). The struggle by the voluntary sector to secure funding for their overhead costs has been recognised by the government, who put in place training for organisations to implement the principle of full cost recovery when bidding and working at a local level by 2006. However, with limited budgets many funding bodies are faced with the choice of funding fewer services or fewer organisations locally and some voluntary organisations are reluctant to submit fully costed bids for fear of pricing themselves out of the market. Intelligent commissioning practice therefore should spend time getting to understand the needs of service users and consult with third-sector organisations before commissioning as well as considering the longer-term outcomes as well as costs.

Understanding the role of social work in the contracting process

Understanding how contracts work is an essential part of the overall commissioning task. A contract is an agreement between two parties, usually written, where one agrees to provide a service for payment. It is a formal way of ensuring that services are provided to a certain standard, specification and cost. There are two main types of contract in use in social care:

1. **Block contracts** where a large supply of services is agreed in advance, gives greater certainty and continuity for providers and purchasers and is generally cheaper.

2. **Spot contracts** which are used to agree an individual unit of service, for example a single residential placement, and can be designed to meet a specific circumstance or need and be purchased quickly.

Social work assessments are the key activity by which social services gather information to inform their commissioning plan and the type of contracts they need. It is an analytical process by which decisions and plans with service users should lead to an individually tailored care plan. Despite the difficult financial context, care planning provides the opportunity for creative thinking about responses to the user/carer's situation. Studies by Challis et al. (1993) have shown that critical success is dependent on the devolution of control over resources to the lowest level possible to meet the priority needed for the service user. Building relationships with staff and management responsible for delivering care was also seen as essential to the process. Implementation of the care plan requires constantly reviewing with the user that the objectives set remain valid, and whether they need to be modified in the light of experience. This is essential to monitoring quality and enhancing service-user involvement. The monitoring and reviewing of care plans is central to the development of needs-led approaches to service delivery and should be formalised, documented and fed back to managers and others in the organisations responsible for commissioning and contracting. Multi-disciplinary assessment and good working relationships with providers are also important to the process and these ingredients should promote best use of resources and value for money. Social workers have an important role to play in advocating for services to meet users' needs and bringing to the attention of their managers any issues that compromise the service users' rights or quality of service provision. This includes highlighting unmet needs or inequalities in delivery.

Funding and service user control

Direct payments and individualised budgets go even further to delegating financial control on the continuum of resource management. The Community Care (Direct Payments) Act

1996 gave LAs the power to make cash payments to disabled people under 65 years assessed as needing a community care service. Individuals use this money to purchase support to meet their assessed needs and this was extended to include older people in 2000 and to carers and parents/carers of disabled children in 2001. Research by Zarb and Nadash (1994) into the cost implications and effectiveness of direct payment schemes found that they offer a higher degree of choice, control and reliability and user satisfaction than direct service provision. Direct payments were also found to be 30–40 per cent cheaper than equivalent service-based supports. A large share of social care budgets go on devising and administering care plans, but self-directed services cut out much of this bureaucracy and release funding for those with less critical needs. Making direct payments to enable people to purchase and arrange their own support is compatible with the philosophy of both market and user rights. The social justice/rights perspective sees these as empowering by enhancing user choice and control over where, how, when and by whom their support is provided. Market philosophy asserts that cash payments increase consumer power, choice and control to enable people to buy their care from a range of suppliers (including from those personal assistants selling their labour) in a competitive marketplace. This can help relatives provide care and enlarge the number of people working in the care sector (Leece, 2004). If direct payments and individualised budgets are boosted significantly in the future as the government has indicated, there will be a dramatic change in the environment for care organisations. While this will give users more control, it will introduce a more obvious market system and present some real challenges to the model of contracting currently employed. The ability of commissioners to predict what people want and to offer service providers some certainty of income through block contracts may be very different in the future. The importance of developing the infrastructure to build services in the community will also require significant investment as well as attention to the training needs of personal assistance and their regulation to protect vulnerable people (Skills for Care, 2005b).

The impact of personalisation and self-directed care on social workers has shown that introducing a new role of brokerage into work with service users can enable more quality time to be spent with service users and in building up rapport and helping relationships. A brokerage service is one where a team of people either internal or independent of the organisation arrange all the provision once an assessment is complete and may frequently do this following the service users' own self-assessment. This might involve finding services and negotiating costs in complex cases or to help meet a simpler request for a piece of equipment. In Devon for example, Care Direct Plus using telephone assessments were able to resolve 75 per cent of requests within two days using a combination of user-led assessments and delivery of equipment. This has resulted in providing a speedier and better quality service with less staff and by freeing up staff in integrated complex care teams in order to concentrate on quality preventative work (Johnstone, 2008). There are of course some reservations on the extensive use of self-directed care where there is suspicion that direct payments can be seen as more for less and the lure of cost-cutting. In some cases, ceilings placed on packages, call for a greater exploration of the downside of these recent legislative and policy developments. Spandler (2004) for example, has highlighted the potential for individualisation of service provision to undermine collective service provision and be used as a Trojan horse for the introduction of even greater privatisation and penetration of the market forces into the welfare state (cited by Ferguson, 2007). The impact of individual budgets and direct payments on contracted services and providers where service users are enabled to choose freely can also make a powerful statement about the quality of provision. We saw earlier how the use of block contracts can help to control costs, but there are risks to the viability of such contracting practice when service users have the freedom to go elsewhere and commissioners may have a problem in double-funding some services. Further, private purchasers of care services are often able to obtain more flexibility from care providers than is the norm for publicly funded services. This has been found to be extended in the early evaluation of individual budgets with older people. The move towards outcome-based commissioning may help public-funded services to exercise the same freedom and control as a private purchaser but requires changes to commissioning and contracting practice as well as to the way in which individual care plans are written, delivered and monitored.

CASE STUDY

Costing services

We will conclude this chapter by looking at issues around costing individual units of services, which is becoming a skill required by all managers for the following reasons:

- *to develop a basis for the establishment of prices for the external market known as contracting;*

- *to undertake a cost comparison with alternative service providers (as in Best Value processes) or with other services during the contracting process;*

- *to set targets for productivity; number of hours, number of service users receiving services, etc.;*

- *to identify options for cost reduction;*

- *to establish and justify whether the service appears to be good value for money and accountability;*

- *to create an internal market for services and to identify the level of charging.*

*The process of costing individual units of service in the public sector is known as **unit costing**. It is a fairly crude method where the total cost of a service is divided by the number of individual services provided to give an average cost.*

Table 5.1 represents a budget report of Ashanti mental health drop-in centre. The report shows a statement for month 9 of the financial year. Column 1 shows the budget allocated at the beginning of the financial year. Column 2 shows what the expected expenditure should be at the end of month 9 to keep within budget and Column 3 shows the actual expenditure at month 9. Column 4 therefore shows the variance or the difference in planned and actual expenditure using a positive or minus figure.

CONTINUED

Table 5.1: Budget report for Ashanti mental health drop-in centre

Item of Expenditure £	Annual Budget £	Planned Expenditure £ Period 9	Actual Expenditure £ Period 9	Budget Variance £ Period 9
Staff Salaries	Column 1	Column 2	Column 3	Column 4
1.Management	60,000	45,000	48,320	–3320
2.Social Workers	192,000	144,000	120,188	23,812
3.Administrative	22,500	16,875	16,875	0
4.Temporary Cover	10,000	7,500	35,000	–27,500
	284,500	213,375	220,383	–7,008
Building Costs				
5.Rent	2,000	1,500	2,000	–500
6.Rates	450	337.5	337.5	0
7.Cleaning	131	98.25	320	–221.75
8.Maintenance	200	150	150	0
	2,781	2,085.75	2,807.5	–721.75
Sundries				
9.Photocopying	560	420	320	100
10.Stationery	1,086	814.5	710	104.5
11.Furniture	2,000	1500	5,369	–3,869
	3,646	2,734.5	6,399	–3,664.5
TOTALS	£290,927	£218,195.75	£229,589,5	£–11,598.75

ACTIVITY 5.3

Examine Ashanti's budget report and see if you can establish whether this budget is a healthy one. (Do this with a colleague if you find this difficult.) Can you identify any specific areas of concern? Which expenditure or costs do you think are controllable and which costs you think are less easy to control?

Hopefully you will have identified from Column 4 that there is already an overspend of £11,598.75 which needs to be addressed by reducing expenditure to an equivalent amount within the next three months to make the budget balance by the end of the financial year. The main areas of concern seem to be the temporary staffing budget (row 4, column 3) and a large expenditure on furniture (row 11, column 3). Both of these were not budgeted for.

Expenditure on staffing is generally a difficult area to control and in provider services is often dictated by the registration and regulation process. Delays in staff recruitment, unplanned staff absence and increasing salaries can also make expenditure unpredictable. The point of this exercise is to raise your awareness of the sometimes unpredictable nature of budget management and to increase your skills in contributing to decision-making. Managers may involve staff in making decisions about ways of reducing expenditure or delivering services arising from such exercises.

In order to effectively manage budgets, managers and staff need to develop an awareness of costs, particularly the cost of the elements that contribute to service provision. We are now going to establish the unit cost of the drop-in service for Ashanti using the informa-tion provided in its budget report. Firstly, we would need to define what a 'unit' represented before trying to measure or cost it. A unit of Ashanti's service could be defined as the cost of a session attended by a service user, e.g. a half-day or full day, or by the number of activities provided or attended.

Formula for working out service costs

So let us try to estimate the cost of the drop-in service on the basis that a minimum unit that a service user would attend is a half-day. We will proceed to make our calculations using this basic assumption.

The number of average days provided by Ashanti annually is 253 after deducting the days closed for public holidays (10) and weekends (102).

The annual budget is £290,297.

Let us assume that if the centre is working to maximum capacity, there are 32 service users attending at any one time (am and pm).

Therefore the unit cost can be calculated as follows:

253 days $\times$ 32 service users = 8096

This can then be divided into the overall cost of the service = 8096 divided into £290,297. This would give us a unit cost of approximately £35.86 per day. If there were fewer service users attending than the centre could cater for, then the cost would increase. If service users only attended one session or half-day, then the cost would be approximately half = approximately £18. Of course this is a very crude measure but it helps to give you an idea of how service costs are identified.

ACTIVITY 5.4

What do you think the main problems are with this approach to costing individual services?

What issues do you think are hidden in the cost calculated?

Can you think of any other information that would be required to consider alongside the cost of this service in a mental health drop-in? What else needs to be considered when using this information to evaluate the cost of the service?

One of the main problems with this approach to unit costing would be that it is an 'aver-age' cost which masks a wide variety of variables. The quality of the service provided and unpredictability of who 'drops in' as well as equality issues about who is accessing or using the service are not taken into account. Similarly, the preventative nature of a service means that by attending the centre, people may be less at risk of having more severe breakdowns in their mental health. This may result in fewer admissions to hospital or use of other more expensive services such as residential care or drug treatment, not to men-tion the quality-of-life issues enshrined in this approach. The above budget does not include other relevant but hidden costs such as additional hours worked by staff, their training costs, equipment and time spent dealing with crises, etc. There may also be a need to apportion overhead costs such as strategic management or legal costs if the day centre is part of a larger organisation, in order to calculate the true costs of the service.

The aim of a costing system is to charge as accurately as possible to each chosen unit the cost incurred in producing it. Costing systems are used to aid planning, control and decision-making. Each of these purposes requires a different approach to costing and you can read further about these in the recommended further reading. Suffice to say that one of the problems of costing units in social care is the lack of homogeneity, for example where different levels of services are provided according to different needs. Defining appropriate units of service for costing purposes to reflect diversity is equally important. Examples of possible units of services are:

- costs per hour of services (e.g. counselling service or domiciliary care);

- costs per consultation, as for family therapy cost per specialist assessment;

- costs per treatment or activity (e.g. family therapy session, providing an item of equipment, support service in a day centre);

- costs per bed per day (residential care or re-ablement services).

Unit costs are used to negotiate contracts and, as you can see, can be very arbitrary. Block contracts are often used to drive down unit costs and can have unfair advantages on smaller organisations that contract to deliver services.

C H A P T E R   S U M M A R Y

This chapter has covered a range of issues in relation to the resource management of social care services from both the purchasers' and providers' perspectives. You may have found this quite challenging but nevertheless it is an introduction to some of the broader socio-economic and political concepts involved in decision-making in social care, and the opportunity to do so can help you understand wider issues about resource management in social care. You will be more aware of the factors which impact on the commissioning and purchasing of services in the mixed economy of care and more recent developments in personalised care, and be able to ask your manager more specific questions about the way in which these systems operate in your organisation.

FURTHER READING

More detail on how effective joint commissioning and funding can be managed within children's services can be found in a best practice guide: *Better outcomes for children's services through joint funding*, August 2007, available from
www.everychildmatters.gov.uk/planningandcommissioning/jointfunding/

The Care Services and Improvement Partnership publishes a number of evaluations on personalisation and individual budgets and these can be found on their website
www.integratedcarenetwork.gov.uk/personalisation/

Robinson, J and Banks, P (2005) *The business of caring*. London: King's Fund. This documents an extensive inquiry into care service for older people in London and the major shortcomings in current arrangements. It links social policy, market development and resource issues with recommendations for future investment in care services.

Chapter 6
The organisational equalities framework

This chapter will help you achieve the following National Occupational Standards and General Social Care Council's Code of Practice.

Key Role 2: Plan, carry out, review and evaluate social work practice, with individuals, families, carers, groups, communities and other professionals.

- Interact with individuals, families, carers, groups and communities to achieve change and development and to improve life opportunities.
- Address behaviour which presents a risk to individuals, families, carers, groups and communities.

Key Role 3: Support individuals to represent their needs, views and circumstances.

- Advocate with, and on behalf of, individuals, families, carers, groups and communities.

Key Role 6: Demonstrate professional competence in social work practice.

- Manage complex ethical issues, dilemmas and conflicts.

General Social Care Codes of Practice

Code 5: As a social care worker, you must uphold public trust and confidence in social care services, in particular, by not discriminating or condoning unlawfully or unjustifiably against service users, carers or colleagues.

It will also introduce you to the following academic standards as set out in the social work subject benchmark statements:

3.1.1 Social work services and service users

- The nature of social work services in a diverse society, with particular reference to concepts such as prejudice, inter-personal, institutional and structural discrimination, empowerment and anti-discriminatory practices.

3.1.3 Values and ethics

- The complex relationship between justice, care and control in social welfare and the practical and ethical implications of these, including roles as statutory agents and in upholding the law in respect of discrimination.

3.2.2.3 Analysis and synthesis

- Consider specific factors relevant to social work practice such as risk, rights, cultural differences and linguistic sensitivities, responsibilities to protect vulnerable individuals and legal obligations.
- Analyse and take account of the impact of inequality and discrimination in work with people in particular contexts and problem situations.

3.2.4 Skills in working with others

- Act with others to increase social justice by identifying and responding to prejudice, institutional discrimination and structural inequality.

Introduction

This chapter looks at equalities and inequalities in social care from the organisational perspective. In particular, we will examine the concept of institutional discrimination and how it might manifest itself in social work and social care organisations. Discrimination and **oppression** at the institutional level are not a new phenomenon. Growing insight supported by research has documented the ways in which health and social care has been, and continues to be, provided in ways which are at best inappropriate to people's needs and at worst collude with and perpetuate inequalities (Dominelli, 1988, 1989; Oliver, 1990; Thompson, 2003; Butt et al., 2005). The provision of social work services should at the very least do no harm to service users, carers and their communities. Relationships between stakeholders, employees and managers within an organisation are important to ensure that there is a clear process of accountability around equality issues.

We will begin by examining the strategic framework for promoting equality in service provision with reference to relevant legislation and policies. This will enable us to define what we mean by terms such as 'institutional discrimination', 'equal opportunities', 'direct' and 'indirect discrimination' and 'diversity'. We will review some of the ways in which organisations strive to achieve equality through their mission or vision statements, the policies, procedures and guidelines given to staff to help them implement **anti-discriminatory** and **anti-oppressive practice**. There will be an evaluation of the research evidence relating to the under- or over-representation of oppressed groups in care services as well as employment practices in organisations which illustrates the presence and impact of **discrimination** at the institutional level. Uncovering and understanding the experiences of the diverse individuals and groups who use or deliver social care services is one step towards providing safe and effective social care. Equally important is the development of a model of practice that incorporates the cultural knowledge, understanding and interpersonal skills needed to respond appropriately to a diverse community and which also takes account of social policy and structural issues in providing access to services.

Management and organisational structures and cultures compatible with the above ideals can help to provide an environment for promoting anti-discriminatory and anti-oppressive professional practice. Likewise, organisational power relationships and dynamics can reflect the structural dimensions of oppression in the social care workforce whereby the organisation itself becomes a microcosm of society. We will look at some of these workforce issues. Building on your knowledge of structure, culture, leadership and change management, we will conclude by examining a case study to help you identify how management practice is an important tool to promote equality in the workplace and to develop a checklist of recommended best practice essential to championing equality issues.

Theoretical models of discrimination

Throughout your training you will be critically evaluating your own values, attitudes and prejudices towards oppressed individuals and groups in society and will be asked to consider philosophical and **epistemological** values of the different approaches to anti-discriminatory and anti-oppressive practice and how this coincides with your own personal and political consciousness and value base. In developing such awareness, you may eventually be drawn to work in certain types of social work organisations which may reflect your own value base and aspirations towards professional practice. You will also begin to develop a deeper knowledge and understanding of the structural issues that affect social work practice. These social, economic, political and cultural issues impact on organisations and the work that goes on within them. The study of social work disciplines such as social policy, sociology, economic theory or politics will make you aware of how these factors impact and act as constraints on people's lives, which in turn can be perpetuated by the availability or accessibility of services to them. According to Thompson (2003, p. 182), social policy and legislation can be an asset in tackling discrimination through the provision and dissemination of supportive policies and practices; alternatively, they can be a major source of discrimination or exacerbate existing inequalities.

Through developing our social work skills and knowledge, we can aspire to challenging the impact of structural constraints on service users' lives. This requires energy, tenacity, understanding and the development of political skills (Nutley and Osborne, 1994, p. 73). It is insufficient to place responsibility for discrimination with one's individual prejudices alone. The routinisation of discriminatory practices and the oppression arising from these within organisations such as social care can institutionalise prejudice. Therefore, social work theorists have designed and offered a number of multi-dimensional theoretical frameworks for understanding anti-discriminatory practice at different levels in society and these can be useful when examining discrimination at the institutional level (Keating, 1997; Thompson, 2003; Dhillon-Stevens 2005).

Multi-dimensional models

Thompson talks about three separate but interrelated levels: the personal, cultural and structural (Thompson, 2003). As stated earlier, the belief that discrimination is based on the attitudes and behaviours of an individual alone does not go far enough to explain why certain groups in society become marginalised. To analyse this further, we must consider the culture within which a person operates, i.e. the prevailing norms, cultures and language that act as a vehicle for transmitting discriminatory ideas and meaning, which Thompson terms the cultural (p. 15). The cultural level also has limitations as an explanatory framework as it is embedded in the social structure comprising the macro-level influences and social, political and economic constraints. Structural oppression arises from the way the social system itself is structured. Therefore, if you were to make a distinction between structural oppression and the oppressive behaviour of individuals you would need to consider the power base that they hold and the source or authority for that power. As social workers, we work with groups of people with the least power in society and are simultaneously employed by the state either directly or indirectly. Within a statutory organisation, social workers are given specific formal powers derived from legislation or as a result of their professional status and access to resources. If you agree that the social work agenda is determined to a large extent by the state and powerful interest groups, then developing anti-discriminatory approaches to practice does not always square up with social work's explicit commitment to social justice:

The social work profession promotes social change, problem solving in human relationships and the empowerment and liberation of people to enhance well-being.

(International Federation of Social Workers, 2004)

In working with other people we enter a complex world of interactions and structures. This can lead to a positive outcome for all concerned or it can lead to a serious exacerbation of the situation. Consequently, we have to recognise the potential for social work to do harm as well as good.

(Thompson, 2000, p.68)

In conclusion then, many people using social care services experience problems directly related to structural inequalities in society. The challenge is how to work with those individuals without seeming to treat their problems as if they were purely individual difficulties.

Keating (1997) offers a similar explanatory model of oppression encompassing the socio-political, socio-cultural and psychological. At the socio-political level oppression is legitimated and institutionalised and the level at which power is used to dominate and assign different status to groups. The socio-cultural level is the level at which oppression is transmitted and propagated in society and is mediated through language and the way in which we construct meaning. Keating points in particular to the way in which we define difference, as a cornerstone upon which oppression is built. The psychological level refers to the ways in which an individual is affected by oppression and to the ways in which those experiences impact upon an individual's life. Ideas and assumptions about asylum seekers are one example of how these different levels of oppression interrelate.

RESEARCH SUMMARY

Research done into social work's involvement in internal immigration controls has been used to argue that social workers have been increasingly drawn into being part of the surveillance process and have become complicit in implementing social policies that are degrading and inhuman. According to Humphries (2004), the uncritical roles taken on by social workers as inquisitors and reporters to the Home Office are blatantly at odds with principles held by the profession and pose a threat to their more progressive future.

One study found that social work teams working with asylum seekers were operating well below the standards seen as acceptable for UK citizens. Workers were found to have had little experience or expertise in working with unaccompanied asylum-seeking children and regarded the duty to check immigration status as another bureaucratic irritation rather than a major ethical dilemma (Duvell and Jordan, 2000).

In the field of mental health, researchers found teams unwilling to acknowledge their duty towards asylum seekers because they said they did not have the resources to deal with post-traumatic stress disorder (Humphries, 2005).

Within community care, there was evidence that local authorities are likely to interpret immigration criteria in the narrowest possible way, resulting in harsh judgements against people facing destitution and from seeking help (Humphries and Mynott, 2002).

CONTINUED

Finally, research by Jones (2002) found that the commitment to promote the family does not apply to families where immigration control leads to disruption of family life and has damaging effects on children. She found social services departments, voluntary agencies and government bodies responsible for children's welfare to be complicit in the creation of disadvantage and discrimination against families involved in immigration proceedings.

As the research cited above illustrates, social work in itself is capable of being oppressive in relation to the level at which it operates and this needs to be taken very seriously. This involves somehow getting to a place in our minds where oppression is simply not something 'out there' but something we have a sense of from the inside (Beckett and Maynard, 2005). In the organisational context, a basis for mobilising strategies towards developing anti-oppressive practice should be built on the idea of interdependence which actively promotes participation of service users and staff within the structures and institutions they are working. As employees of an organisation we are bound by the agency's constraints as part of our employment contract. Dominelli (2002) points out that the strength of commitment of individuals towards their agency will be conditional on how far personal value systems coincide with organisational ones and this may be tested out in our relationships with managers, co-workers and service users and is dependent on the support available to us (Dominelli, 2002). In statutory settings, legislation is an important aspect of organisational structure and whilst working within the legislative framework we may also have to challenge organisational 'norms'. This means coping with the contradictory nature of trying to develop helping relationships on the one hand in an environment with as many controlling elements on the other (Dominelli, 2002; Thompson, 2003). Developing an understanding of the legislation and how this operates is crucial to developing anti-oppressive social work practice.

The legislative framework

Article 14 of the Human Rights Act 1998 specifically prohibits discrimination. Growing legislation places responsibilities on public sector bodies to actively combat discrimination and applies equally to independent, private and voluntary social care provision where these are providing a service on behalf of a public authority. Anti-discriminatory legislation covers key areas of provision such as goods, services, employment, education and housing. It is frequently accompanied by detailed guidance spelling out employers' duties to demonstrate how they have taken action to prevent discrimination and actively promote equality (DTI, 2004; DoH, 2005c).

Table 6.1 gives a brief overview of the relevant legislation. More detailed information can be found in Johns (2007) or in any comprehensive social work law textbook.

You should familiarise yourself with the specific requirements that relate to equality issues contained in government policy guidance on other key social work legislation. The Children Act 1989 and 2004, NHS and Community Care Act 1993, the Mental Health Act 1983 and 2007, the Mental Capacity Act 2005 and the Criminal Justice Act 1991 all refer

Table 6.1

Legislation	Summary of duties
Equal Pay Act 1970	Eliminates discrimination as regards pay, terms and conditions between men and women doing equal work.
Sex Discrimination Act 1975	Prohibits discrimination in relation to employment including sex, gender reassignment, married persons and victimisation.
Race Relations Act 1976	Prohibits discrimination in relation to employment, education, housing, provision of goods and services. General duty to promote equality of opportunity and good relations between different racial groups in policy-making, service delivery, employment practice and other functions.
Race Relations (Amendment) Act (2000) and RRA 1976 Regulations (2003)	Duty to publish a race equality scheme which assesses, monitors functions and policies to see how they affect race equality, publish findings, consult public and train staff in new duties.
Disability Discrimination Act 1995 (DDA) DDA (Amendment) Regulations (2003)	Prohibits discrimination against disabled people in relation to less favourable treatment and duty to make reasonable adjustments in certain circumstances in relation to education, employment, provision of goods, facilities and services. The Disability Discrimination Bill (2006) provides a general duty to promote equality of opportunity for disabled people.
Employment Equality (Sexual Orientation) Regulations 2003 and the Equality Act (Sexual Orientation) Regulations 2007	Prohibits direct, indirect discrimination and harassment on grounds of sexual orientation in employment and vocational training and less favourable treatment in relation to the regulations. The Sexual Orientation Regulations, introduced as a consequence of the Equality Act 2006, provide protection to LGBT people against discrimination in the provision of 'goods, facilities and services', essentially almost any activity in which either business or public providers are engaged.
Employment Equality (Religion or Belief) 2003 belief	Prohibits direct, or indirect discrimination and harassment on grounds of religion or in employment and vocational training. Follows regulations of sexual orientation.
Employment Equality (Age) Regulations (2006) and amended Regulations (2008)	Prohibits any direct or indirect discrimination and harassment in relation to an employee's age
Equality Act 2006	Introduced to level up protection against the equality strands and established the Commission for Equality and Human Rights (CEHR) now responsible for promoting understanding of equality and human rights issues and for challenging unlawful discrimination.

to specific duties in relation to anti-discriminatory practices in the implementation of these acts. You will also recall that the National Service Frameworks referred to in Chapter 3 are all underpinned by an equalities framework integral to the specific standards for each particular service user group.

Specific commissions have been appointed by government to oversee and support the implementation of anti-discriminatory legislation. The Commission for Racial Equality, the Disability Rights Commission and the Equal Opportunities Commission have separately and together promoted best practice, and represented individuals to challenge and obtain rights of redress following complaints of discrimination. These commissions have developed codes of practice for employers and public bodies and have acted as a monitoring body on behalf of the government and lobbied in key areas of discrimination. Following the Equality Act 2006, the Commission for Equality and Human Rights was established, bringing together the work of the previous commissions and as a single body to act as an authoritative champion for tackling discrimination on multiple grounds through one single access point. The CEHR has responsibility for providing information, advice and guidance on the full breadth of equality and human rights issues, in promoting improvements to the delivery of public services and in taking a more coherent approach to enforcing discrimination legislation (DTI, 2004).

Despite the presence of protective legislation, discrimination in key areas of social care continues to be documented. This can manifest itself through evidence of over- or under-representation of certain groups in service delivery and we will return to examine this later on. Some of these arise as a direct consequence of social workers exercising their powers within the legislative framework. Minimal intervention and maximising partnership are therefore key principles for social work practice to minimise discrimination (Dalrymple and Burke, 2003).

Terminology used in legislation

You will come across specific terms associated with the grounds covered by anti-discrimination law, and these are:

- **Direct discrimination** – treating a person less favourably because of his/her racial background, gender, disability, sexuality or age.

- **Indirect discrimination** – the application of conditions or criteria that disadvantages an individual or group.

- **Victimisation** – treating a person less favourably once they have raised a concern or complaint under the legislation, for example by allocating excessive workloads or not speaking to them. This is a term frequently used in organisational policies and procedures to deal with discrimination at work and will be found in 'Discrimination, Victimisation and Harassment' policies under the disciplinary procedure.

Harassment is an issue which lies on the boundary between law and organisational policy. If harassment policies are not valued or enforced, then an individual may be forced to leave their job before making such complaints. Research shows that some members of socially oppressed groups are likely to suffer worse repercussions than their actual harasser, resulting in individuals making calculated decisions not to take any action in cases of discrimination for fear of recriminations.

Promoting equal opportunities

Besides the legal framework, individual organisations publish mission statements, policies, procedures and guidelines to demonstrate that they are acting lawfully. Organisations are also obliged to make public their duties to provide equality in services they provide with a statement of how they intend to achieve this. Statements or policies on equal opportunities serve as one means of doing this. Equal opportunities can be defined as:

> *the elimination of discrimination in society. It is about effective use of human*
> *resources and positive action measures to ensure employment opportunities and*

service provision are bias free and made readily available to people from within a target group. Equality of opportunity involves the breakdown and removal of discriminatory structures, biased policies and prejudicial practices in organisations. It seeks to replace processes that perpetuate inequality with better and more effective ways of working which will provide equal access for all service and employment opportunities.

(Nutley and Osborne, 1994, p. 57)

The above excerpt acknowledges that discrimination is twofold, relating to service provision and employment practice, both of which form a cornerstone of policy within social

---

ACTIVITY **6.1**

Review what has been discussed so far and clarify your own thoughts about why we need equal opportunities policies. Why are they necessary and what should a policy contain?

---

care organisations.

You may have come up with some or all of the following reasons:

- to comply with legislation;
- as an expression of the organisation's ethical belief in equality;
- to promote better use of resources, for example by having a policy that states clearly what someone is entitled to and what their rights are;
- to encourage diversity in the workforce, which in turn contributes to diversity in perspectives on service provision;
- as a measure which acknowledges the pervasive nature of overt and covert discrimination in social care;
- to provide an opportunity for organisations to publicise any emphasis on marginalised or disadvantaged groups or their intention to provide services in an anti-oppressive way.

A number of public service organisations have been granted specific awards, accreditations and national charter marks to demonstrate their achievements in diversity in relation to the workforce. Stonewall's Diversity Champion programme is Britain's good-practice forum in which employers can work with Stonewall and each other, to promote lesbian, gay and bisexual equality in the workplace. Diversity Champion brings together employers who are at the cutting edge of delivering diversity in business and public services and focuses on the new challenges and opportunities for employers addressing issues of diversity in the workplace. The Positive About Disabled People charter mark represented by the symbol of two ticks (✓✓) can also be given to organisations who have agreed to make certain positive commitments regarding the employment, retention, training and career development of disabled people (www.directgov.uk) and who demonstrate compliance with the disability equality scheme. Age Positive (www.agepositive.gov) is a further scheme where the organisation has signed up to promoting the benefits of employing a mixed-age workforce that includes older people and has developed strategies and policies to support people making decisions about working and retirement.

One criticism of equal opportunities policies is the discrepancies revealed by research between the rhetoric on agencies' priorities and expectations, with the evidence of how these are achieved in practice. It is when these two areas do not correlate then institutional discrimination can begin to develop. In order to explore this concept further, we will start by looking at one aspect of institutional discrimination, institutional racism, a term that was systematically adopted and accepted by the government in 1999.

Institutional racism

The Race Relations Act 1976 made discrimination on the grounds of race unlawful and monitoring its effectiveness relied heavily on the burden of proof or ability of individuals to make complaints and seek personal redress. The racist murder of black teenager Stephen Lawrence and the reports of Lord Macpherson into the circumstances of his death formally introduced the term 'institutional racism', defining it as:

> *the collective failure of an organisation to provide an appropriate and professional service to people because of their colour, culture or ethnic origin. It can be seen or detected in processes, attitudes and behaviours which amount to discrimination through unwitting prejudice, ignorance, thoughtlessness and racist stereotyping which disadvantage minority people.*

(Home Office, 1999, para 6)

Macpherson provided evidence that racism is endemic in the public sector. This was not only a concern for the police but had strong implications for other sectors such as social care, the criminal justice system and health services. Moreover, evidence of institutional racism has continued to accrue and remains a matter of concern.

RESEARCH SUMMARY

David Bennet, a 39-year-old African-Caribbean patient, died in 1998 in a medium secure psychiatric unit whilst being restrained face down on the floor for 25 minutes. The independent inquiry into his death identified many failings in the system as a result of racial discrimination. The DoH response to the inquiry involved developing an action plan for tackling issues that affect black and minority ethnic mental health patients (DoH, 2005c).

An inquiry into the murder of Zahid Mubarek in a young offending institution highlighted ignorance and poor practice in dealing with racist behaviour and the lack of supportive environments for black and minority offenders.

(www.zahidmubarekinquiry.org.uk)

A review by the Social Exclusion Unit (2004) found that black and minority ethnic disabled people share two of the characteristics of those who have benefited least from policies and initiatives to combat social exclusion. In March 2006, the government established a formal inquiry into the relationship between young black people and the criminal justice system focusing on the reasons for young black people's overrepresentation in the system. It found substantial evidence to support allegations of direct or indirect discrimination in

CONTINUED

policing and the youth justice system and also found that despite public perception there was no evidence that young black people committed crime more than any other group.

Institutional racism is about customary attitudes, mind sets and ways of behaving which can be perpetuated by the myth of how things are usually done within an organisation. This approach allows individual prejudice to go unchallenged and to take root in the fabric of the organisation. The Race Relations (Amendment) Act 2000 places a general duty on all public authorities to promote equality. These duties include a requirement of employers to monitor by ethnic group, their existing staff, and applicants for jobs, promotion and training. In organisations with 150 staff or more, employers must also monitor grievances, disciplinary action, performance appraisals, training and dismissals for racial bias and disadvantage (Dimond, 2004). In essence, employers must now take direct responsibility for racial discrimination or racial harassment within their organisations and design and implement schemes to tackle institutional racism and find ways of responding to the needs of black and minority ethnic people which value diversity, respect human rights and promote independence. Local authorities have taken racial equality schemes further by extending provisions to all areas of discrimination affecting their local communities, by developing equality audit tools to review and evaluate their achievements.

RESEARCH SUMMARY

In a northern English town, Chinese and Vietnamese residents were socially and culturally isolated from the rest of the local community. A proactive contact programme was set up to encourage wider community engagement, particularly in the areas of regeneration and neighbourhood planning.

A residents' group was set up to allow Chinese and Vietnamese residents to communicate directly with the city council to raise any concerns, and contacts were promoted through local schools, luncheon clubs, community centres and home visits. Building up trust with people who had not traditionally engaged with the rest of the community to a great extent was difficult, but persistence and determination helped to forge links. The programme used a Chinese facilitator and translator when working with the Chinese community, which proved very successful.

(Race Equality Unit, *Breaking down barriers*, www.reu.org.uk, undated)

Butt (2005) has pointed out that care must be taken not to view black and minority ethnic communities as passive victims of racism and disadvantage. We also need to take account of the activity by people with significant support needs from these communities to shape and maintain their own lives, including the development of social and support networks.

Institutional discrimination

Institutional racism is one form of discrimination in terms of key issues within social care. The remainder of this chapter will consider characteristics of social care organisations that successfully promote diversity and explores further research on barriers to promoting diversity and which institutionalise a range of discriminatory practices. Institutional discrimination is defined as:

> *A system of beliefs, policies, institutions and culture that systematically*
> *discriminate against and demean women, black people, people with disabilities,*
> *lesbians and gays, working-class people and other oppressed groups.*

> (Banks, 2001, p. 132)

Institutional racism is one instance of structural oppression and can incorporate an approach that treats people all the same and generalises about their needs. It can also stereotype people and their needs by attaching labels to them and acting on these labels without genuine respect by accepting differences both at an individual level and at the level of structures, policies and institutions. According to Butt (2005), recognising that people in different circumstances and with different backgrounds have different needs as well as a contribution to make which will benefit society or the organisation, is crucial to effective management of diversity. Butt goes on to remind us that diversity means taking account of the complexities of the lives of individuals and of groups of people, and the impact of these complexities on their experience of discrimination and disadvantage.

ACTIVITY 6.2

It has been suggested that social workers are not adequately meeting the social care needs of lesbians and gay men. Before we look at some of the evidence for this, try to identify the areas in which you think gay and lesbian citizens might experience discrimination in relation to social work practice or using social care services.

It is only recently that issues relating to sexual orientation have begun to find their way on to the social work agenda (Brown, 1998; Bayliss, 2000). As these issues are explored, the effects of multiple oppression have become more apparent. You may have identified that in working with gay, lesbian and bisexual service users, there are issues relating to a lack of visibility. Sexual orientation may not be immediately apparent and can be compounded by viewpoints about gays or lesbians as members of a homogenous service user group such as mental health, learning disability or older people. Research into the experiences of gay and lesbian people using social care services has identified the following barriers and difficulties:

- The design and use of referral or assessment forms which reflect these assumptions by perhaps enquiring about marital status (Bayliss, 2000) or by not giving parity to friendship networks, partners and children in gay and lesbian relationships (Pugh, 2005).

- The lack of awareness of particular issues which face people in same-sex partnerships, for example, pension rights, inheritance rights leading to financial or housing problems following the death of a partner (Lavin, 2004).

- The emotional issues surrounding bereavement where a relationship is not acknowledged, is denied or concealed (Manthorpe, 2003).

- A lack of gay, lesbian and bisexual issues in the social work literature (Hardman, 1977) and lack of reflection and critical analysis in the workplace that help to identify their needs and the impact of heterosexism and homophobia on the lives of gay and lesbian service users (Bayliss, 2000).

- Assessment based on heterosexist assumptions about a service user.

- The provision of services which do not reflect or support people in the lifestyle of their choice (Abbott and Howarth, 2005), particularly for older people living in institutionalised care environments (Hafford-Letchfield, 2008).

- Discrimination against the rights of lesbian couples to receive IVF treatment in the same way as other infertile couples.

The Equality Act (Sexual Orientation) Regulations 2007 prohibit both direct and indirect discrimination on the basis of sexual orientation and against others associated with them. The Civil Partnership Bill (2005) has meant, among other things, that lesbian and gay couples can acquire rights and responsibilities which reflect their commitment and it provides help to organise their lives together. This includes joint treatment for income-related and state pension benefits, recognition for immigration purposes as well as encouraging proper respect for partners in relation to care arrangements and the implications of these. The recent development of guidance documents (DoH, 2007b; CSCI, 2008a) on good practice in assessment, person-centred planning and self directed service provision within the LGBT community is an important foundation for ensuring the personalisation of services appropriate to those from LGBT communities.

Currently, there is relatively sparse literature on transgender people, although 2,237 transsexual people applied for legal recognition in 2005–07 via registration with the Gender Recognition Panel. This Panel was set up under the Gender Recognition Act 2004 to ensure that transsexual people enjoy the rights and responsibilities appropriate to their acquired gender (www.grp.gov.uk). Using social care services can cause immense fear for transgender individuals, particularly when using personal care, which can be a terrifying prospect and needs sensitive handling. Given that legislation against discrimination on grounds of gender identity is planned but not yet in place, good-practice guidance with clear policies and procedures can do much to promote equality in service provision (CSCI, 2008a). People who are transgender often face very similar issues in relation to discrimination as those from the LGB community. When trans people start to live permanently in their new gender role, they and their families, partners and spouses are likely to experience great stress. Many trans people also suffer discrimination in the workplace and for these, the Sex Discrimination Act provides protection in employment before, during and after the transition process (DoH, 2007c). CSCI have offered the following best practice pointers in supporting transgender people using social care services:

- Ensure that policies, procedures and publicity include transgender people when talking about equality issues, including addressing transphobia from staff or other people using services.

- Ensure that staff training on equality includes issues for transgender people.

- Ensure that staff and managers have access to resources on transgender issues. National organisations of transgender people are a useful starting point for information.

- Develop equality policies that enable transgender staff to feel confident that they will be treated equally are likely to have a positive impact on equality and diversity in service provision.

- If none of the people using your service has come out as transgender, consider consultation with local groups of transgender people or LGBT groups as people who could potentially use your service.

- Use the name and title (eg Mr, Ms, Mrs, Miss) that the person prefers.

- Allow transgender people access to appropriate single-sex facilities which are in line with their gender identity.

- Be aware that some transgender people may have specific personal care needs and handle these sensitively; for example, trans women who have transitioned later in life may still need to shave regularly. Trans people who need assistance going to the toilet or bathing require support from workers who understand that their body may not match their gender identity.

- Transgender people may need support if they face prejudice from other people using the service or their family.

- Confidentiality around someone's transgender status is very important. Whether someone wishes other people to know about their status may change over time, particularly if the person is in transition.

- Support transgender people who want to maintain contacts with other transgender people or the broader LGBT community as this is important for identity and self-esteem.

(CSCI, 2008a, p. 37)

Over- and under-representation of service users in services

Now that you have an understanding of the concept of institutional discrimination, we are going to take a snapshot of the many ways in which it manifests itself in service delivery, before turning our attention to the social care workforce issues. There is a wide range of documented research and I have highlighted just a few examples here which may raise your awareness or help you to come up with your own examples:

- The links between young women living in or leaving care and involvement in prostitution or at risk of sexual exploitation have been attributed to the psychological and emotional aspects of being in care as well as the multiple and frequent placement moves that hampered their ability to develop meaningful relationships and self-esteem (O'Neil, 1995).

- Social services have been shown to have played a minimal role in the development and maintenance of racial and ethnic identity, and in equipping young people to deal with racism (Barn et al., 2005).

- Research that explored patterns of decision-making for children whose lives were affected by domestic violence, found that social workers had a tendency to focus intervention/responsibility on the mother, whilst either avoiding or working ineffectively with fathers, which placed women in situations where their needs were not met or were even ignored (Humphreys, 2000).

- Scrutiny of sexuality in social work practice has been shown to be underpinned by stereotypes about the need for supervision or control, for example with people with learning disabilities living in institutional care (Carabine, 2004).

- The increase in community prescriptions of anti-psychotic drugs and the failure to review the increasing chemical management of older people in care homes (Sone, 2000).

- Until the amendment to the Health and Social Care Bill in 2008, more than 300,000 elderly people and an estimated 35,000 younger adults with disabilities were residing in private care homes which were not covered by the Human Rights Act 1990.

The social care workforce

The government's agenda for transforming services emphasises requirements for services to assess the future impact of changes in service delivery, skill mix and technology in order to improve planning of future workforce requirements (CWDC, 2008 and SfC, 2008). Strategies concerned with social care needs of the population, views of service users and tackling inequality are inextricably linked with workforce developments (Drennan et al., 2004). Ensuring the workforce reflects the diverse nature of communities it serves and developing an organisational culture in which diversity is systematically acknowledged, valued and effectively managed are likely to determine increased access to quality services at an operational level (Friday and Friday, 2003).

Research into career prospects of different people working in social care highlights under- and over-representation of some groups at different levels in an organisation. Findings suggest that black and minority ethnic staff are less likely to be in management and supervisory positions. For those already in management, they are less likely to receive supervisory support, training and development opportunities and high-quality feedback than other managers and are more likely to miss out on important development opportunities that could help career progression (IDeA, 2004). The children's workforce has a higher than average proportion of part-time workers and is predominantly female, although, at management level, the proportion of men is higher (CWDC, 2008, p. 2).

Fragmentation of services during change can also affect opportunities for promotion and career progression. The metaphorical barrier used to describe the exclusion of employees from black and minority ethnic groups, women and people with disabilities from achieving promotion, particularly to senior levels in social care, has been termed the 'glass ceiling' (Davidson and Cooper, 1992). Obstacles to career development include a lack of formal qualifications and training, the availability of permanent posts, subverted hostility from subordinates and colleagues, and many other subtle discriminatory attitudes. There is evidence that women experience discrimination at the selection process for senior posts, particularly from elected members (Foster, 2001). At the other end of the spectrum there is a predominance of women in lower-paid posts away from higher influential positions. There is evidence of over-representation of black staff subject to disciplinary procedures (Coulshed and Mullender, 2001).

As discussed earlier, oppression is built into the very structures of organisations because of the fundamental thinking on which they are based. Managerialist environments can be dominated by rules, regulations and procedures which emphasise maximum efficiency over other priorities. This puts the contribution of staff in terms of their unique backgrounds or diversity outside of the organisational boundaries so that issues such as gender, sexuality, reproduction and emotionality are minimised (Harlow, 2004). Staff from different social backgrounds who do not fit the prevailing culture may not be valued for the strengths of what they have to offer in terms of life experience or diversity of contribution by those managing or in a position to recruit or promote them. Taking into account what staff can potentially bring because of their empathic approach and personal understanding and consideration of service users' own experiences can help to put diversity issues firmly on the organisational agenda.

Some studies have argued that certain workers from the same background as service users bring 'cultural knowledge' or 'cultural competence' to service provision. However, this can perpetuate stereotypes, and debates should continue as to the whole range of professional expertise that these workers bring and which should be valued and supported both in specialist and mainstream provision (Butt, 2005). There is evidence that black and minority ethnic workers appear to make a difference to frontline practice in a way that emphasises the catalytic effect they can have on organisations by sparking wider changes in the way an organisation operates (Harris and Dutt, 2005). This in turn relies on good support of black and minority staff as they are also more likely to experience direct and indirect discrimination in the workplace. Support groups, mentoring schemes and access to good training and supervision are essential ingredients for retaining staff from traditionally marginalised groups (Hafford-Letchfield, 2005).

ACTIVITY 6.3

Viraj is a 58-year-old care assistant of Indian origin. She has worked for Ashton day centre for people with learning disabilities for 16 years and has recently been asked by her manager to undertake the NVQ Level 2 in Care. Viraj is not keen as she has never done any formal study before and feels that she does a good job anyway, even though she hasn't had any training for years; besides which, Viraj is looking forward to retiring in two years' time.

At a compulsory health and safety training day, Viraj reveals to the trainer that she has recently been bitten, scratched and verbally abused by some of the service users with challenging behaviour. This happens on a frequent basis. When she reported this to the day centre supervisor she was told that the service user 'couldn't help it' and as she is not their key worker, she should just try to avoid contact with the service users involved. Viraj has started to develop headaches and a rash and recently took time off. On her return to work, her manager stopped her in the corridor and said that she was extremely concerned about her recent absences and requested a formal meeting with her.

Analyse the above case study and make notes of your responses to the following questions:

1. Can you identify any discriminatory elements to this case? Be as specific as you can.

2. Do you think there are any institutional features to these? Again be specific.

3. What changes to the working practices in Ashton day centre might reduce discrimination for individuals there?

4. What specific management strategies would help to reduce barriers to discrimination and deal with those already in place?

I am now going to conclude this chapter by referring to strategies which you may have managed to identify yourself when working through the above case study. These will highlight characteristics of organisations successful in promoting equality and link these to effective professional and management practices which support this.

Policies, procedures and rights in practice

Assessment and service provision

By implementing a needs-led approach which incorporates effective service user involvement, organisations can become more accurate in deciding priorities, developing services and identifying appropriate outcomes that meet users' self-defined needs. The funding of and use of appropriate advice and advocacy services drawn from a wide range of backgrounds to reflect the communities worked with, can increase the visibility and voice of specific groups who have been traditionally disadvantaged. All staff and advocates should also be trained in cultural and diversity awareness and made aware of the specific rights of individuals, especially where legislation restricts their rights or liberties. Tools for assessment should be based on an exchange model and start with service users by facilitating them to articulate their own needs and facilitate their decision-making capacity. Likewise, risk assessments should collect and organise information in partnership with people and consider sources of both stress and support within the cultural context for individuals. This will help point towards building capacity in local communities and to develop collective responses alongside individual ones (Robinson and Banks, 2005). The personalisation of care services emphasises the importance of self-assessment where the role of social workers is focused on advocacy and brokerage, rather than assessment and gatekeeping (DoH, 2008b). This model of care that is person-centred should enable people to design the support or care arrangements that best suit their specific needs and provides greater opportunity for users to participate as active and equal citizens, both economically and socially.

Both the Children's Plan, 2007 and Putting People First 2007 provide the tools, through individualised budgets and integrated commissioning for social workers, managers and employing agencies to engage with local issues affecting service users. By taking an ecological approach and connecting with poverty issues and social factors that affect people via local consultation groups and partnerships, they should be able to work more effectively with all the relevant agencies to develop more coherent responses (Jack, 2000). Likewise, social care organisations can support or fund local research into resilience and effectiveness of early intervention schemes. The commissioning and contracting process can engage the local community to help develop more culturally compatible services as well as to ensure that mainstream services are accessible. Mainstream services should be able to meet service users' linguistic and cultural requirements and be adjusted to realise this.

Responding to discriminatory incidents

All organisations should have written policies for dealing with specific incidents of discrimination which are actively disseminated to all members of staff and displayed to service users. Policies should be strictly monitored with a written record kept of breaches, with clearly defined sanctions. Managers need to take responsibility for sensitively implementing any action to counter or respond to incidents of discrimination. Service users and staff need to know that they will be cared for in a safe environment that reflects their culture and needs and senior managers should take direct personal responsibility for this (DoH, 2005c). Internal support via consultation, focus and self-support groups that assist communication between managers and staff about issues that affect them can help to develop any new initiatives and address issues proactively. Staff should also be encouraged to join unions or professional support associations to increase opportunities for collective bargaining and to seek rights of redress.

Training and supervision

We will see in the next chapter that a workforce with the right skills, knowledge and commitment can help to promote equality and diversity in the workplace. The way in which organisational learning resources are prioritised and distributed should include the effective use of positive action and mentoring schemes as well as ongoing professional development. Regular supervision which includes active and critical reflection can encourage learning and the development of competence and confidence in staff around equality issues. It also ensures accountability between staff and managers. For members of a diverse workforce, mechanisms within teams that facilitate their contribution, value and recognise the experiences they bring to the delivery of the appropriate support to service users should be developed and reviewed. Understanding and celebrating diversity should assist us in making psychological contact with people who have experienced life differently. Staff teams can help to develop work cultures within which there is an openness and a willingness to participate in new learning, which in turn can result in skilled performance.

Monitoring and evaluation

Standards of good practice set out by the GSCC, regulatory and inspection bodies, and legislative guidance can provide an effective basis for ensuring that employers develop procedures to protect service users' rights. Organisations should implement these within local policies and provide a monitoring framework to promote diversity and equality which includes a statement of the specific aims and objectives. The strategy for implementation should include a system of accountability where people regularly collect meaningful and useful information which informs the organisation about where they are getting it right or where plans need to be reviewed. The use of meaningful performance indicators, as we saw in Chapter 3, can help in this process led by service user and staff groups. Ongoing publicity on the achievements and failures of the organisation should be shared with the community and staff with agreed mechanisms and processes as to how these will be followed up.

C H A P T E R   S U M M A R Y

Issues of discrimination within organisations are complex and make serious and searching demands on us as practitioners who are confronting and challenging these within very demanding environments. At the same time, there is clear evidence that change can be achieved towards producing better outcomes for the users of services, employees and social care organisations. These can occur through a number of mechanisms.

- Strong leadership in equality issues and prioritising and deploying resources by being creative and developing initiatives that articulate and practically support the moral, legal and business reasons for equality.

- Understanding the national levers and drivers that can create opportunities for taking positive action where discrimination occurs.

- Developing an evidence base on which social work practice can reflect and respond through continuous critically reflective practice. This includes questioning and challenging the culture in our organisations and taking responsibility for our own continuous professional development.

- Striving towards increasing service user involvement and participation strategies.

- Acknowledging the relationships between wider political, economic and social factors and social work practice with individuals. This includes advocating for individual service users with our managers and using influential professional groupings from within the organisation to voice concerns about the way in which service users experience services.

FURTHER READING

Thompson, N (2003) *Promoting equality: Challenging discrimination and oppression* (2nd edition). Basingstoke: Palgrave Macmillan.

This is a highly respected text which addresses issues of inequality, discrimination and oppression in all aspects of theory, policy and practice.

Chapter 7
Dignity at work

This chapter will help you achieve the following National Occupational Standards and General Social Care Council's Code of Practice.

Key Role 4: Manage risk to individuals, families, carers, groups, communities, self and colleagues.
- Assess, minimise and manage risk to self and colleagues.
- Work within the risk assessment and management procedures of your own and other relevant organisations and procedures.
- Plan, monitor and review outcomes and actions to minimise stress and risk.

Key Role 5: Manage and be accountable, with supervision and support, for your own social work practice within your organisation.
- Use professional and managerial supervision and support to improve your practice.
- Deal constructively with disagreements and conflicts within relationships.

Key Role 6: Demonstrate professional competence in social work practice.
- Use professional assertiveness to justify decisions and uphold professional social work practice, values and ethics.
- Identify and assess issues, dilemmas and conflicts that might affect your practice.

General Social Care Code of Practice
Code 3: Promote the independence of service users whilst protecting them as far as possible from danger or harm
- Following practice and procedures designed to keep you and other people safe from violent and abusive behaviour at work.
- Complying with employers' health and safety policies, including those relating to substance abuse.

Code 4: Respect the rights of service users while seeking to ensure that their behaviour does not hurt themselves or other people

It will also introduce you to the following academic standards as set out in the social work subject benchmark statements:

3.1.3 Values and ethics
- The conceptual links between codes defining ethical practice and the regulation of professional conduct.

3.1.4 Social work theory
- Models and methods of assessment, including factors underpinning the selection and testing of relevant information, the nature of professional judgement and processes of risk assessment.

3.2.5 Skills in personal and professional development
- Identify and keep under review your own personal and professional boundaries.
- Manage uncertainty, change and stress in work situations.
- Handle inter-personal and intra-personal conflict constructively.

Introduction

This chapter introduces the concept of dignity at work by exploring conditions within which good social work practice can flourish and promote the achievement of positive outcomes for managers, staff, service users and carers. Since the late 1990s, the government's attention to developing the health and social care workforce has highlighted the types of strategies and practices that social work organisations need in place in order to recruit and retain high-quality staff. According the ADSS (undated report), to be a 'good employer' means that social care organisations must pay explicit attention to how staff at all levels in the organisation are subject to the same values and principles expected by members of the public who use services.

In line with other employers in the UK, social care employers must comply fully with all aspects of legislation relating to staff employment. We will start this chapter by outlining the legal responsibilities of public bodies under health and safety legislation to meet these requirements. The establishment of the GSCC and the code of practice for social care workers and their employers embed these responsibilities further within the organisation's operational culture. Compliance with legislation as well as professional ethics is both important to the retention of staff and to organisational morale. We will go on to examine stress management, bullying and aggression and violence to staff as particular areas of concern to social workers in the above context. We will explore policies and procedures that organisations have in place to support the development of safe working conditions. The efforts that an organisation makes to put these in place as well as implementing and monitoring their effectiveness are a clear demonstration of the value an organisation places on its staff. The robustness of the risk-management process to ensure staff safety should also include not only concerns about environmental and physical risks but also systems of safe working that encompass emotional and psychological risks to staff. Therefore, the management team need to be well trained to deliver risk assessment (ADSS, undated, p. 11).

Since the late 1990s, there have been a number of government-sponsored investigations into issues affecting the social care workforce resulting in the emergence of **workforce strategies**. These have targeted particular sectors and staff groups with particular issues and provide the vision and prescribed action needed to employ, manage and develop people essential to further support an organisation's ability to maximise potential to deliver effective and appropriate services. The types of organisational arrangements used to support workforce development rely on good quality supervision, appraisal and analysis of training needs and provision of staff development opportunities, a topic we will return to in our final chapter. Nationally there have been clear identifiable concerns about the quality and continuity of staffing arrangements (SCIE, 2005) and critics of the status of social care staff and their employment conditions often refer to the limited time allowed for employees to meet users' individual needs. Recommendations for strong managerial, professional and political leadership at a local level based on power sharing with users and carers in a non-hierarchical relationship are essential to ensure that appropriate workforce development strategy is not some 'add on' to the new vision for services but an integral element in its realisation (SCIE, 2005). In Chapter 2, we identified that in the transition period of major change, staff will find their performance level and work rate reduced because many of the cues which they use, often unconsciously, to assess situations and keep on track are no longer available or appropriate and decision-making becomes more laboured and less confident, with work being less fluent and demanding more attention (Eraut, 2004). These changes can result in disorientation, exhaustion and vulnerability of staff in the organisation and lead to the quality of the workplace culture deteriorating, affecting respect and dignity for colleagues and subordinates. Staff can respond in two ways: firstly, by organising themselves to take collective action to address issues in the workplace, and we will touch on the role of professional bodies and trade unions in promoting rights and dignity at work. Secondly, staff can respond to changes and new policies with passive resistance; for example, by adopting a negative attitude towards their job or devoting less effort to it. To help you avoid this less desirable strategy, this chapter will conclude with an opportunity for you to construct an individual and personal action plan to ensure that your own work–life balance is maintained and respected.

Health and safety at work

Legislation

In line with other employers, social care organisations have a duty under the Health and Safety at Work Act 1974 and subsequent regulations to ensure, so far as is reasonably practicable, your health and safety, welfare and well-being at work. In general this means:

- making your workplace safe and without risks to health;

- ensuring that any environment, equipment or substances you use are safe and that procedures are put in place which set out how this can be followed;

- providing adequate welfare facilities and support;

- providing you with sufficient information, training and supervision necessary for your health and safety.

Detailed government health and safety regulations spell out how the above provisions must be implemented but in particular your employer must:

- assess the risks to your health and safety and make and record the arrangements for implementing health and safety measures identified from the assessment;

- appoint somebody competent to assist with health and safety responsibilities including emergency procedures;

- co-operate and consult on health and safety with employees and allow employees to make representations about matters affecting health and safety.

(www.hse.org.uk)

Employees also have responsibilities under the law to take reasonable care of their own health and safety and that of others and are obliged to follow any instructions or procedures that promote these. Social workers registered with the GSCC must inform employers or the appropriate authority about any physical, mental or emotional difficulties that might affect their ability to do their job competently and safely; and to seek the necessary supervision and training. Unions and professional organisations have a significant contribution to make to developing solutions to challenges faced in creating a safe working environment in social care. Following work done by Bostock et al. (2005) on risk management, recommendations were made by SCIE that organisations adopt a systems approach which shifts attention away from a focus on individual practice and puts the spotlight on the systems that support practice. The systems approach is a more supportive framework for staff because it acknowledges both human and systems error, emphasising why incidents occur, away from blaming individuals. This depends on fostering an open and fair culture in any organisation which encourages all staff and other stakeholders such as politicians and policy-makers to understand their role in decision-making and preventing errors in relation to areas of risk assessment and management. Now that we have established the legal responsibilities and roles of employers and employees, we will go on to look at specific areas in which risk assessment and management are relevant to social work, starting with the topic of occupational stress, its causes and effects.

Stress and social work

The content of social work can have a traumatising effect on practitioners, no matter how well trained or experienced. Much of social work practice demands that we draw extensively on our own personal resources and on the capacity to understand and support the personal, social and emotional needs of service users, their carers and informal supporters in a person-centred way. Occupational stress has been acknowledged as a significant factor contributing to difficulties in recruiting and retaining social workers in the public and independent sectors. Social work vacancy rates (which have been monitored since 2003) have consistently shown recruitment and retention difficulties in the profession. More than 25 per cent of councils reported difficulties, with some reporting increasing difficulties in recruiting to social work posts in adult services, where there is an average turnover rate of 11 per cent (SfC, 2008a). There is a similar picture within the children's workforce where retention difficulties vary and employers are adopting distinctive patterns of response to tackle the issues, including the development of career pathways, workforce planning and succession planning (CWDC, 2008). In social care as a whole, vacancy rates are about twice as high as those for the totality of all private and public-sector business activity in England despite being significant to the economy, with 5 per cent of employers being in social care (SfC, 2007). Whilst studies of the social care workforce show that commitment to the goals and values of the profession in serving users and carers underlies some of the reported motivations for staying in the job or resulting in a high intrinsic job satisfaction, the experience of functioning in the context of unsympathetic economic and political constraints and constant media criticism of social work can also be a powerful deterrent (Huxley et al., 2005). McLean and Andrew (2000) found that stress was highest for those social workers who felt that they lacked support and felt undervalued. This can lead to social workers themselves being out of sympathy with the way services are run, with a tendency to burnout: the combination of emotional exhaustion, depersonalisation and low personal accomplishment. A ministerial task force reporting in 2005 examined the principal causes of sickness absence from work in the public sector and identified a number of stress-related disorders. Depression and anxiety

(30%) and musculoskeletal disorders (40%) alongside violence to staff (14%) were found to be responsible for an average of 16 days' absence per person per year in local authority social services departments. 'Presenteeism' is also a problem referring to the scenario where people physically attend work but, because of negative factors in the workplace, actually contribute little or perform badly.

Definitions and causes

Stress is defined as the adverse reaction people have to excessive pressures or other types of demand placed upon them (www.hse.gov.uk/stress/standards). There is a distinction between pressure, which can create a 'buzz' or act as a motivating factor, and stress, which occurs when pressure becomes excessive and when the ability to cope is affected or diminished. In defining 'occupational stress', Storey and Billingham (2001) identified an array of interrelated factors including: the effect of environmental stressors and the influence of moderating factors such as personality traits on an individual's perception, for example the ability to adapt to stress; and the availability of support. Traditional belief that stress was an individual problem was officially challenged when in 1995, John Walker, a social worker, made legal history. The High Court ruled that Northumberland County Council was responsible for his two nervous breakdowns by exposing him to impossible workloads and Walker was awarded £175,000 in an out-of-court settlement on stress grounds. The basis of the case was that Walker had an excessive workload and following an initial breakdown, his employers, who were alerted to his vulnerability, failed to provide adequate support to alleviate the pressures on him. This negligence led to a wider examination of the causes and effects of stress within social work teams and organisations and highlighted a range of issues that need to be explored. Referring to such a framework, we will now investigate the types of circumstances that give rise to stress.

CASE STUDY

Ted, an experienced social worker, has been working with the Tears, a very chaotic family. There are frequent allegations and concerns about neglect and physical abuse of the children and this has churned up memories and feelings of Ted's own upbringing. Ted's father died two years ago and the anniversary is coming up. The parents of the family he is working with have been consistently verbally abusive and unco-operative. Last week Mr Tear physically threatened Ted and Ted has not been sleeping well at night, partly due to an irritating skin rash developing in his groin area. Ted is unable to take on any new cases because his workload is falling behind. He runs the risk of losing his outstanding annual leave with so many deadlines to meet. Ted is aware of the resentment building up from some of his team members, who see themselves as 'carrying him'. A long-awaited opportunity for promotion to practice supervisor has recently come up and Ted feels that his managers, whilst outwardly supportive, have doubts about his readiness and ability to cope with the extra responsibilities. Ted needs the extra income because his partner, Maggie, is pregnant and whilst they are both pleased, it was not ideal timing.

In order to analyse Ted's situation we will first look at the six areas identified by the Health and Safety Executive (HSE, 2004) where stress at work may occur. These are:

- **Demands** – emanating from workload, work patterns, and the work environment.

- **Control** – the level of influence or say that a person has in the way in which they do their work.

- **Support** – the level of encouragement, sponsorship and resources provided by the organisation, line management and colleagues.

- **Relationships** – as social work usually takes place in team contexts, these can provide a potential resource for alleviating stress and empowering staff as well as a structure to deal with unacceptable behaviour.

- **Roles** – people need to understand their role within the organisation and the organisation should ensure that they do not have conflicting roles.

- **Change** – the structure and climate of organisations and involvement in decision-making processes can determine the environment for nurturing or alienating staff.

(www.hsa.gov.uk/stress/standards)

Other researchers into stress in social work have added to our understanding of areas in which stress may be exacerbated by acknowledging the implications of individual differences in response to stress. Storey and Billingham (2001) included personality characteristics of the person experiencing stress, their attitudes, past experiences, life circumstances and life stages or education. You may be familiar with these ideas from theories of human growth and development (Walker and Crawford, 2003). Public images and expectations of social work and the interface between work and home life are equally significant, not to mention the institutional factors such as those we explored in Chapter 6. For example, how an organisation responds to individuals' experiences of discrimination and harassment will further determine how an individual may be equipped to respond to stress at work.

ACTIVITY 7.1

How do you think Ted's circumstances fit with the key areas identified by the HSE and with the other theories described above? What internal and external stressors can you identify in the case study? What factors are present that add to or detract from Ted's ability to cope?

Once you have identified these, list any strategies that could be adopted by Ted. What could be done by his team colleagues and manager to help him break the cycle of demands on him and to relieve his current level of stress?

At a personal level Ted is experiencing loss and bereavement, violence and abuse, and potential changes in his personal life may result in increased demands on him emotionally, physically and financially. At a practice level Ted appears to have an unmanageable workload with a high proportion of difficult cases, some of which are mirroring his own personal past experiences. He is subject to regular abuse and his self-confidence may be diminished if he feels that his practice is under further scrutiny or being criticised. At a team level, Ted is in danger of being undervalued by his team, resulting in potential scape-goating, bullying or by putting him in direct conflict with his colleagues which can undermine potentially supportive relationships. Ted's prospects of promotion could be a motivator or a further threat to his self-esteem and confidence depending on whether he is successful or not.

As well as identifying Ted's internal stressors, you may have concluded from your analysis of Ted's situation that stress has accumulated from all parts of the organisational system in which he works. Stress can move around a system in both directions as the worker can accumulate stress from each of the areas outlined above whilst also acting as a stressor to other parts of the system (Brown and Bourne, 1996). The role of supervision is central to Ted's survival, as is the deployment of a risk-assessment model that identifies both short- and long-term issues needing attention in order to avoid further detriment to his well-being. Ted is already showing physical and emotional symptoms of stress and distress and the consequences for not actively managing and responding to Ted's situation could be disastrous. Short-term objectives should aim to improve Ted's capacity to do the job effectively by providing a supportive environment with support to utilise immediate prac-tice skills and emotional support to help him cope with the current demands on him. The threats of violence and his direct experiences of abuse need to be immediately dealt with. Without such support it is inevitable that his service users will also suffer and without a proactive approach, the pressure on the agency may become overburdening and result in a bureaucratic, minimalist style of management (Brown and Bourne, 1996).

> *This inquiry saw too many examples of those in senior positions attempting to*
> *justify their work in terms of bureaucratic activity rather than outcomes for*
> *people.*

> (Lord Laming, Victoria Climbié Inquiry; Home Office, 2003)

Working cultures that foster blame and promote defensiveness can create circumstances in which errors of practice are more likely. Such defensiveness is often referred to as 'cov-ering your back' and is often linked to issues of poor leadership and individualistic attitudes towards making mistakes or poor practice and ultimately bullying approaches as opposed to problem-solving. One explanation given by Menzies-Lyth (1988) for the emer-gence of procedurally dominated practice lies in its role as a defence against the anxiety inherent in emotionally charged professional practice. Instead of utilising relationship-based and reflective approaches as viable responses to the anxiety-provoking nature of social work, the enforcement of systems of accountability and control paradoxically give the impression that child care, or any other social work for that matter, is predictable. Clarity of work policies and availability of good, relevant professional advice can greatly reduce anxiety and facilitate a work focus. Inconsistency in these areas will inevitably cause stress. The DoH found that tendencies towards wanting to blame someone was found to be profoundly unhelpful in tackling the problem of violence and abuse in social care and that workers often blame themselves, are blamed or feel blamed by their man-agers despite the presence of policies and procedures in these areas (DoH, 2000d).

RESEARCH SUMMARY

In her study of social work practice in cases of child neglect, Horwath (2005) found that variations in the interpretation of the task and process appeared to be influenced by workload pressures, resources and local systems, with teams focusing either on immediate safeguarding issues or on both safeguarding and the longer-term welfare of the child. For example, in cases where there were alleged concerns about both carers, a minority of aggressive men appeared to use their position to proactively contact workers to keep them away from their families.

Respondents to a questionnaire were asked whether or not they agreed with the statement 'whether we like it or not, if one of the carers is physically aggressive we may tolerate standards of care that we would not accept among less aggressive carers'. Practitioners and managers had very different views. Practitioners were fairly evenly divided on these issues but managers generally disagreed with the statement, indicating that managers may be less aware of the way in which aggressive carers can influence social work practice.

When looking at the impact that management had on assessment of child neglect cases, Howarth's analysis of the files demonstrated that very few cases contained comprehensive advice written on the file that gave the social workers directions as to how to progress the assessment. In focus groups, all participants noted that supervisors are under pressure and supervision is constantly cancelled or interrupted and when it does take place the focus is on cases in crises. In this context, one can understand why ongoing concerns of child neglect are likely to be marginalised in supervision in favour of more crisis-driven cases.

(Horwarth, 2005)

The above research demonstrates that staff supervision involves complicated organisational dynamics and multiple accountabilities to various parties both within and outside of the organisational context. At the same time, our training as social workers encourages us to become reflective practitioners and develop reflective capabilities. Moon (1999) points out that reflective practice requires time and space to question assumptions, develop new ideas and make connections. A safe and non-threatening environment includes someone to motivate and work with and emotionally support us alongside clear roles for managers and agencies in how aggression and violence are dealt with.

Aggression and violence in social work

Violence from service users can significantly affect social workers' capacity to carry out their work effectively and their commitment to that work. The government's national taskforce on violence against social care staff (DoH, 2000d) reported that research into the management of violence and abuse against social care staff has been impeded by problems of inconsistent definition. They suggested adopting the following definition of violence:

Incidents where persons are abused, threatened or assaulted in circumstances relating to their work, involving an explicit or implicit challenge to their safety, well-being or health.

(European Commission DG-V (3))

This definition includes verbal abuse or threats, threatening behaviour, any assault and serious or persistent harassment including racial or sexual harassment, and extends from what may seem to be minor incidents to serious assaults and murder, and threats against the worker's family. No longer is violence seen as 'part of the territory', or 'something that you might expect from service users'; the government identified clear principles to bring about effective change to workplace culture and to obtain an accurate picture of the levels of abuse, aggression and violence that staff are experiencing in social care. Additionally, through the provision of clear guidelines translated into organisations' local policies and procedures, the opportunities for local managers and individual workers as well as service users to misinterpret policy should be reduced.

ACTIVITY 7.2

Why do you think that violence and aggression are so common in social work practice and what are the main triggers behind its occurrence?

What elements of workplace culture can help to reduce these and what responses do you think social workers should expect from their teams, managers and colleagues when aggression and violence occur?

Potential triggers associated with violence at work can be identified as lack of privacy or boredom for service users. Service users may feel that they are not being listened to or able to communicate their concerns. Social workers are often the bearers of 'bad news' or have to exercise control or gate-keep resources. For staff, a lack of direct time with service users, working under pressure and feeling powerless or being part of the delivery of poor-quality services or practice sometimes involving other agencies can contribute to situations where aggression escalates.

The national taskforce on violence against staff recommended that the General Social Care Council code of practice should include a standard which makes clear the responsibilities of all social care employers for the safety of their staff. This was adopted but recent criticisms that the government failed to follow through other recommendations to inspect social care employers against this standard have been made following a number of serious and fatal attacks against staff working in social care. Responsibilities to implement the government's action plan continue to remain at a local level whereas within the NHS £97m has been pledged to tackle violence against NHS staff from 2007–11 (Ahmed, 2008).

Positive work cultures

Messages from frontline workers, service users and research all point to the possibility of creating a culture in organisations that reduces the incidence of violence and provides support to staff and service users when it happens. According to the DoH (1995b), a positive work culture is one in which:

- the upset and harm caused by different forms of violence and abuse, including verbal abuse, sexual and racial harassment and assault, as well as damage to property and theft, are clearly acknowledged;

- there is a clear definition of violence which takes into account severity, perceptions and professional discretion in reporting and dealing with incidents;

- the definition of violence has been agreed in consultation with staff, and, where possible, with service users;

- agency strategies are fully supportive of staff and encourage reporting of incidents, including minor ones;

- policies on violence and abuse clarify what is expected from workers and managers;

- there are straightforward mechanisms for reporting, recording and following up incidents, which take account of the victim's view, particularly on possible improvements;

- regular monitoring and reviewing of procedures takes place on the basis of the incident report system;

- there is easy access to post-incident support and counselling for affected staff;

- there is appropriate, regularly updated training for all staff on how to deal with violence and abuse.

(DoH, 1995)

Workplace culture is often seen by social care staff as something established by the senior management team. The presence or absence of policies in themselves can give a clear indication of the way in which staff are valued. However, as we have seen in previous chapters, workplace culture is often influenced at a more local level and is dependent on the social work profession becoming clearer about the nature of relationships at work. Schofield (1998) and Ruch (2005) state that prevailing trends which emphasise reductionist understandings of human behaviour and narrowly conceived bureaucratic responses to complex problems need to be reclaimed by social work practitioners. The ability to hold together the cognitive, emotional and practical aspects of a service user's life is to provide a sense of security and therefore reduce anxiety (Schofield, 1998). All these factors can help to reduce the potential for aggression. On a more formal level, violence can also be reduced by assessing the risks staff are experiencing and wherever possible taking action or establishing processes to either eliminate or control the risks. These are usually done using a device or format to record the risks assessed, the information from which then informs how risks will be managed by specifying and following up on the action required.

Risk assessment – a model

A risk assessment generally comprises five key stages and invariably involves the consideration of three elements: the service user, the environment and the staff involved. A simple version of this is as follows:

Stage 1 – identify the risks.

Stage 2 – decide who may be harmed and how.

Stage 3 – evaluate the level of risk as high, medium or low.

Stage 4 – identify the measures taken to reduce or eliminate the risks.

Stage 5 – review and assess the effectiveness of the measures taken.

Using our earlier case study to apply this model, we will examine the aspects of Ted's situation regarding risk of aggression and violence from Mr Tear. At **stage 1** we would need to establish a recording system to gather information about the incidents that had already occurred and ensure that there is a documented discussion with Ted about their effects on him. Organisations usually have an incident report form designed to capture this information. There are clear risks to Ted's physical and mental well-being. A threat has been made and there is continuous verbal abuse. At **stage 2**, whilst Ted is the main subject of risk, it should be noted that any employee working with this family may also be affected. Ted is at particular risk because of the role and power he holds. He may need to use legal authority to safeguard the Tear children, which could escalate the potential for violence. Already, evidence of the effects of aggression on Ted have manifested in his skin rash and insomnia and there is further potential for physical harm from Mr Tear. At **stage 3**, the level of risk would be identified as 'high' given the current escalation of threats from verbal to physical harm. Action is required to reduce this level of risk which at **stage 4** could employ the following measures:

1. Giving a verbal and written warning to Mr Tear with appropriate sanctions if his behaviour does not cease and involving the police if necessary.

2. Considering alternative venues for interviewing Mr Tear, and supporting Ted to avoid working alone with him. Joint visits with colleagues with prior agreed strategies to deal with any situations, assessing the environment for potential hazards or weapons, ensuring a clear exit, using an alarm or mobile phone and dressing appropriately are all recommended common-sense precautions. Local policies and procedures about lone working or visiting service users in their own homes already in existence will apply to Ted's situation.

3. The provision of training to staff on dealing with violence and aggression is important as well as identifying any areas of practice and skills that might help Ted and his team work more effectively with the Tear family. Careful supervision is important, as we saw earlier in the research (Howarth, 2005), with attention to giving Ted emotional support and helping him in debriefing and managing the case to the best of his ability. Counselling support following any incidents of aggression and violence would be appropriate. Resources issues often come up at this stage of the risk assessment but they are irrelevant in law if Ted is found to be knowingly put at risk due to resource limitations.

Finally, at **stage 5**, the manager would review and assess further whether the arrangements were sufficient to safeguard Ted's well-being and this could also be discussed in supervision and team meetings to include peer support. Senior managers should be kept up to date on any measures being taken and their effectiveness. Risk assessments should be reviewed regularly, at least at six-month intervals until the risk is demonstrably reduced if not eliminated.

So far we have discussed stress, aggression and violence and the importance of workplace culture in providing support for social workers. I would now like to turn to a less openly discussed form of aggression or stress injury: bullying and harassment at work. This is not specifically covered under health and safety legislation but nonetheless good practice dictates that organisations provide appropriate policies and procedures aimed at eliminating it.

Bullying at work

Bullying at work involves repeated negative actions and practices that are directed at one or more workers. The behaviours are unwelcome to the victim and undertaken in circumstances where the victim has difficulty in defending themselves. Bullying behaviours may be carried out as a deliberate act or unconsciously and cause humiliation, offence and distress to the victim.

(CIPD, 2004, p. 18)

Bullying is a specific form of harassment and insidious by nature in the sense that it usually develops gradually but has a cumulative, entrapping effect on the individual to whom it is targeted. Organisations that leave themselves open to the creation of a bullying environment usually find low levels of morale among employees, high rates of sickness absence and an unusually high turnover of staff. Wright and Smye (1997) discuss three types of abusive work cultures. First is the win/lose culture, where there is a highly competitive atmosphere and poor teamwork. Second there is the blame culture, which we looked at earlier. Third there is the sacrifice culture, in which people put their jobs before their social and personal lives to an extent which damages their health. This is now widely recognised and good organisations will have in place policies which address issues of **work–life balance**.

The Employment Act 2002 (Dispute Resolution) Regulations were introduced in October 2004 to encourage employers and staff to resolve more disputes in the workplace. At the same time, the DTI announced a project to tackle bullying and discrimination at work. Under these proposals, all employers need to have a minimum three-step disciplinary and grievance procedure which consists of an initial letter, a face-to-face meeting and a further meeting to consider an appeal if necessary.

RESEARCH SUMMARY

The Chartered Institute of Personnel and Development found that a significant amount of conflict in the workplace results from personal behaviour and that positive behaviour of line managers is the most significant factor in an organisation's success in tackling bullying/harassment at work by dealing with it quickly. Those accused of bullying in UK organisations are more likely to be men (60%) than women (40%) and likely to be the victim's line manager (38%). When asked to rate their line managers' effectiveness, the public sector provided a more pessimistic picture, with 14% of managers seen as 'poor', 2% as 'excellent' and 57% as 'average'. Despite poor rating, training is more likely to be carried out in the 71% of public sector organisations, with managers spending an average of 5.9 days per year managing disciplinary and grievance cases. By focusing on the law, employers' motivation for tackling bullying at work still appears to be compliance based rather than on other benefits such as improving performance or absence. Finally, positive support from the top in building a culture that doesn't support bullying/harassment at work has been shown to be an important success factor.

(CIPD, 2004)

Bullying often involves an abuse of power or perceived power and you might find it useful to go back and remind yourself of the sources of power identified by French and Raven (1958) discussed in Chapter 2.

ACTIVITY 7.3

What examples can you think of of bullying in social care organisations, either from your own observations or experiences or what you have read so far?

You may have identified any of the following:

- Shouting at individuals or groups, humiliating them or making them subject to constant or unjustified negative criticism including the use of sarcasm or inappropriate humour.

- Imposing unreasonable or continually changing workloads or deadlines.

- Harassment or unwanted attention because of somebody's race, culture, religion, gender or sexuality. This can be invasive behaviour or more subtle, for example by misusing personal information.

- Excluding people from training, work activities and social events through bogus scheduling or deliberately withholding information or consent to requests for leave, training, etc., without justification.

- Being inconsistent in behaviour, withholding supervision, constructive feedback and support and undermining someone's authority or professional reputation.

Braithwaite (2001) has offered the following suggestions for staff affected by bullying to help them regain some control over a situation.

1. First of all acknowledge that you may be bullied rather than taking on a 'victim' mentality, as feeling less capable or competent in our work can have the effect of confirming the bully's power.

2. Keep a record of the incidents, dates and times to build up a picture that will help you identify that you are not over-reacting, as well as keeping any evidence which may include witnesses.

3. Try not to be alone with the bully and build networks with other staff that are also affected or can support you.

4. Practise using assertive responses to gain more control over your situation and learn how to say 'no'.

5. Take time off or time out to reflect and rethink your situation or plan how you can develop any coping strategies.

6. Do not suffer in silence but talk it over with a senior member of your department for advice and support. Use the agency's policies and procedures on bullying, harassment and complaints or the grievance or whistleblowing procedure. Find out if there is a designated person in your agency under these procedures who can investigate and take action on your behalf.

7. Involve your union, who may already be aware of the issue and can provide someone to support you through any complaints procedure. You may ultimately wish to take legal action against your employer or seek redress through an industrial tribunal if your situation is not resolved within a reasonable time or process.

8. You may wish to consider leaving your job for an organisation with a more positive and supportive culture. Do not think that this automatically constitutes a failure on your part if you have tried other approaches and at the end of the day you should make sure you give yourself the appropriate praise for managing your situation regardless of the outcomes.

(Braithwaite, 2001)

The role of trade unions and professional bodies

Staff groups, professional bodies and trade union groups can offer support and active involvement of employees can help to promote collective bargaining and representation of employees' rights and an atmosphere of mutual respect and communication. Other forms of support for employees can be sought from the human resource department, staff welfare and counselling services and occupational health. Familiarising yourself with human resource policies in your organisation will enable you to identify your rights at work and understand the roles and responsibilities of both employers and employees so that you can refer to these later on if necessary. These may include drug and alcohol policies, whistleblowing policies and procedures for responding to harassment and bullying. You should ensure that you receive regular supervision and appraisal, as research shows that for the first year of employment, social workers may only reach 60 per cent of their full work capacity (Huxley et al., 2005).

Since the implementation of the new degree, there has been much discussion about how newly qualified social workers (NQSWs) might be better supported in their first year of employment. The CWDC has been asked by the Department of Children, Schools and Families (DCSF) to develop a three-year pilot programme for NQSWs working in children's services to help them strengthen their skills, knowledge and confidence. Starting in September 2008, a year of supported and structured induction will be given to 1,000 newly qualified children's social workers working for both statutory and voluntary sector organisations across England underpinned by a set of outcome statements outlining what is expected at the end of their first year of employment. Funding will also be offered to ensure that NQSWs receive a reduction of 10 per cent of their workload.

Other sources of support may come from staff and colleagues themselves. Look out for any forums where staff from particular groups such as women, black and minority ethnic staff, gay, lesbian and bisexual staff can meet to discuss their particular issues as these groups are often useful for consultation with management and for advising on organisational issues in these areas. Organisations genuinely committed to improving dignity at work will conduct regular staff surveys and undertake audits of supervision and appraisal systems, as well as provide informative staff newsletters and team briefings. Manager and staff forums, away-days and team-building events are also evidence of the way in which organisations and teams deal with issues in a planned, constructive and respectful way.

ACTIVITY **7.4**

Take some time to consider what you think are the necessary ingredients to achieve a work–life balance. Using three headings – personal, career, team/peers – identify any issues or problems arising for you in this area contributing to stress. Then based on what you have already read, identify any positive steps you can take to get support or overcome issues.

Below are some further tips that may assist you currently or in the future.

Personal

If you are a carer or have caring responsibilities, get support with these and tell those responsible for agreeing more flexible working and studying patterns where possible.

Eat well and try to avoid strategies to deal with stress such as increasing smoking, drinking, using substances or reverting to any compulsive behaviour that can cause you further harm. Spending time on hobbies, relaxation and taking time out are important ingredients to keeping life in perspective. Keep in touch with friends, family and other supportive relationships. Physical exercise can help to burn up the chemicals and hormones associated with stress.

Career

Take advantage of any training or personal development opportunities and research into the best tools that suit you to reflect regularly on your professional practice and make it a habit. Plan and utilise any available study leave and set yourself realistic objectives in developing your professional career, for example, by thinking about where you see yourself in five years' time and the manageable steps towards achieving this. Take advantage of any learning opportunities or project work where you can extend your expertise, knowledge and skills. Make the most of supervision and practise assertiveness skills. Be clear about where to go if issues need discussion and resolving, and develop networks. Planning regular breaks and time out are essential to recharge your batteries and reflecting on your achievements.

Team/peers

It is likely that some of your issues or problems will be shared with your colleagues at work or university. Communicating and talking to those around you about your experiences, feelings and needs can help to find solutions and get feedback. Regular team meetings and time out in your team are important to reflect on practice and to keep conflict to a minimum.

Finally, it is important to have fun at work, maintain a sense of humour and celebrate your achievements no matter how small.

CHAPTER SUMMARY

Organisational structures and cultures can create and sustain dignity at work in a variety of ways. Adopting and employing proactive measures aimed at creating an environment in which good-quality relationships and communications can be maintained are at the heart of effective and helpful social care. Attracting staff with the right values and attitudes is the first step to meeting service users' needs and attaining outcomes, but from there on, developing skills and good people management are crucial components in the development and retention of good-quality staff. This means modelling these to service users, managers and colleagues to instil a sense of well-being and job satisfaction, which will in turn translate into greater productivity. We have looked at many of the negative aspects of organisational cultures and some of the strategies that managers and staff utilise to combat these. It is essential that you prioritise your health and well-being at work and you should make yourself familiar with the relevant policies and procedures on these as soon as you begin to work for any organisation. Skills for Care (2005a) identified six contributory factors to social care job satisfaction which you could assess and advocate for in your own organisation by discussing them in your teams and with other stakeholders. These are:

- interactions and relationships with service users and carers;

- working with and learning from a team of colleagues;

- feeling valued by management, government and society as a whole;

- a manageable workload and acceptable hours;

- worthwhile procedures, administration and paperwork;

- fair pay.

Research has shown that the quality of human resource management in the public sector is linked to staff morale, effective recruitment and retention and that this is only just beginning to be systematically developed in the social care sector, as we shall see in our final chapter. Strong management development that also takes account of diversity is vital to workforce development (Hafford-Letchfield, 2005).

FURTHER READING

Braithwaite, R (2001) *Managing aggression*. London: Routledge in association with Community Care. This comprehensive text combines theory and practice skills with common sense in relation to all aspects of aggression at work. It clarifies the roles and responsibilities of everyone involved and helps to find workable solutions to practical problems in this area.

Hughes, L and Pengelly, P (1997) Staff supervision in a turbulent environment. London: Jessica Kingsley. Drawing on work done by the Tavistock Institute, supervision is explored from a conceptual framework which focuses on the interaction between supervisor and supervisees in the agency context.

The Health and Safety Executive have set out core standards for managing stress in the workplace and tools to help managers assess, plan and improve the management of stress at work. Generally this website has a lot of useful information for managers and staff about health and safety at work. **www.hse.gov.uk/stress/standards/downloads**

Unison is a public sector union which actively campaigns and supports staff and has produced a number of publications useful in the area of health and safety, obtainable from **www.unison.org.uk/resources/**

Chapter 8
Learning organisations

A C H I E V I N G A S O C I A L W O R K D E G R E E

This chapter will help you achieve the following National Occupational Standards and General Social Care Council's Code of Practice.

Key Role 5: Manage and be accountable, with supervision and support, for your own social work practice within your organisation.

- Carry out duties using accountable professional judgement and knowledge-based social work practice.
- Use professional and managerial supervision and support to improve your practice.
- Contribute to identifying and agreeing the goals, objectives and effectiveness of the team network or system.

Key Role 6: Demonstrate professional competence in social work practice.

- Research, analyse, evaluate and use current knowledge of best social work practice.
- Work within agreed standards of social work practice and ensure own professional development.
- Contribute to the promotion of best social work practice.

General Social Care Code of Practice

Code 6: Be accountable for the quality of your work and take responsibility for maintaining and improving your knowledge and skills

- Recognising and respecting the roles and expertise of workers from other agencies and working in partnership with them.
- Undertaking relevant training to maintain and improve your knowledge and skills and contributing to the learning and development of others.

It will also introduce you to the following academic standards as set out in the social work subject benchmark statements:

2. Defining principles

- Social work, both as occupational practice and as an academic subject, evolves, adapts and changes in response to the social, political and economic challenges and demands of contemporary social welfare policy practice and legislation.
- Acquire and apply the habits of critical reflection, self-evaluation and consultation, and make appropriate use of research in the evaluation of practice outcomes.

3.1.5 The nature of social work practice

- The processes of reflection and evaluation, including familiarity with the range of approaches for evaluating welfare outcomes and significance for development of practice and the practitioner.

3.2.5 Skills in personal and professional development

- Take responsibility for your own further and continuing acquisition of knowledge and skills.

Introduction

This chapter will identify which characteristics of organisations providing social care are significant or crucial to our analysis and understanding of what constitutes a **learning organisation**. As the concluding chapter of this book, it aims to help you reflect back on issues and themes developed in previous chapters and to evaluate the relevance of these to enhancing or hindering an organisation's capacity for learning and its future development. We will begin by defining what we mean by the concept of 'learning organisation' and then go on to look at some of the more positive aspects of organisational structure and culture in social care conducive to providing formal and informal learning and support for managers, staff, users, carers and stakeholders. Within social work, the interest in reflective learning has emerged broadly at the same time as the development of the concept of the learning organisation. We will look at the strategies which enable people to access resources and support in order to become reflective learners and practitioners. This includes examining the role of supervision, appraisal and formal and informal sources of learning from the organisational perspective. We will look at contextual factors in promoting or impeding informal learning at work and define exactly what we mean by informal learning. We will explore the idea of the organisation as a learning system, or community of practice. Within the complexity of social work and social care provision, staff need to constantly optimise their own potential for developing expertise and specialist knowledge and, as indicated in Chapter 4, to be able to capitalise on expertise coming from service users themselves. Organisations in social care that demonstrate the characteristics and cultural values of a learning organisation will be able to deliver substantial quality improvements in service delivery. We will therefore conclude with an overview of the government's national quality strategy which highlights the principle of continuous and lifelong learning and the post-qualifying framework for social work.

Theory of the learning organisation

Literature on the learning organisation is relatively recent and builds on a longer sociological tradition of theorisation of the relationship between organisational structure and behaviour. In Chapter 1, we looked at scientific views of organisations where individuals were trained to perform specific tasks within a highly standardised system and the subsequent development of theories within the human relations school and systems theory. The latter developments are helpful for any organisation to adapt through learning to meet the changing demands of its environment. Simultaneously the emergence of management development theory has challenged managers to accept that change has become a continuous reality and one which has to adapt through learning to the changing demands created by its environment (Handy, 1993).

According to Gould (2000), at the heart of organisational theory is the problematic concept of learning: what it means, how it relates to organisational structure and behaviour and whether there are any real differences between the concept of 'organisational learning', defined as the processes through which learning takes place, and 'the learning organisation', defined as the characteristic of an organisation that learns. Gould points out that two fundamental premises underpin these concepts: first, that individual learning is a necessary but not sufficient condition for organisational learning; and second, that the learning experience is more pervasive and takes place across multiple levels within the organisation.

ACTIVITY 8.1

Review what you have already learnt about organisational structure and culture, management and leadership styles from previous chapters. What positive aspects of these do you think can contribute to a learning organisation? Can you give any specific examples of the type of good practice that might feature in a learning organisation?

SCIE (2004) identify five areas under which characteristics of a learning organisation in social care can be demonstrated:

1. **Organisational structure**

   - Service user and carer feedback and participation are actively sought, valued and resourced, and used to influence and inform practice.

   - Team working, learning and making the best use of all staff skills are integral to the organisation.

   - There is cross-organisational and collaborative working.

2. **Organisational culture**

   - There is a system of shared beliefs, values, goals and objectives.

   - The development of new ideas and methods is encouraged.

   - An open learning environment allows learning from mistakes and the opportunity to test out innovative practice.

   - Messages from research and new evidence are thought about and incorporated into practice.

3. **Informational systems**

   - There are effective information systems, for both internal and external communication.

   - Policies and procedures are meaningful and understood by everybody (based on a human rights and social justice approach).

4. **Human resource practices**

   - There is continuous development for all staff including a clear supervision and appraisal policy.

5. **Leadership**

   - There is capacity for the organisation to change and develop services over and above day-to-day delivery.

   - Leadership at all levels embodies and models the key principle of a learning organisation.

   (SCIE, 2004, card no 2)

As we have already covered a number of these areas, we will now look at the role of staff development policies, specifically, supervision.

The role of supervision

In Chapter 3 we concluded that checking performance and introducing measures to coerce behavioural changes to secure performance improvements may have a counterproductive effect. Managers' fear of falling short on measured performance also leads to a disinclination to innovate and can lead to game-playing or distortion within a system rather than developing genuine conversations amongst stakeholders away from methodological-driven agendas. Practice therefore needs to be proactive in seeking out and advancing their own knowledge and organisational approaches to professional ethical practice in the workplace and investigating support networks. One vehicle for achieving this is supervision, a system we will examine from an organisational perspective. For a more comprehensive account of how supervision can enhance practice learning and practice competence during your social work training, you are referred to Parker (2004). Tsui (2005) argues that staff supervision differs greatly from student supervision as it involves complicated organisational dynamics, hierarchies of administrative authority and multiple accountabilities to various parties inside and outside of the organisation. From a holistic point of view, supervision involves four parties: the agency, the supervisor, the supervisee and service users. It should be an enabling process which mirrors direct social work practice and parallels social work intervention. Short-term objectives of social work supervision are to improve the worker's capacity to do the job effectively by providing a healthy work environment, stimulate professional knowledge, practice skills and provide practical and emotional support. Social work supervision has been identified as one of the most significant factors in determining the job satisfaction levels of frontline social workers and is possibly the most crucial determinant of safeguarding the quality of service provided. In the previous chapter, we learnt that this process can often be interrupted or impacted on by other dynamics and more negative relationships within the organisation. In social care organisations, supervision models often reflect the level of control exercised by the agency: at one extreme, the casework model, which is based on a high level of administrative accountability, and at the other, the autonomous practice model where there is high level of professional autonomy. Tsui (2005) identified group and peer supervision as being between these two extremes. The supervisory process involves the use of authority, exchange of information and expression of feelings. These aspects correspond to the three widely recognised functions of supervision: administrative, educational and supportive, identified by Morrison (2002) and other writers on supervision. In learning organisations, the basic principle of effective supervision is essentially humanistic and at the root of good social work practice.

> *Frontline managers are the keystones of the organisation. They have a key role in determining whether standards of practice are consistently maintained, in supporting staff engaged in complex, personally demanding practice, and ensuring staff are continually developed in knowledge-based practice. Without this, they can add to the separation that can occur within an organisation and the poor or non-existent collaboration with others.*

(Chief Inspector of Social Services, DoH/SSI, 2000e)

The importance of positive role-modelling by managers cannot be overstated and is put starkly by Morrison (2002, p. 2), who states that making a difference depends not just on the existence of supervision *per se* but what is necessary is good supervision. As we have seen throughout this book, the experience of organisations and staff is one of being stretched to the limits by unprecedented levels of demand, rising public expectations, resource constraints, turbulent circumstances and a crisis in workforce management. The evolution of flatter management structures in organisations has also delegated decision-making much closer to the front line, resulting in increased administrative responsibilities for front-line managers and encroaching on their personal capacity to provide supervision. Morrison points to the paradox in that at the very time when supervision has never been more important to the process of managing change, it may also be one of the first casualties.

RESEARCH SUMMARY

Tsui (2005) conducted focus groups with 40 experienced social work supervisors in Hong Kong. He identified five guidelines for supervision from the emerging data. First, supervisors should be ethical and dedicated. Second, supervisors should have a sense of professional and social responsibility and balance social work values with administrative requirements. Third, supervisors should have a positive attitude towards themselves, their supervisees and their clients. Fourth, supervisors should be rational and logical. Finally, supervisors should be continuous learners, always ready to refresh their knowledge and skills, seek advice from top management, obtain support from and exchange ideas with colleagues, and benefit from the expertise of external consultants.

(Tsui, 2005)

The quality of supervision depends on several factors, including the relationships among individual parties, the contract, format and developmental stages of the supervisory process, the balance amongst the various supervisory functions and the relationship between the features of supervision and the external environment. You should make sure that you familiarise yourself with your organisation's supervision policy and its requirements so that you can assert your rights to supervision. Both the CWDC and SfC have continued to assert effective supervision as a central tool within workforce development and policy direction for supervision established within documents such as *Options for Excellence* (DfES and DoH, 2006b) and the *Leadership and Management Strategy for Social Care* (SfC 2008c). We saw from SCIE's definition above that learning organisations respond to feedback from staff and have a high level of stakeholder participation. Staff influence can be exerted in two ways: by taking individual or collective action, or by staff responding to management or organisations' policies with passive resistance, for example by adopting a negative attitude towards their job or devoting less effort to it. Supervisors can act as change agents by advocating for and asserting the rights of staff as well as providing a buffer between management and frontline staff. Supervision is also a management tool for providing access to further learning resources to enable people to cope and to apply other human resource policies such as training and staff development. The integration of services and the evolving nature of what professionals do and the development of new roles in social work and social care have led to the notion of inter professional supervision. It is much more commonplace for specialists and generic workers within organisations to be supervised by managers from a different professional back-ground. Multi-disciplinary teamwork and collaboration are not only beneficial for effective service provision but can be advantageous to the well-being of team members (Ovretveit, 1993). From the perspective of service users, interprofessional supervision can facilitate the sharing of skills and information that contributes to continuity in care, the development of effective protection plans and the apportionment of clear responsibilities and accountabili-ties (Townend, 2005). Interprofessional supervision enables better co-ordination of resource allocation and deployment of expert resources as well as creating rich opportuni-ties for learning and practice development. We will now turn our focus on to the importance of learning opportunities within learning organisations for enabling potential to be developed to meet both formal and informal learning needs.

Staff learning and workforce development strategies

Back in 1999, the Training Organisation for the Personal Social Services (TOPSS), now known as Skills for Care, published the first national training strategy in response to a survey of the qualifications and training needs of the social care workforce. The *Quality Strategy for Social Care* (DoH, 2000f) initially set out the government's requirements for improving the skills and competencies through a new qualifications framework which would provide consistency and help with performance management of the workforce. Since then, there have been major workforce development initiatives focused on the two differentiated strands of the social care workforce. Within children's services we have had the *Options for Excellence* review (DfES and DoH, 2006b); the Children's Workforce Strategy (DfES, 2005); Care Matters: Time for Change (DfES, 2006c); the *Children's Plan* (DfES, 2007); *Building Brighter Futures: Next Steps for the Children's Workforce* (DfES, 2008), and many other related initia-tives around recruitment and retention across the sector as a whole. Within adult services the vision for a personalised approach to adult social care has huge implications for the workforce of the future, given population and workforce demographics, as well as rising expectations of people using services. The workforce will have to change radically. Whereas strategies since 2001 have focused on vocational and professional qualifications within par-ticular service specific groups of staff, local workforce development strategies need to be more co-produced, co-developed, co-provided and co-evaluated with private and voluntary sector partners as well as users and carers (DoH, 2008a). A set of Common Core Principles to Support Self Care (SfC, 2008) in adult services has been developed to capture best practice in order to support service reform and promote choice, control and independence and partici-pation of people who use services. Implementing these seven principles is a challenge for workers at all levels and the principles are designed to be consistent with the seven out-comes set out in *Putting people first* (HM Govt, 2007b). These will be used alongside existing tools such as national workforce competencies, national occupational standards and the knowledge and skills framework in order to provide 'added value' For organisations, this means embedding the seven principles in service delivery, appraisal, supervision and devel-opment planning (SfC, 2008b) and provides a framework for staff development and to support new ways of working.

Achieving reliable information about the social care workforce has long been a source of frustration to individual organisations as well as nationally as this information is essential to understand the provision of social care and to assess how workforce development can meet future needs. In 2005, the National Minimum Data Set for Social Care was developed as a data collection system for social care's major players and onging annual collection and analysis of workforce data has enabled the government to collect a bespoke data set on both adults' and children's services.

Formal and informal learning

Paragraph 3 of the GSCC code for employers says:

> *As a social care employer, you must provide training and development opportunities to enable social care workers to strengthen and develop their skills and knowledge. This includes providing induction, training and development opportunities to help social care workers do their jobs effectively and prepare for new and changing roles and responsibilities.*

> (www.gscc.org.uk/codes_practice.htm)

Whilst current learning frameworks are heavily biased towards education and formal training, most qualifications in social care incorporate work-based learning or work-related learning which is at the heart of personal and team development in social care.

ACTIVITY 8.2

What do you think the main differences are between formal learning and informal learning? Try to give some examples of opportunities for both types of learning.

Formal learning may be characterised as being planned and externally organised or prescribed and delivered by designated educators using prescribed outcomes which are academically or vocationally accredited. Informal learning, on the other hand, may be planned or unplanned, is usually incremental and is based on an approach emphasising experiential, informal and self-directed learning methods, thus facilitating personal as well as organisational development. Examples of informal learning are mentoring, shadowing or project work and can assist in learning through change or within interdisciplinary contexts (Hafford-Letchfield and Chick, 2006). Formal education and training have been shown to provide only a small part of what is learnt at work and the transfer of learning is a complex process influenced by the learner or individual, the task being undertaken and the context (Macaulay, 2000).

Kirkpatrick and Ackroyd (2003) identified the following factors as conducive to informal learning within learning organisations:

- sufficient variation in the tasks, for example the opportunity to participate in temporary groups;

- opportunities to consult experts inside and outside the workplace, changes in duties and work roles that stimulate learning;

- work roles that allow for peripheral participation in communities of practice where informal communication, problem-solving and innovation play a big part;

- structures and incentives for knowledge sharing, job mobility and working autonomously.

Understanding the factors affecting learning is particularly important, because it suggests ways by which changes might enhance people's learning. Feelings and emotions are an integral part of the learning and critical thinking process and individual learning and employee development will only be successful within a learning organisation whose culture and process promote and support it. Whatever opportunities an organisation creates for learning, developing practice-based career pathways for both qualified and unqualified staff is beneficial for staff retention, morale and in ensuring that investment in training is used to maximum effect. The organisation's workforce development plan must follow an integrated system of appraisal and individual development planning on the basis of life-long learning, post-qualifying training and continuous professional development which become part of integrated planning rather than stand-alone issues.

Continuous professional development

After training for a degree in social work you will inevitably go on to perform additional, more complex functions as your career progresses, and developing your skills and knowledge by building on the core standards and benchmarks you have already demonstrated. This will necessitate attention to your continuing professional development (CPD), which is a requirement for all registered social workers underpinned by the GSCC's Codes of Practice. Registered Social Workers (RSWs) provide a validated record of their training and learning in order to re-register with the GSCC after the initial three-year period. This is not necessarily focused on formal learning, as discussed earlier, but can include many different sorts of learning, such as reading, project work, attending conferences and unaccredited training courses as well as gaining a post-qualifying award. Needless to say, keeping skills and knowledge up to date is key to delivering high-quality care to people who use services, and to their carers.

One way of maintaining and extending your knowledge and skills in order to remain registered is by working towards GSCC-approved post-qualifying (PQ) awards under the PQ framework established in 2007. The PQ framework allows social workers to continue their education and training in a flexible and modular way. There are three academic levels for you to progress through, which correspond to different stages of professional and career development.

- Post-Qualifying Award in Specialist Social Work.

- Post-Qualifying Award in Higher Specialist Social Work.

- Post-Qualifying Award in Advanced Social Work.

There are currently five specialisms, focusing on: mental health; adult social care; practice education; leadership and management; and children and young people, their families and carers. The implications for you as a qualified social worker are that you will be relying on supervision and appraisal systems in your organisation to ensure that you are able to continue your CPD. You should continue to keep a portfolio of your professional development in order to provide evidence against the relevant standards as any learning provider in relation to a programme of PQ learning will bring together your work-based learning and assessment with the required academic work to provide a holistic picture of your competence.

> *Social work should be clear and confident about the expertise it has developed, the distinctive contribution it makes and the features of its work particularly valued by people who use its services. It also has a responsibility to feed its knowledge, values and approaches into the work of joint teams to inform their culture and widen their frame of reference. Professionals working together in multi-disciplinary settings, in children's centres or community mental health teams, for instance, are likely to become familiar with one another's areas of expertise, and able to apply a common core of knowledge, whilst recognising when a particular professional's skills are required. Social workers who are outposted still need access to good professional supervision, learning and development opportunities, up-to-date knowledge support and links to relevant policy and practice developments.*

(GSCC, 2008, p. 18)

C H A P T E R   S U M M A R Y

High-quality services depend upon a high-quality workforce. The changing expectations of people who use services and of carers require a workforce which is highly skilled and supported and able to work in flexible ways. Throughout this book we have referred to the policy drivers, government initiatives and linked practice issues which will all have an impact on the national training and workforce development strategy in social care. These strategies will support the expansion and co-ordination of integrated service delivery for the different service user groups within the government's whole-systems approach to service delivery. In this chapter we have had an opportunity to reflect on how the themes covered in this book are relevant to the concept of learning organisations and the roles and responsibilities of different stakeholders within it. Effective management and inspiring leadership are essential in contributing to an active and supportive learning environment which facilitates professional, safe and accountable practice with the best possible outcomes for service users based on evidence, up-to-date knowledge and research.

FURTHER READING

Following developments around integration of social care services with other partners, a statement was drawn up about the changing role of social work in this environment. Produced by the General Social Care Council in association with the Commission for Social Care Inspection, the Children's Workforce Development Council and the Social Care Institute for Excellence and Skills for Care in March 2008, it can be downloaded from the GSCC website. **www.gscc.org.uk**

General Social Care Council (2008) *Social work at its best: A statement of social work roles and tasks for the 21st century*. March. London: General Social Care Council in association with the Commission for Social Care Inspection; the Children's Workforce Development Council; Social Care Institute for Excellence; Skills for Care.

For a good theoretical and practical guide on different types of supervision styles in different contexts, try:

Hawkins, P and Shohet, R (2006) *Supervision in the helping professions*. Maidenhead: The Open University Press with McGraw-Hill.

WEBSITES

Skills for Care for keeping up to date with issues to do with workforce development in the adult sector. **www.skillsforcare.org.uk**

Children's Workforce Development Council for keeping up to date with issues to do with children's services. **www.cwdc.org.uk**

Conclusion

This book has covered a number of topics in relation to the organisations and organisational frameworks in which social workers may practise. The nature of contemporary social work practice requires the profession to engage actively in current debates about the role of social work within a constantly shifting social, legislative, political and economic environment. Your education and training as a social worker require that you develop an understanding and appreciation of the issues having a direct impact on social work practice at the organisational level.

At the beginning of this book, we examined the nature of organisations delivering social work and social care and we then went on to examine specific developments that have influenced the way in which organisations have evolved to meet the demands for the delivery of high-quality services. We considered the impact of the market economy and business cultures, their relevance to social care and identified specific governmental policies driving initiatives aimed at improving the quality and measuring performance of public services. Most importantly, we considered the impact of the service user movement and the existence of policies and decision-making processes in these areas that can help organisations be successful in their service user participation strategies. Throughout this book, we have constantly highlighted the leadership of service users and carers in developing alternative organisational responses to delivering social care services and support.

The second half of this book has focused more on particular ethical issues and dilemmas arising for management and staff in relation to particular issues in the organisational context. We examined the context in which social care is resourced and delivered and considered the complexity of balancing needs, demands, costs and quality with reference to the relevant legislative and policy frameworks. In our evaluation of research findings and through case studies, we identified evidence of inequality at the institutional level and discussed some of the ethical dilemmas that can arise for managers and staff if these issues are not actively addressed or strategies and supportive policies are not put in place. You will have observed that the importance of developing healthy, transparent and supportive work cultures has been a consistent theme throughout this book and, in particular, those that respect and harness or maximise the potential of staff, service users and stakeholders. Effective management and inspiring leadership are essential contributory factors for active and supportive learning environments that facilitate safe and accountable professional practice with the best outcomes for service users based on evidence, up-to-date knowledge and research. This became evident in the concluding chapter on what constitutes a learning organisation.

Collaboration between staff, managers, service users and stakeholders is crucial to the successful delivery of social care services, especially within its increasing interdisciplinary context. Linking the topics in this book to the GSCC codes of practice and key roles of social work acknowledges the interdependence of these to enable everyone involved to meet the high standards that social work must achieve in sometimes very difficult circumstances. Each chapter has incorporated basic knowledge, some key research using case studies and reflective learning exercises to enable you to meet the requirements of the social work degree.

I hope you have acquired an enthusiasm for more knowledge and feel more confident in translating theory, concepts and ideas into a framework for your future practice, which will be activated in the organisations you choose to work in. Truly professional social workers need to engage in current debates about the nature of problems in society and the structures within which solutions are developed and implemented. This means keeping under review ideologies subscribed to and your own professional and personal values to increase your potential for influencing judgements and decision-making in a fair, equal and consistent way. Being constantly aware of the roles that these factors play in organisational structure and culture will help you understand what is often the root cause of dysfunctional organisations and management teams as well as healthy ones.

Glossary

Advocacy Originating from skills used by the legal profession, advocacy seeks to represent the interests of people who are seen as less powerful and addresses this by speaking for them, interpreting their views and wishes, and presenting on their behalf to other powerful individuals or social structures.

Anti-discriminatory practice Refers to practice that makes use of the legislative framework to challenge discrimination experienced by particular marginalised or vulnerable groups. Anti-oppressive and anti-discriminatory practice can complement each other and according to Thompson are more or less synonymous (Thompson, 2000).

Anti-oppressive practice A radical approach adopted by social workers informed by humanistic theories and values of social justice and which takes account of the experiences and views of oppressed people themselves. It is based on a theoretical understanding of the concepts of power, oppression and inequality and their impact on relationships at all levels, in particular, personal and structural relations in social care.

Audit A cyclical activity which leads to continuous improvement through using standards and means of measuring practice against these. Audit activity is useful to managers as a process to systematically review activities and to know at any one time what the strengths and areas for development are within the team and to identify staff training and development needs.

Benchmark The process of measuring or comparing performance of a product or service against the best as a means of competing or meeting changing customer requirements.

Best value A method of reviewing and evaluating services founded on the 'four Cs': **challenge** why the service is needed; **compare** cost and quality with other 'like' services; **consult** with public and service users to test the validity of conclusions; **compete** to ensure the best way of providing the service. The process of best value is inspected and assessed using best value performance indicators, and authorities must show a significant stepped-up improvement and continuous improvement. One of the advantages of best value has been the thematic value of reviewing services across different agencies and services within the authority itself.

Block contract Provision of a given service in a large number, for example the supply of meals, residential beds, where the service, payment and performance monitoring arrangements are agreed in advance. The advantages are simple administration, lower unit costs and better value for money. Block contracts create greater certainty and stability over the supply of the service and referral arrangements and are the basis of strategic partnerships between purchasers and providers.

Budget A detailed financial plan which gives details on income, the resources available to the organisation and departments within it, and expenditure, the uses to which these resources will be put.

Care trust A single, multi-purpose legal body to commission and be responsible for all local health and social care.

Civil society Groups of people who form informal organisations as an alternative sector to government or business.

Commissioning The strategic approach to arranging and purchasing services and resources to meet needs using a clear plan to get the best from available resources.

Commission for Social Care Inspection Launched in April 2004, CSCI was the single, independent inspectorate for all social care services in England created by the Health and Social Care (Community Health and Standards) Act 2003. CSCI had total overview of the whole social care industry and its primary function was to promote improvements in social care through a regime of registration and inspection, reporting directly to the government. CSCI will merge with other inspectorates in 2007 to reflect the separate needs of adult and children's services.

Communitarianism Refers to collective strategies where people in existing social groups organise themselves to meet their own need, gain control over their own resources and issues. It is the basis of community work and community development.

Contracting A legal term which involves forming a legally binding agreement between those that purchase or buy a service, and those that provide the service. A contract between them is based on a specification of the services that have to be provided. This is negotiated and defined in the purchasing process.

Contracting out The process to replace a service that a statutory service might have previously provided itself but chooses for another body in the independent sector to provide it instead. This is done by putting out to tender and inviting organisations to bid for the contract to provide the service against a specification.

Discrimination An action that makes a distinction between people or groups based unjustly on grounds of race, religion, gender, sexual identity, age, etc. It has a negative meaning in that it is unfair or illegal.

Emotional intelligence The ability to identify, integrate, understand and reflectively manage one's own and other people's feelings.

Epistemology The science of science, it deals with the nature of knowledge and studies the grounds for and modes of knowledge acquired.

Ethics A term used to refer to the actual norms people follow concerning what is right or wrong, good or bad (sometimes referred to as morals). The development of ethics can help us to understand how we make moral judgements and respect people's rights in social work practice.

Governance A framework used by organisations to systematically develop accountability and continuous improvement of the quality of services.

Grant A one-off sum of money given to an agency or body with or without conditions. These are likely to be accompanied by a service-level agreement or be ring-fenced to be used for a specific purpose or to meet a specific need. Grants are common features of new policy initiatives from central government to help implement a new initiative and usually have specific reporting requirements.

Independent sector A term coined during the market reforms to social care in the 1980s where both the voluntary sector and the private sector were described as 'independent' from statutory services for contracting purposes.

Joint Review A team co-owned by the Audit Commission (the regulatory body overseeing local government) and the Social Services Inspectorate (the regulatory body overseeing social services). They jointly review and inspect social services authorities in England and Wales as a result of legislation in 1996. Joint reviewers attempt to evaluate social services provision within the context of the local authority's structures and cultures and its community and democratic context. Readers should note that the Commission undertook this regulatory function for Social Care Inspection (CSCI) prior to its further merger in 2007.

Learning organisation An organisation with the following characteristics: firstly, a structure that seeks and utilises service user and carer participation, team working and learning across the organisation and in collaboration with others; secondly, a culture based on clear shared beliefs, values and objectives and which uses a range of sources of evidence to learn from; thirdly, effective communication systems widely shared and understood; fourthly, continuous development of staff within clear supervision and appraisal policies; and lastly, clear leadership at all levels within the organisation.

Lifelong learning A term coined in the 1920s by Yeaxlee and Lindeman to describe the intellectual basis for a comprehensive understanding of education as a continuing aspect of everyday life. In recent years this has become focused on interest in informal learning and the value placed on the learner's experience. Lifelong learning is a process that carries on throughout life past developing competencies for employment on the basis that education is life and life is education.

Managerialism A term used to describe the adoption of approaches used in the business sector to the public sector to achieve increased productivity, efficiency or value for money.

Mixed economy of care Care provision that is drawn from the private, voluntary and statutory sectors and thought to provide a greater range of consumer choice through competition and the application of market principles away from monopoly of state service provision.

National Service Framework A coherent set of national standards and objectives for social care focused on a particular service user group or service area, such as mental health, older people, children. The framework sets out the vision, organisational arrangements and specific minimum standards that should be achieved. It includes specific targets and statements of quality expected. Timescales and indicators set to measure progress are also included.

Neo-liberalism A political term which promotes a market-led process of social and economic restructuring. In the public sector, it involves privatisation and the use of commercial criteria for delivery services. It is believed that given the right opportunities, those disadvantaged individuals will be able to break free of the culture of dependency.

Oppression Inhuman or degrading treatment of individuals or groups, hardship or injustice brought about by the dominance of one group over another.

Organisational effectiveness A concept which is multi-dimensional and uses a range of different indicators, both qualitative and quantitative, used by stakeholders to measure the effectiveness of an organisation.

Organisational operator A term coined by Neil Thompson which describes an individual who has the knowledge and skills required to work effectively and with a positive influence within an organisation in order to maximise opportunities for promoting equality by challenging discrimination and oppression.

People First An organisation run and controlled by people with learning difficulties who work to improve the lives of people with learning difficulties by speaking up for themselves with help and support and information about their rights.

Performance indicator A measurement of the nature and characteristic of a service standard and of how far this has been met. Performance indicators enable the area being measured to be reviewed and evaluated against agreed statements within the service standard. They are a source of information drawn upon for the purposes of external quality assurance, as to whether threshold standards are met, as well as evidence of good practice. They are generally not used in isolation but combined with a broad range of other evidence and reference points to support judgements of quality.

Performance management The system used to describe how performance is managed in an organisation based on a structure of agreed standards, measurements and indicators.

Pluralism A term that refers to the concept of many and often conflicting interests arising for an idea.

Positive discrimination A term used to describe acts of discrimination that have a reverse effect and redress discrimination by taking positive steps. An example may be through training or recruiting under-represented staff in an organisation from under-represented groups. This is permissible under the Race Relations Act 1976.

Power The ability of a person or group of people such as in an organisation to shape, frame and direct the actions of others, even against resistance. Power in organisations can be positively or negatively used, informal or formal.

Private finance initiative (PFI) A scheme which shifts capital expenditure on public buildings such as schools, hospitals, homes, etc., from the public to the private sector which can include not only the cost of building but also the provision of services, maintenance, staffing and continued ownership. The state can pay to lease the building or own it but contract with the private agency to run it. Many combinations are possible.

Professional power A source of power arising from a person's status, knowledge and expertise, which they can use for the good of people they work with. It can also be misused to deny access to services, persons' rights, or to directly abuse or neglect those without professional power. Professionals in health and social care are guided by codes of practice and ethics to try to minimise the abuse of professional power.

Providing The provision of services from public, private or voluntary sector agencies. It is subject to a form of agreement, which may take the form of legally binding contracts, service agreements or grant conditions dependent on the nature and scale of service provided.

Purchasing The process of acquiring goods or services at an agreed price, defined quality and to a specific timescale.

Quality A product that is fit for purpose with features and characteristics that enable it to satisfy all aspects of customers' needs.

Quality assurance A chain of activities or system within an organisation which embodies aspects of quality during the process of delivering a particular product.

Quasi-markets This term was coined by Le Grand and his colleagues in the early 1990s to refer to developments of the market economy in social care. In the separation of service purchasing from service provision and the need to spend 85 per cent of budgets in the independent sector, LAs delivered services outside in a competitive marketplace of independent sector providers referred to as the 'quasi' or 'not quite pure' market.

Service level agreement A written agreement between providers and users of the service which covers the level of provision, the specified standard of quality and performance, the predetermined agreed costs and the period of time the service will be delivered over.

Shaping Our Lives A national user network which started as a research and development project for people with mental health issues and became independent in 2002.

Social capital The idea of developing the social and economic infrastructure to provide an important resource for contemporary society.

Social democracy A system within national and local government that assumes and builds on participation of the public in public and social issues.

Social model of disability This was developed in the 1970s by disabled activists from the Union of the Physically Impaired Against Segregation (UPIAS) and later advanced by Michael Oliver, who stated that 'Disability is the disadvantage or restriction of activity caused by a contemporary social organisation which takes little or no account of people who have physical impairments and thus excludes them from participation in mainstream social activities.'

Spot contract The purchase of a single or individual unit of service, for example a single residential placement in a geographical location to meet a choice. Spot contracts are designed to meet a specific set of circumstances and needs that are personal to the individual and more flexible and relatively quick to establish. Performance measurement is easily established as it can be derived from the satisfaction of the user with the service delivered.

Stakeholder Anyone who is involved or interested in how the organisation operates and who may be affected by any changes or programme of changes. This may include funders, representatives from partner organisations, employees, service users and carers.

Strategy The process by which a longer-term policy and action plan with realistic targets and timescales is seen to extend beyond the year in question.

Transformational leadership A type of leadership, the features of which are charisma, inspiration and intellectual stimulation. Transformational leaders can communicate high expectations and express purposes in simple ways dealing mainly with abstract and intangible concepts. These are ideal people to have during a major organisational change because they have staying power and provide energy and support through the change process.

Unit cost The total cost of a single service or unit of service. This is usually calculated by looking at the total cost of services within a budget or cost centre divided by the number of services provided.

Valuing People A government White Paper published in 2001 to herald an ambitious new approach to improving services for people with learning disabilities based on four principles: rights, independence, choice and inclusion. A national forum of people with learning disabilities was set up with a taskforce to advise the government of the best ways of implementing change at regional and local levels.

Workforce strategies A plan or approach to develop the workforce to support the implementation of improved services based on the legislative and policy drivers from government to achieve its key objectives. Workforce development strategies include identifying and meeting training needs, establishing a set of competencies and national occupational standards, progression pathways and pay strategies. A strategy needs resources, timescales and predicted outcomes in anticipation of change being achieved.

Work–life balance Having a measure of control about when, where and how you work and being able to enjoy an optimal quality of life. Work–life balance is achieved when an individual's right to a fulfilled life inside and outside of paid work is accepted and respected as the norm and is seen as a mutual benefit to the individual, the employer and the society.

References

Abbott, D and Howarth, J (2005) *Secret loves, hidden lives? Exploring issues for people with learning disabilities who are gay, lesbian or bisexual.* Bristol: The Policy Press.

Adams, R (2002) Quality assurance, in Adams, R, Dominelli, L and Payne, M (eds) *Critical practice in social work.* Basingstoke: Palgrave.

Age Concern Policy Unit (2005) *Opportunity age, meeting the challenges of ageing in the 21st century.* Age Concern Policy Papers.

Ahmed, M (2008) DH failed to act on key recommendations of violence task force. *Community Care,* 22 April.

Association of Directors of Social Services (undated) *Round pegs – round holes? Recognising the future of human resource management, a discussion paper on how organisations learn.* Report by Linda Tapey published by the ADSS. Available at **www.adss.org.uk/publications**

Association of Directors of Social Services (2005) *Independence, well-being and choice: The ADSS response to the Green Paper on adult social care.* July. Available at **www.adss.org.uk**

Ahearn, K, Ferris, GR, Hochwater, WA, Douglas, C and Ammeter, A (2004) Leader political skill and team performance. *Journal of Management,* 30 (3) June, 309–27.

Audit Commission (1986) *Making a reality of community care.* London: HMSO.

Audit Commission (1993) *Citizen's charter indicators.* London: HMSO.

Audit Commission (2002) *Recruitment and retention: a public service workforce for the twenty first century.* London: Audit Commission.

Audit Commission and Social Services Inspectorate (2000) *People need people; releasing the potential of people working in social services.* London: Audit Commission.

Audit Commission and Social Services Inspectorate (2004a) *Old virtues, new virtues.* London: Audit Commission.

Audit Commission and Better Government for Older People (2004b) *Older people – independence and well-being; The challenge for public services.* Available at **www.bgop.org.uk**

Audit Commission and Social Services Inspectorate (undated) *Making ends meet – financial management: A website for managing the money in social services.* **www.joint-reviews.gov.uk/money/Financialmgt**

Badham, B and Eadie, T (2004) Social work in the voluntary sector: Moving forward whilst holding on, in Lymbery, M and Butler, S (eds) (2004) *Social work ideals and practical realities.* Basingstoke: Palgrave Macmillan.

Bailey, K (2004) Learning more from the social model: linking experience, participation and knowledge production, in Barnes, C and Mercer, G (ed) *Implementing the social model of disability: theory and research.* Leeds: The Disability Press.

Ball, C and Connolly, J (2004) *Something to complain about,* **www.communitycare.co.uk** 15–21 January.

Bamford, T (2001) *Commissioning and purchasing.* London: Routledge, in association with Community Care.

Banks, P (1999) *Carer support: time for a change of direction? A policy discussion paper.* London: King's Fund.

Banks, S (2001) *Values and ethics in social work.* Basingstoke: Palgrave.

Barn, R, Andrew, L and Mantovani, N (2005) *The experiences of young care leavers from different ethnic groups. Findings, informing change,* July. Joseph Rowntree Foundation. Available at **www.jrf.org.uk**

Barnard, C (1938) *The functions of the executive.* Cambridge, MA: Harvard University Press.

Barnes, C and Mercer, G (eds) (2004) *Disability policy and practice: applying the social model.* Leeds: The Disability Press.

Barnes, C, Mercer, G and Morgan, H (2000) *Creating independent futures: Stage one report.* Leeds: The Disability Press.

Bayliss, K (2000) Social work values, anti-discriminatory practice and working with older lesbian service users. *Social Work Education,* 19 (1).

Beck, U (1992) *Risk society.* London: Sage.

Beckett, C and Maynard, A (2005) *Values and ethics in social work: an introduction.* London: Sage.

Beresford, P (2004) Madness, distress, research and a social model, in Barnes, C and Mercer, G (eds) *Implementing the social model of disability: theory and research.* Leeds: The Disability Press.

Beresford, P and Campbell, J (1994) Disabled people, service users, user involvement and representation. *Disability and Society,* 9 (3), 315–25.

Beresford, P, Green, D, Lister, R and Woodward, K (eds) (1999) *Poverty first hand: poor people speak for themselves.* London: Child Poverty Action Group.

Better Regulation Task Force Report (2004) *Bridging the gap – participation in social care regulation.* Government Response, 1 December.

Blair, T (1998) *The third way.* London: Fabian Society.

Blair, T (2000) *Transforming the welfare state,* Speech to the Institute for Public Policy Research, London, 7 June.

Blueprint Project (2004) Young people as partners in the Blueprint project pack including project report and *Try it a different way* help sheets published by Voice for the Child in Care, National Children's Bureau, obtainable at **e.blueprint@vcc-uk.org** or **www.vcc-uk.org**

Bostock, L, Bairstow, H, Fish, S and Macleod, F (2005) *Managing risk and minimising mistakes in services to children and families. Children and families' services report 6,* published by Social Care Institute for Excellence, September. Available at **www.scie.org.uk**.

Boydell, T, Burgoyne, J and Pedler, M (2004) Suggested development. *People Management*, 10 (4), 32–4.

Braithwaite, R (2001) *Managing aggression*. London: Routledge in association with Community Care.

Braverman, H (1974) *Labour and monopoly capital: The degradation of work in the twentieth century*. New York: Monthly Review Press.

British Association of Social Workers (2003) *Code of ethics for social workers*. Available at **www.basw.org.uk**

Brown, A and Bourne, I (1996) Stress and trauma: the supervisor's response, in *The social work supervisor*. Buckingham: Open University Press.

Brown, HC (1998) *Social work and sexuality: working with lesbians and gay men*. Basingstoke: Macmillan.

Buchanan, D and Huczynski, A (2004) *Organisational behaviour: an introductory text* (5th edition). Harlow: Pearson Education.

Butt, J (2005) Are we there yet? Identifying the characteristics of social care organisations that successfully promote diversity, in Butt, J, Patel, B and Stuart, O *Race equality discussion papers*. Social Care Institute for Excellence, June 2005, available in print and online from **www.scie.org.uk**

Butt, J, Patel, B and Stuart, O (2005) *Race equality discussion papers*. Social Care Institute for Excellence, June 2005, available in print and online from **www.scie.org.uk**

Cabinet Office (2000) *Wiring it up: Whitehall's management of cross-cutting policies*. London: Performance and Innovation Unit, January.

Campbell, J and Oliver, M (1996) *Disability politics: Understanding our past, changing our future*. London: Routledge.

Carabine, J (ed) (2004) *Sexualities: personal lives and social policy*. Bristol: The Policy Press in association with the Open University.

Carmichael, A (2004) The social model, the emancipatory paradigm and user involvement, in Barnes, C and Mercer, G (eds.) *Implementing the social model of disability: theory and research*. Leeds: The Disability Press.

Carr, S (2004) *Has service user participation made a difference to social care services?* Position Paper no 3. Social Care Institute for Excellence, **www.scie.org.uk**

Cass, E (2005) *Act of guidance*, **www.communitycare.co.uk** 27 October–2 November.

Challis, D, Chesterman, J, Darton, R and Traske, K (1993) Case management in the care of the aged, in Bornat, J, Pereira, C, Pilgrim D and Williams F (eds) *Community care: a reader*. Basingstoke: Macmillan.

Chandler, AD (1962) *Strategy and structure: chapters in the history of the American industrial enterprise*. Cambridge, MA: MIT Press.

Charles, M and Butler, S (2004) Social workers' management of organisational change, in Lymbery, M and Butler, S (eds) *Social work ideas and practice realities*. Basingstoke: Palgrave Macmillan.

153

Children's Workforce Development Council (2008) *The state of the children's social care workforce*. Leeds: CWDC.

CIPD (2004) *Managing conflict at work, a survey of the UK and Ireland*. Chartered Institute of Personnel and Development, Survey Report October 2004, obtainable from **www.cipd.co.uk**

Citizens' Charter Task Force (1994) *Access to complaints systems*. Cabinet Office, HMSO.

Clarke, J (ed) (1993) *A crisis in care: challenges to social work*. London: Sage.

Clarke, J (2004) *Changing welfare, changing states, new directions in social policy*. London: Sage.

Clarke, J and Newman, J (1997) *The managerial state*. London: Sage.

Clegg, S, Kornberger, M and Pitsis, T (2005) *Managing and organisations, an introduction to theory and practice*. London: Sage.

Commission for Social Care Inspection (2007) *Experts by experience make inspections better*. Available at **www.csci.org.uk/about_us/news/experts_by_experience_make_ins.aspx**

Commission for Social Care Inspection (2008a) *Putting people first: providing appropriate services for lesbian, gay, bisexual and transgender people*. Available at **www.csci.org.uk/PDF/putting_people_ first_equality_and_diversity_matters_1.pdf**.

Commission for Social Care Inspection (2008b) *The state of social care in England 2006–07*. Executive summary. London: CSCI.

Commission for Social Care Inspection (2008c) *Health and social care bill; briefing note by the Commission for Social Care Inspection for the House of Lords second reading debate*. London: CSCI.

Conn, D. (2007) The children's champions. Available at **www.cyc-net.org/features/ft-lilac.html**

Cooper, A (2004) Surface and depth in the Victoria Climbié inquiry report. *Child and Family Social Work*, 10, 1–9.

Corrigan, P and Leonard, P (1978) *Social work practice under capitalism: a Marxist approach*. Basingstoke: Macmillan.

Coulshed, V and Mullender, V (2001) *Management in social work* (2nd edition). Basingstoke: Palgrave.

CWDC and SfC (2006) *Leadership and management strategy for social care*. London: CWDC and SfC.

Dalley, G (1996) *The ideologies of caring* (2nd edition). Basingstoke: Macmillan.

Dalrymple, J and Burke, B (2003) *Anti-oppressive practice, social care and the law*. Buckingham: Open University Press.

Davidson, MJ and Cooper, CL (1992) *Shattering the glass ceiling: the woman manager*. London: Paul Chapman Publishing.

Davis, A and Garrett, PM (2004) Progressive practice for tough times: social work, poverty and division in the twenty-first century, in *Social work ideas and practice realities*. Basingstoke: Palgrave Macmillan.

Department for Children, Schools and Families (2007) *Building brighter futures: Next steps for the Children's Workforce*. London: DCSF.

Department of Health (1995a) *An introduction to joint commissioning*. London: DoH.

Department of Health (1995b) *Child protection: messages from research*. London: The Stationery Office.

Department of Health (1998a) *Modernising social services, promoting independence, improving protection, raising standards*. CM 4169. London: The Stationery Office.

Department of Health (1998b) *Caring for children away from home: messages from research*. London: Department of Health, John Wiley & Sons.

Department of Health (1998c) *Quality protects circular: Transforming children's services, Local Authority circular LAC (98) 28*. London: DoH.

Department of Health (1999) *The government's objectives for children's social services (Quality Protects)*. London: The Stationery Office.

Department of Health (2000a) *The NHS: A plan for investment, a plan for reform*. London: DoH.

Department of Health, Department for Education and Employment and the Home Office (2000b) *Framework for the assessment of children in need and their families*. London: The Stationery Office.

Department of Health (2000c) *Listening to people*. **www.doh.gov.uk/listen.htm**

Department of Health (2000d) *A safer place: report of the task force and national action plan on violence against social care staff*. London: The Stationery Office.

Department of Health (2000e) *Working together to safeguard children: a guide to interagency working to safeguard and promote the welfare of children*. London: DoH/HO/DfEE and The Stationery Office.

Department of Health (2000f) *A quality strategy for social care*. London: DoH.

Department of Health (2001) *The national service framework for older people: modern standards and service models*. London: DoH.

Department of Health (2002a) *Guidance on the single assessment process*. HSC 2002/001: LAC (2002) 1.

Department of Health (2002b) *Achieving fairer access to adult social care services*. LAC (2002) 13 **www.dh.gov.uk**

Department of Health (2004a) *Every child matters: change for children*. London: DoH.

Department of Health (2004b) *All our lives: social care in England 2002 – 2003*. A joint report from the three partner organisations, Joint Review, SSI, NCSC. London: DoH.

Department of Health (2004c) *Learning from complaints: consultation on changes to the social services complaints procedure for adults*. October. Available at **www.doh.gov.uk**

Department of Health (2005a) *Independence, well-being and choice: The vision for the future of social care in England*. Green Paper. London: DoH.

Department of Health (2005b) *Best practice guidance on the role of the director of adult social services*. London: DoH.

Department of Health (2005c) *Delivering race equality in mental health care and the government's response to the independent inquiry into the death of David Bennet.* **www.dh.gov.uk/**

Department of Health (2005d) *Personal social services expenditure and unit costs: England: 2003 –2004.* London: DoH.

Department of Health (2005e) *Self-care – a real choice.* London: DoH.

Department of Health (2006) *Our health, our care, our say: a new direction for community services.* London: DoH.

Department of Health (2007a) *National service framework for children, young people and maternity services: Core standards.* Available at **www.dh.gov.uk/en/Publicationsandstatistics/ Publications/PublicationsPolicyAndGuidance/Browsable/DH_4094329**

Department of Health (2007b) *Being the gay one: Experiences of lesbian, gay and bisexual people working in the health and social care sector.* Available at **www.dh.gov.uk/en/ Managingyourorganisation/Equalityandhumanrights/Sexualorientationandgenderidentity/ index.htm**

Department of Health (2007c) *Transgender experiences: Information and support.* Information leaflet available at **www.dh.gov.uk/en/Publicationsandstatistics/Publications/ PublicationsPolicyAndGuidance/DH_081579**

Department of Health (2007d) NHS: *Next stage review.* Interim report summary, October. Available at **www.ournhs.nhs.uk/fromtypepad/283411_ourNHS_summary_v2acc.pdf.**

Department of Health (2008a) *Making experiences count: The proposed new arrangement for handling health and social care complaints – response to consultation,* February. Available at **www.dh.gov.uk/en/Publicationsandstatistics/Publications/PublicationsPolicyAndGuidance/ DH_082714**

Department of Health (2008b) *Transforming social care.* Local Authority Circular 1. Available at **www.dh.gov.uk/en/Publicationsandstatistics/Lettersandcirculars/LocalAuthorityCirculars/ DH_081934**

Department of Trade and Industry *The original quality gurus.* **www.dti.gov/quality/gurus**

Department of Trade and Industry (2004) *Fairness for all: A new commission for equality and human rights.* White Paper. London: The Stationery Office. Available at **www.tso.co.uk/bookshop**

DfEE (2004) *Providing effective advocacy services for children and young people making a complaint under the Children Act 1989; Draft regulations and guidance.* Available at **www.dfee.gov.uk**

DfES (2005) *Youth matters.* London: Department for Education and Skills, The Stationery Office.

DfES (2006a) *Getting the best from complaints: Social care complaints and representations for children, young people and others.* Available at **www.everychildmatters.gov.uk/_files/ 09CC656B2B98A12A9905CAADA055ACAA.doc**

DfES and DoH (2006b) *Options for excellence: Building the social care workforce of the future.* London: The Stationery Office.

DfES (2006c) Care matters. Green Paper. Available at **www.dfes.gov.uk**

DfES (2007) *The children's plan: building brighter futures*. Available at **www.dfes.gov.uk/ publications/childrensplan/downloads/The_Childrens_Plan.pdf**

Dhillon-Stevens, H (2005) Personal and professional integration of anti-oppressive practice and the multi oppression model in psychotherapeutic education. *The British Journal of Psychotherapy Integration*, 1(2), 47–62.

Dimond, B (2004) Race relations in the UK: the implications for health and social care of recent changes in the law. *Diversity in Health and Social Care*, 1 (7), 7–12.

Directgov (undated) The disability symbol. **www.direct.gov.uk/en/DisabledPeople/ Employmentsupport/LookingForWork/DG_4000314**

Dominelli, L (1988) *Anti-racist social work*. Basingstoke: Macmillan.

Dominelli, L (1989) *Feminist social work*. Basingstoke: Macmillan.

Dominelli, L (1997) Feminist theory, in Davies, M (ed.) *The Blackwell companion to social work*. Oxford: Blackwell.

Dominelli, L (2002) *Anti-oppressive social work theory and practice*. Basingstoke: Palgrave Macmillan.

Donabedian, A (1980) *The definition of quality and approaches to its assessment, explorations in quality assessment and monitoring, volume I*. Ann Arbor, MI: Health Administration Press.

Drennan, V, Levenson, R, Goodman, C and Evans, C (2004) Developing the health and social care workforce. *British Journal of Health Care Management,* 9 (11).

Duvell, F and Jordan, B (2000) *'How low can you go?' Dilemmas of social work with asylum seekers in London*. Exeter: Department of Social Work, Exeter University.

Ejo, Y (2004) Managing practice in black and minority ethnic organisations, in Statham, D (ed.) *Managing front line practice in social care*. Research Highlights in Social Work 40. London: Jessica Kingsley.

Eraut, M (2004) Editorial: Learning to change and/or changing to learn. *Learning in Health and Social Care*, 3 (3), 111–17.

Everitt, A and Hardiker, P (1996) *Evaluating for good practice*. BASW Practical Social Work Series. Basingstoke: Palgrave.

Felton, K (2005) Meaning-based quality-of-life measurement: A way forward in conceptualising and measuring client outcomes? *British Journal of Social Work*, 35, 221–36.

Ferguson, I (2007) Increasing user choice or privatising risk? The antinomies of personalisation. *British Journal of Social Work*, 37, 387–403.

Fook, J (2004) Critical reflection and organizational learning and change: A case study, in Gould, N and Baldwin, M (eds) *Social work, critical reflection and the learning organization*. Aldershot: Ashgate.

Foster, G (2004) Managing front line practice, women and men: The social care workforce, in Statham, D (ed.) *Managing front line practice in social care*. Research Highlights in Social Work 40. London: Jessica Kingsley.

Foster, J (2001) Networking: a personal view, in Baxter, C (ed.) *Managing diversity and inequality in health care*. Edinburgh: Balliere Tindall.

Foster, P and Wilding, P (2003) Whither welfare professionalism?, in Reynolds, J, Henderson, J, Seden, Charlesworth, J and Bullman, A (eds) *The managing care reader*. London: Routledge, Open University Press.

French, JRP and Raven, BH (1958) The bases of social power, in D Cartwright (ed.) *Studies in social power, Institute for Social Research*. Ann Arbor, MI: University of Michigan Press.

Friday, E and Friday, S (2003) Managing diversity using a strategic planned change approach. *Journal of Management Development*, 22, (10), 863–80.

Gallagher, B, Brannan, C, Jones. R and Westwood, S (2004) Good practice in the education of children in residential care. *British Journal of Social Work*, 34, 1133–60.

Gender Recognition Panel website **www.grp.gov.uk**

General Social Care Council (2005) *The post qualifying framework*. **www.gscc.org.uk**

General Social Care Council (2008) *Social work at its best: A statement of social work roles and tasks for the 21st century*. March. London: General Social Care Council in association with the Commission for Social Care Inspection; the Children's Workforce Development Council; Social Care Institute for Excellence; Skills for Care.

Glasby, J (2004) Social services and the single assessment process: early warning signs? *Journal of Interprofessional Care*, 18 (2), May.

Glendinning, C and Means, R (2004) Rearranging the deckchairs on the *Titanic* of long-term care – is organisational integration the answer? *Critical Social Policy*, 24 (4), 435–57.

Glennester, H (2003) *Understanding the finance of welfare, what welfare costs and how to pay for it*, Bristol: The Policy Press and the Social Policy Association.

Golightley, M (2008) *Social work and mental health* (3rd edition). Transforming Social Work Practice series. Exeter: Learning Matters. **www.learningmatters.co.uk**

Gould, N (2000) Becoming a learning organisation: a social work example. *Social Work Education*, 19 (6).

Griffiths, R (1988) *Community care: Agenda for action*. London: HMSO.

Hafford-Letchfield, T (2005) On the up. *Community Care*. 14–20 April. **www.communitycare.co.uk**

Hafford-Letchfield, T (2008) What's love got to do with it?: Developing supportive practices for the expression of sexuality, sexual identity and the intimacy needs of older people. *Journal of Care Services Management*, 2 (4).

Hafford-Letchfield, T and Chick, N (2006) Talking across purposes; the benefits of an inter-agency mentoring scheme for managers working in health and social care settings in the UK. *Work based learning in primary care*, 4: 13–24.

Hales, C (1993) *Managing through organisations*. London: Routledge.

Hampshire Centre for Integrated Living (HCIL) (1990) *Consumer consultation*. Available at www.leeds.ac.uk/disability-studies/archieveuk/index.html

Handy, C (1993) *Understanding organisations*. London: Penguin.

Harding, T and Beresford, P (1993) *The standards we expect: What service users and carers want from social service workers*. London: National Institute for Social Work.

Hardman, KLJ (1997) Social workers' attitudes to lesbian clients. *British Journal of Social Work*, 27, 545–63.

Harkin, J and Huber, J (2004) *Eternal youth demos. How the baby boomers are having their time again*. York: Joseph Rowntree Trust.

Harlow, E (2004) Why don't women want to be social workers anymore? New managerialism, post feminism and the shortage of social workers in social services departments in England and Wales. *European Journal of Social Work*, 7 (2), pp 167–79.

Harris, V and Dutt, R (2005) *Meeting the challenge: A good practice guide for the recruitment and retention of black and minority ethnic workers*. London: Race Equality Unit.

Harrison, R (2005) *Learning and development* (4th edition). London: Chartered Institute of Personnel and Development.

Hasler, F (2003) *Users at the heart: User participation in the governance and operation of social care regulatory bodies*. Social Care Institute for Excellence, Report no 5. Available at **www.scie.org.uk**

Hayman, R (2001) Young people in care, in Cull, LA and Roche, J (eds) *The law and social work*. Basingstoke: Palgrave, Open University Press.

Healy, K (2002) Managing human services in a market environment: What role for social workers? *British Journal of Social Work*, 32, 527–40.

Health and Safety Executive (2004) *Tackling stress; the management standards approach*. London: Health and Safety Executive. Available at **www.hse.gov.uk/publications**.

Henwood, M (2005) What's driving reform? *Community Care*, 21–27 July, 32–3, **www.communitycare.co.uk**

HM Government (2004) *Opportunity age. Volume two. A social portrait of ageing in the UK*.

HM Government (2005) *Statutory guidance on the duty of local authorities to promote the educational achievement of looked after children under Section 52 of the Children Act 2004*. Nottingham: DfES Publications.

HM Government (2007a) *Strong and prosperous communities: The local government White Paper*. October. Department for Communities and Local Government, CM 69394. Available at **www.communities.gov.uk/publications/localgovernment/strongprosperous**

HM Government (2007b) *Putting people first: a shared vision and commitment to the transformation of adult social care*. DoH. Available at **www.dh.gov.uk/en/Publicationsandstatistics/Publications/PublicationsPolicyandGuidance/DH_081118**

Home Office (1999) *The Stephen Lawrence Inquiry, Report of an inquiry by Sir William Macpherson of Cluny*. London: The Stationery Office.

Home Office (2003) *The Victoria Climbie Inquiry Report.* London: The Stationery Office.

Hood, C, Rothstein, H and Baldwin, R (2000) *The government of risk: understanding risk regulation regimes.* Oxford: Oxford University Press.

Horner, N (2006) *What is social work? Context and perspectives* (2nd edition). Exeter: Learning Matters. **www.learningmatters.co.uk**

Horwath, J (2005) Identifying and assessing cases of child neglect: learning from the Irish experience. *Child and Family Social Work*, 10, 99–110.

House, RJ (1995) Leadership in the twenty-first century, in Howard, A (ed) *The changing nature of work*, pp. 411–50. San Francisco, CA: Jossey-Bass.

Hudson, B (2005) Will reforms suit users? *Community Care*, 28 July – 3 August, 30–1, **www.communitycare.co.uk**

Huhne, C (2007) Taking back the initiative. Private finance initiatives have had their day. Let's get back to honest finance and proper accounting. *Guardian*, 27 November. **www.guardian.co.uk**

Humphrey, JC (2003a) Joint reviews: the methodology in action. *British Journal of Social Work*, 33 (2), 177–90.

Humphrey, JC (2003b) Joint reviews: judgement day and beyond. *British Journal of Social Work*, 33, 727–58.

Humphreys, C (2000) *Social work, domestic violence and child protection: challenging practice.* Bristol: The Policy Press.

Humphries, B (2004) An unacceptable role for social work: Implementing immigration policy. *British Journal of Social Work*, 34, 93–107.

Humphries, B (2005) Refugees, asylum seekers, welfare and social work, in Hayes, D and Humphries, B (eds) *Social work and immigration controls.* London: JKP.

Humphries, B and Mynott, E (eds) (2002) *From immigration controls to welfare controls.* London: Routledge.

Huxley, P, Evans, S, Gately, C, Webber, M, Mears, A, Pajak, S, Kendall, T, Medina, J and Katona, C (2005) Stress and pressures in mental health social work: the worker speaks. *British Journal of Social Work*, 35, 1063–79.

IDeA (2004) *Prospects.* Improvement and Development Agency co-funded by Leadership Research and Development Ltd. **www.IDeA.org.uk**

Iff Research Ltd (2007) *Third sector market mapping.* Research Report, February. Commissioned by the Department of Health. Available at **www.dh.gov.uk/en/Publicationsandstatistics/ Publications/PublicationsPolicyAndGuidance/DH_065411**

Information Centre (2008) *Personal social services expenditure and unit costs, England, 2006–07.* National Statistics. Available at **www.ic.nhs.uk/statistics-and-data-collections/social-care/ adult-social-care-information**

International Federation of Social Workers (1994) *The ethics of social work principles and standards.* **www.ifsw.org**

Jack, G (2000) Ecological influences on parenting and child development. *British Journal of Social Work*, 30, 703–20.

Johns, R (2007) *Using the law in social work* (3rd edition). Exeter: Learning Matters **www.learningmatters.co.uk**

Johnstone, D (2008) Can you feel the buzz of care management transformation? *Community Care*, 12 June 2008, p 29.

Jones, A (2002) Family life and the pursuit of immigration controls, in Cohen, S, Humphries, B and Mynott, E (eds) *From immigration controls to welfare controls*. London: Routledge.

Jones, C and Novak, T (1999) *The disciplinary state*. London: Routledge.

Jones, C (2001) Voices from the frontline: State social workers and new Labour. *British Journal of Social Work*, 31 (4), 547–62.

Jordan, B with Jordan, C (2001) *Social work and the third way: tough love as social policy*. London: Sage.

Kearney, P (2004) First line managers, the mediators of standards and the quality of practice, in Statham, D (ed.) *Managing front line practice in social care*. Research Highlights in Social Work 40. London: Jessica Kingsley.

Keating, F (1997) *Developing an integrated approach to oppression*. London: CCETSW.

King's Fund (1992) *Living options in practice, achieving user participation: planning services for people with severe physical and sensory disabilities*. Project Paper No 3. London: King's Fund Centre.

King's Fund Wanless Review Team (2005) Social care needs and outcomes, background paper for the *Wanless Social Care Review*.

Kirkpatrick, I and Ackroyd, S (2003) Transforming the professional archetype? The new managerialism in United Kingdom social services. *Management Review*, 5 (4), December.

Kotter, JP (1996) *Leading change*. Boston, MA: Harvard Business School Press.

Labour Party (2005) *Britain: Forward not back*. The Labour Party Manifesto.

Lavin, N (2004) Long time companion. *Community Care*, 22–28 July. **www.communitycare.co.uk**

Leece, J (2004) Money talks but what does it say? Direct payments and the commodification of care. *Practice*, 16 (3), September.

Lewin, K (ed.) (1951) *Field theory in social science*. New York: Harper & Row.

Linder, S (2000) Coming to terms with the public–private partnership: a grammar of multiple meanings, in Rosenau, P (ed.) *Public–private policy partnerships*. Westwood, MA: Massachusetts Institute of Technology.

Local Government Association (2006) *Social services finance 2005–06; A survey of local authorities. Research briefing 1.06*, London: LGA.

Lonne, B, McDonald, C and Fox, T (2004) Ethical practice in the contemporary human services. *British Journal of Social Work*, 4 (3), 345–67.

Lymbery, M (2004) Responding to crisis: The changing nature of welfare organisations, in Lymbery, M and Butler, S (eds) (2004) *Social work ideals and practical realities*. Basingstoke: Palgrave Macmillan.

Lymbery, M and Butler, S (eds) (2004) *Social work ideals and practical realities*. Basingstoke: Palgrave Macmillan.

Lysons, K (1997) Organisational analysis. *British Journal of Administrative Management*, 16 March.

Mabey, C (2001) *Preparing for change: Context and choice*. Block 3, *Managing change*. Buckingham: Open University Press.

Macaulay, C (2000) Transfer of learning, in Cree, VE and Macaulay, C *Transfer of learning in professional and vocational education*. London: Routledge.

McCullagh, M (2001) Personal communication with Geraldine Cunningham, cited in Cunningham, G, Supervision and governance, in Statham, D (ed) (2004) *Managing front line practice in social care*. Research Highlights in Social Work 40. London: Jessica Kingsley.

McGregor, D (1960) *The human side of enterprise*. New York: McGraw-Hill.

McLean, J and Andrew, T (2000) Commitment, satisfaction, stress and control among social services managers and social workers in the UK. *Administration in Social Work*, 23 (3/4), 93–117.

Malin, N, Wilmot, S and Manthorpe, J (2002) *Key concepts and debates in health and social policy*. Buckingham: Open University Press.

Mann, P, Pritchard, S and Rummery, K (2004) Supporting inter-organisational partnerships. *Public Sector Management Review*, 6 (3), 417–39.

Manthorpe, J (2003) Nearest and dearest? The neglect of lesbians in caring relationships. *British Journal of Social Work*, 33, 753–68.

Manthorpe, J (2004) *Championing older people – making a difference: Summary survey findings from 209 older people's champions*. Better Government for Older People Research Series no.1. Available at **www.bgop.org.uk**

Marinner-Tomey, A (1992) *Guide to nursing management and leadership*. St Louis, MO: Mosby.

Martin, J and Frost, P (1996) The organizational culture war games: A struggle for intellectual dominance, in Clegg, SR, Handy, C and Nord, W (eds) *A handbook of organisational studies*. London: Sage.

Martin, S and Boaz, A (2000) Public participation and citizen-centred local government: lessons for the best value and Better Government for Older People pilot programmes. *Public Money and Management*, 20 (2) April–June, 47–53.

Martin, V and Henderson, E (2001) *Managing in health and social care*. London: Routledge, Open University Press.

Maslow, AH (1954) *Motivation and personality*. New York: Harper & Row.

Mayo, E (1945) *The social problems of an industrial civilisation*. Cambridge, MA: Harvard University Press.

Means, R, Richards, S and Smith, R (2003) *Community care policy and practice* (3rd edition). Basingstoke: Palgrave Macmillan.

Menzies-Lyth, I (1988) *Containing anxiety in institutions: selected essays, volume one*. London: Free Association Books.

Ministerial Task Force for Health, Safety and Productivity and the Cabinet Office (2005) *Managing sickness absence in the public sector, one year on report*. A joint review by the Health and Safety Executive, Cabinet Office, Department for Work and Pensions. Available at **www.hse.org.uk/publications**.

Mintzberg, H (1985) The organisation as political arena. *Journal of Management Studies*, 22, 133–54.

Mintzberg, H (1989) *The structuring of organizations*. Englewood Cliffs, NJ: Prentice Hall.

Mitchell, W and Sloper, P (2003) Quality indicators: Disabled children's and parents' prioritizations and experiences of quality criteria when using different types of support services. *British Journal of Social Work*, 33, 1063–80.

Moon, JA (1999) *Reflection in learning and professional development: theory and practice*. London: Routledge Falmer.

Morgan, G (1987) *Creative organisation theory*. London: Sage.

Morrison, T (2000) Working together to safeguard children: challenges and changes for inter-agency co-ordination in child protection. *Journal of Interprofessional Care*, 14 (4), 2000.

Morrison, T (2002) *Staff supervision in social care: making a real difference to staff and service users*. London: Pavilion Publishing.

Morrison, T (2007) Emotional intelligence, emotion and social work: Context, characteristics, complications and contribution. *British Journal of Social Work*, 37, 245–63.

Munroe, E (2004a) Child abuse inquiries since 1990, in Stanley, N and Manthorpe, J (ed.), *The age of the inquiry, learning and blaming in health and social care*. London: Routledge.

Munroe, E (2004b) The impact of audit on social work practice. *British Journal of Social Work*, 34, 1075–95.

Nocon, A and Qureshi, H (1996) *Outcomes of community care for users and carers, a social services perspective*. Buckingham: Open University Press.

Nutley, S and Osborne, S (1994) *The public sector handbook*. Harlow: Longman.

Obholzer, A (1994) Authority, power and leadership: contributions from group relations training, in Obholzer, A and Zagier Roberts, V (eds) *The unconscious at work, individual and organizational stress in the human services*. London: Routledge.

Obholzer, A and Zagier Roberts, V (1994) *The unconscious at work, individual and organizational stress in the human services*. London: Routledge.

Office of the Deputy Prime Minister (ODPM) (2005) *Statistical release, Local authority revenue expenditure and financing, England*, 2005-06 budget. London: Local Government Finance Statistics division of ODPM.

Office of the Deputy Prime Minister (2006) *A guide to the local government finance settlement*. January. ODPM. Available at **www.local.odpm.gov.uk/finance/0607/simpguid.pdf**

Oliver, M (1990) *The politics of disablement*. Basingstoke: Macmillan.

Oliver, M (2004) The social model in action: if I had a hammer, in Barnes, C and Mercer, G (eds) *Implementing the social model of disability: theory and research*. Leeds: The Disability Press.

O'Neil, T (1995) Juvenile prostitution: the experiences of young women in residential care. *Childright*, no 113, December.

OPSI (2006) *The employment equality age regulations, Statutory Instrument 2006, no 1031*. Available at **www.opsi.gov.uk/si/si2006/20061031.htm**

Ovretveit, J (1993) *Co-ordinating community care: Multi-disciplinary teams and care management*. Buckingham: Open University Press.

Parker, J (2004) *Effective practice learning in social work*. Exeter: Learning Matters. **www.learningmatters.co.uk**

Parsloe, P (1996) Empowerment in social work practice, in Parsloe, P (ed.) *Pathways to empowerment*. Birmingham: Venture.

Partridge, B (1989) The problem of supervision, in K Sisson (ed.) *Personnel management in Britain*. Oxford: Blackwell, pp. 203–221.

Paxton, W and Pearce (2005) *The voluntary sector delivering public services, transfer or transformation?* Study papers: Part I. York: Joseph Rowntree Foundation.

Payne, M (1996) *What is professional social work?* Birmingham: Venture.

Payne, M (2005) *Modern social work theory* (3rd edition). Basingstoke: Palgrave Macmillan.

Peters, T (1995) *The pursuit of WOW! Every person's guide to topsy-turvy times*. Basingstoke: Macmillan.

Pillinger, J (2001) *Quality in social public services*. Luxembourg: European Foundation for the Improvement of Living and Working Conditions.

Pinnock, M (2004) Rage against the machine. *Community Care*, 15–21 April. **www.communitycare.co.uk**

Pollitt, C (2003) *The essential public manager*. Buckingham: Open University Press.

Powell, M and Hewitt, M (2002) *Welfare state and welfare change*. Buckingham: Open University Press.

Preston-Shoot, M (2001) Evaluating self-determination: an adult protection case study. *Journal of Adult Protection*, 3 (1), February.

Procter, S and Mueller, F (eds) (2000) *Teamworking*. Basingstoke: Macmillan.

Pugh, S (2005) Assessing the cultural needs of older lesbians and gay men: Implications for practice. *Practice*, 17 (3), September.

QAA (2000) *Social policy and administration and social work: Subject benchmark statements*. Available at **http://www.qaa.ac.uk**

Reynolds, M and Vince, R (2004) Critical management education and action-based learning: Synergies and contradictions. *Academy of Management, Learning and Education*, 3 (4), 442–56.

Ritzer, G (ed.) (1998) *The McDonaldization thesis: Explorations and extensions*. London: Sage.

Robinson, J and Banks, P (2005) *The business of caring*. London: The King's Fund.

Robson, P, Begum, N and Locke, M (2003) *Developing user involvement: Working towards user-centred practice in voluntary organisations*. Bristol: The Policy Press with Joseph Rowntree Foundation.

Rosen, A (1994) Knowledge use in direct practice. *Social Services Review*, 68, 561–67.

Ruch, G (2005) Relationship-based practice and reflective practice: holistic approaches to contemporary child care social work. *Child and Family Social Work*, 10, 111–23.

Rushton, A and Nathan, J (1996) The supervision of child protection work. *British Journal of Social Work*, 26, 357–74.

Salari, N (2003) Delayed discharges, councils and health bodies plan to reinvest fines to improve services. *Community Care*, 9–15 October. **www.communitycare.co.uk**

Schein, E (1997) *Organisational culture and leadership*. San Francisco,CA: Jossey-Bass.

Schofield, G (1988) Inner and outer worlds: a psychosocial framework for child and family social work. *Child and Family Social Work*, 3, 57–67.

Schön, DA (1991) *The reflective practitioner*. Aldershot: Avebury (first published 1983).

SCIE (2004) *Learning organisations: a self-assessment resource pack*. Social Care Institute for Excellence. Available in print or downloadable from **www.scie.org.uk**

SCIE (2005) *SCIE consultation response to independence, well-being and choice*, **www.scie.org.uk**

SCIE (2007) *Participation – finding out what difference it makes*. SCIE Resource guide 07. London: SCIE.

Scull, A (1993) *The most solitary of afflictions: Madness and society in Britain, 1700 – 1900*. New Haven, CT: Yale University Press.

Seebohm Report (1968) *Report of the committee on local authority and allied personal services*. London: HMSO.

Senge, P (1996) *The fifth discipline: The art and practice of the learning organisation*. New York: Doubleday.

Sheldon, B (1986) Social work effectiveness experiments: review and implication. *British Journal of Social Work*, 16 (2), 223–42.

Simon, K (1995) Views from another angle: the professional perspective, in *I'm not complaining but ...* Joseph Rowntree Trust. Available at **www.jrt.org.uk**.

Skills for Care (2004) *What leaders and managers in social care do: a statement for a leadership and management development strategy for social care*. Statement no 1. Skills for Care. Available at **www.topssengland.co.uk**

Skills for Care (2005a) *The state of the social care workforce 2004. The second skills research and intelligence annual report April 2005*. **www.topssengland.org.uk**

Skills for Care (2005b) *Developing the role of personal assistants*. Report to Skills for Care's New Types of Worker project. **www.skillsforcare.org.uk/projects/**

Skills for Care (2006) *Manage effective supervision. A unit of competence for managers in social care*. Leadership Product no 6. Commissioned from Fran McDonnell and Harry Zutshi, HZ Management and Training Consultancy. Leeds: Skills for Care.

Skills for Care (2007) *The sector skills agreement, summary of stage 1 report: Assessing current and future needs of the adult social care workforce in England*. Leeds: Skills for Care.

Skills for Care (2008a) *The state of the adult social care workforce in England, The third report of Skills for Care's skills research and intelligence unit*. Researched and compiled by Christine Eborall and David Griffiths (February). Leeds: Skills for Care.

Skills for Care (2008b) *Common core principles to support self care: A guide to support implementation*. Leeds: Skills for Care.

Skills for Care (2008C) *Leadership and management strategy update 2008: transforming adult social care*. Leeds: Skills for Care Available from: **www.skillsforcare.org.uk/developing_skills/ leadership_and_ management/leadership_and_management_st**

Smyth, C, Simmons, I and Cunningham, G (1999) *Quality assurance in social work – A standards and audit approach for agencies and practitioners*. London: National Institute for Social Work.

Social Exclusion Unit (2004) *Breaking the cycle: Taking stock of progress and priorities for the future*. London: Office of the Deputy Prime Minister.

Social Exclusion Unit (2003) *A better education for children in care*. September. Available from **www.socialinclusion.org.uk**

Sone, K (2000) What would you do for a quiet life? **communitycare.co.uk**

Spandler, H (2004) Friend or foe? Towards a critical assessment of direct payments. *Critical Social Policy*, 24 (2) 187–209.

Statham, D (ed) (2004) *Managing front line practice in social care*. Research Highlights in Social Work 40. London: Jessica Kingsley.

Storey, J and Billingham, J (2001) Occupational stress and social work. *Social Work Education*, 20 (6), 2001.

Tanner, D (2003) Older people and access to care. *British Journal of Social Work*, 33, 499–515.

Taylor, FW (1911) *Principles of scientific management*. New York: Harper.

Thompson, N (2000) *Understanding social work, preparing for practice*. Basingstoke: Palgrave.

Thompson, N (2003) *Promoting equality, challenging discrimination and oppression* (2nd edition). Basingstoke: Palgrave Macmillan.

Thompson, N, Stradling, S, Murphy, M and O'Neill, P (1996) Stress and organisational culture. *British Journal of Social Work*, 26 (5), 647–66.

Tilbury, C (2004) The influence of performance measurement on child welfare policy and practice. *British Journal of Social Work*, 34, 225–41.

Tomlinson, C (2008) Our escape from 'serviceland'. *Learning Disability Today*, June, 30–2.

Townend, M (2005) Interprofessional supervision from the perspectives of both mental health nurses and other professionals in the field of cognitive behavioural psychotherapy. *Journal of Psychiatric and Mental Health Nursing*, 12, 582–8.

Townsend, P (1981) The structural dependency of the elderly: the creation of social policy in the twentieth century. *Ageing and Society*, 1 (1), 5–28.

Tsui, Ming-sum (2005) *Supervision in social work*. London: Sage.

Tsui, Ming-sum and Cheung, FCH (2004) Gone with the wind: The impacts of managerialism on human services. *British Journal of Social Work*, 34, 437–42.

Unwin, J and Molyneux, P (2005) *Beyond transfer to transformation: barriers and opportunities facing voluntary organisations providing public services*. Study review papers: Part II. York: Joseph Rowntree Foundation.

Vanstone, M (1995) Managerialism and the ethics of management, in Hugman, R and Smith, D (eds) *Ethical issues in social work*. London: Routledge.

Walker, P (2002) Understanding accountability: Theoretical models and their implications for social services organisations. *Social Policy and Administration*, 36, 62–75.

Walker, J and Crawford, K (2003) *Human growth and development*. Exeter: Learning Matters **www.learningmatters.co.uk**

Weber, M (1976) *The Protestant ethic and the spirit of capitalism*, London: Allen & Unwin.

Weinberg, A, Williamson, J, Challis, D and Hughes, J (2003) What do care managers do? A study of working practice in older people's services. *British Journal of Social Work*, 33, 901–19.

Wittenberg, R, Pickard, L, Comtas-Herrera, A, Davis, B and Darton, R (2001) Demand for long-term care for older people in England to 2031. *Health Statistics Quarterly*, 12, 5–17.

Wright, L and Smye, M (1997) *Corporate abuse*. New York: Simon & Schuster.

Zagier Roberts, V (1994) The organisation of work: contributions from open systems theory, in Obholzer, A and Zagier Roberts, V (eds) *The unconscious at work, individual and organizational stress in the human services*. London: Routledge.

Zarb, G and Nadash, P (1994) *Cashing in on independence: comparing the costs and benefits of cash and services*. London: British Council of Disabled People/Policy Studies Institute.

Index

Transforming Social Work Practice – titles in the series

To order, please contact our distributor: BEBC Distribution, Albion Close, Parkstone, Poole, BH12 3LL. Telephone: 0845 230 9000, email: **learningmatters@bebc.co.uk**. You can also find more information on each of these titles and our other learning resources at www.learningmatters.co.uk